What Emergency?

Second Edition

"Oh, what a tangled web we weave when first we practice to deceive."
Sir Walter Scott, 1808

There is an old adage among lawyers that says,
"If you have the facts on your side, pound the facts; if you have the law on your side, pound the law; if you have neither the facts nor the law, pound the table."
Martin A. Davis, Jr., Thomas B. Fordham Institute, 2/21/2007

What Emergency?

Guns!
Alcohol!
Children!

Second Edition

A.L. Dickason

Mystic Circle Books

Table of Contents

Preface

After the publication of the first edition of *What Emergency? Guns! Alcohol! Children!*, I initiated several steps to further raise public awareness of the dangers of mixing guns, alcohol, and children at a live-fire shooting facility, the misconduct of Duncanville narcotics detective and ECSC leagues manager Dan Hunt, ECSC leadership, and five attorneys who had represented Dan Hunt and the Ellis County Sportsmans Club. Within this *Second Edition*, I detail my subsequent actions in a new chapter, *Aftermath*.

In my professional opinion, mixing guns, alcohol, and children is a topic of public concern. This book details the events that occurred after I attempted to speak out about the inherent dangers of mixing guns, alcohol, and children at a Texas gun club. The Desoto Gun Club d/b/a Ellis County Sportsmans Club (ECSC) is a not-for-profit corporation located south of Dallas, near Waxahachie, Texas.

This is a book every member of a gun club, guest, or parent of a child participating in events sponsored by a gun club should read. First, to raise awareness of the critical importance of club leadership's duty to its members by implementing sound gun safety policies and procedures, then recognizing the importance of appointing qualified, competent individuals to oversee live-fire shooting events. Second, to understand what can happen when a club member is intentionally harmed by another club member's misbehavior and false accusations, and such misconduct is intentionally condoned by club leadership.

Starting in 2018, Danny Garth Hunt, a vindictive Duncanville, Texas, Police Department narcotics detective and unqualified ECSC leagues manager, set in motion a series of events leading to an appalling pattern of unprincipled conduct within the leadership of the Ellis County Sportsmans Club.

On July 2, 2018, at thirty-four minutes preceding midnight, some three hours after the conclusion of a regularly scheduled ECSC monthly board meeting, one in which Dan Hunt agreed to a confidentiality agreement, Dan Hunt, acting in his official capacity as ECSC leagues manager, sent a malicious, defamatory email titled, *Immediate resignation,* to nearly one hundred unsuspecting club members, guests, and even children.

Within his lengthy diatribe, Dan Hunt falsely accused Shawn George and me of abuse and causing harm to his family. As a Defendant in my lawsuit, Dan Hunt continued his false, malicious accusations in his future court filings to the 443rd Ellis County District Court and the Court of Appeals, Tenth District of Texas. Accusations Hunt failed to support with any notarized, signed affidavits or evidence. Yet, Dan Hunt never mentioned to the Courts his libelous email or any of the malicious accusations he spread to nearly one hundred members, guests, and children.

Considering Dan Hunt's malicious, vindictive email, *Immediate resignation* exposed Hunt and the ECSC to a lawsuit, it was a telling omission. One that, in my professional opinion, was a damning indictment of Danny Garth Hunt's character.

I wrote this book to expose Dan Hunt's false accusations, and what I believe was the 2018 ECSC Board of Directors' reckless, negligent attitude toward the safety of their members, guests, and children. A gun club allowing gun safety infractions, the consumption of alcoholic beverages, and, in my opinion, condoning the deliberate misconduct of their incompetent, unqualified, vindictive leagues manager, Dan Hunt, was inexcusable.

I am a retired, twenty-two-year veteran of the Dallas Police Department. I served as a state and federal certified Field Sobriety Testing and Drug Recognition Expert (DRE) instructor for approximately eighteen years. I have twenty-plus years of experience in NRA high-power rifle competitions. In my professional and competitive experience, mixing guns, alcohol, and children at a live-fire shooting facility is unwarranted, foolhardy, and downright dangerous.

The ECSC conducts numerous live-fire competitions, allowing substantial numbers of young people and inexperienced shooters to compete on their property through the Scholastic Clay Target Program (SCTP), 4H, DIVA WOW for women, and ECSC sponsored events.

After I attempted to warn ECSC elected leadership about the dangers of mixing guns, alcohol, and children, gun safety issues, and the inappropriate behavior with a loaded firearm by their leagues manager, Dan Hunt, I was maligned, falsely accused of cheating, and my paid membership rights to participate in club-sponsored events wrongly suspended.

Throughout the events described within this book, Duncanville narcotics detective and ECSC leagues manager Danny Garth Hunt and the ECSC Board of Directors demonstrated an inexcusable pattern of contempt for their Bylaws, Texas laws, a mediated, signed contract, and First Amendment Rights.

Introduction

This book details the malicious, vindictive, intentional misconduct of a Duncanville, Texas, Police Department narcotics detective and ECSC leagues manager Danny Garth Hunt.

This book details how seven individuals, in elected positions of authority, presided over by a highly educated Texas Doctor of Veterinary Medicine (DVM), the former council member and past mayor of Cedar Hill, Texas, ECSC Vice President Christopher Lyons Rose, took it upon themselves to wrongfully destroy the reputations of two innocent competitors, myself and Shawn George.

The arrogance of ECSC elected officers knew no bounds. The depths to which they stooped to discredit me and refuse me the opportunity to defend myself was appalling. I believe their actions were an attempt to keep me from speaking out about the unsafe gun infractions I observed at the Ellis County Sportsmans Club—a gun club mixing guns, alcohol, and children.

I will show how Dan Hunt and the ECSC Board of Directors reneged on a contract they signed, *Rule 11 and Settlement Agreement*.

I will show how Dan Hunt and the ECSC Board of Directors continued their false facts, false accusations, and defamation within two court filings, two hearings before the 443rd Ellis County District Court, and in *Appellees' Brief* filed with the Court of Appeals, Tenth District of Texas. None of Defendants' court filings were ever supported by any signed, notarized affidavits from ECSC leagues manager Dan Hunt or the ECSC Board of Directors, verifying their truthfulness.

Excerpts from the transcripts of two hearings before the 443rd Ellis County District Court will show how Defendants' attorneys reiterated Defendants' false, misleading statements and false accusations to, I believe, unduly influence the Court.

You will learn about the laissez-faire attitude within the Ellis County Sportsmans Club leadership and their advertised **Saftey** *and Education,* as misspelled for years on the ECSC website. I observed the social atmosphere at this gun club was far more important to ECSC leadership than the safety of the individuals using their facility.

I refused to follow their status quo. I refused to look the other way. I refused to ignore the inherent danger to ECSC members, their families, and guests from the mixing of guns, alcohol, and children. I believe the 2018 ECSC Board of Directors didn't want me rocking their happy-go-lucky boat. I became persona non grata.

The 2018 Board of Directors attempted to silence me by exploiting the misconduct and false accusations by Danny Garth Hunt, their arrogant, vindictive, incompetent, unqualified, hothead leagues manager, through their *Board Meeting-Emergency Meeting,* a meeting of which I had no prior knowledge, in reality, a kangaroo court.

At great personal expense, I stood my ground. This book details my fight to obtain the evidence to clear my name and expose the truth about the dangerous practice of mixing guns, alcohol, and children at the Desoto Gun Club d/b/a Ellis County Sportsmans Club, a not-for-profit corporation in the state of Texas.

The details, statements, and opinions within this book are based on my professional knowledge and experiences, training, expertise, observations, and documents I obtained, some only with the help of an expensive judicial proceeding.

The Stage Is Set

Chapter One

It all began on the evening of June 28, 2018, the final night of the Desoto Gun Club d/b/a Ellis County Sportsmans Club (ECSC) Spring trap league. While my lawsuit was never about two properly contested points in a poorly managed, bordering on unsafe, haphazardly overseen ECSC live-fire shooting competition, two incidents occurred that evening, setting the stage for what would follow.

The first incident happened before the trap league started, pointing a weapon toward the staging area where competitors were gathering. On numerous occasions, I observed this egregious gun safety infraction of covering others with their shotguns at the ECSC. I informed ECSC Treasurer Rusty Porter of the ongoing problem. Per Texas law, this is a criminal act. Mistakes with guns can lead to injury or death. How many people have been killed due to a belief the weapon was unloaded?

In this case, a highly specialized, across-the-course, competition target rifle was in the hands of an individual, Dan Hunt, for which there was no excuse. Danny Garth Hunt, a Duncanville narcotics detective, Texas license to carry (LTC) instructor, ECSC shoot management and leagues manager, was known to parents and children as Coach Dan.

Shawn had brought a highly specialized, twenty-plus-year-old NRA, across-the-course match rifle (competition target rifle) to the gun club to show to a fellow club member considering the purchase of something similar. Dan Hunt eventually joined them. Shawn explained the type of rifle it was, its expensive micrometer sights, and how it was developed to shoot 200, 300, and 600-yard NRA High Power Rifle competitions. The target rifle has a very distinctive, approximately 4" in diameter, red toymaker's sticker on the right side of the buttstock, which Hunt asked about. Shawn explained that when his friend, a gunsmith and one of the best competition rifle and pistol shooters in Texas, created these target rifles in the early 1990s, they were referred to as spaceguns. This design was a big step forward for across-the-course competitions. Hunt grasped the target rifle, astounded at how much it weighed. He then shouldered it, pointing it toward the staging area where competitors began assembling as his league was about to start, then placed his finger on the trigger.

Despite the fact the target rifle was unloaded with a yellow safety flag in the breech, Shawn immediately grabbed the fore-end of the target rifle, raised its muzzle to the sky, turned Dan Hunt in a safe direction away from the staging area, and told him to keep his finger off the trigger. All to the chagrin of ECSC shoot management and leagues manager Dan Hunt.

Pointing a firearm *at or in the direction of another* is a Class A misdemeanor as defined by the *Texas Penal Code: Deadly Conduct*.

Texas Penal Code

Sec. 22.05

Deadly Conduct

(a) A person commits an offense if he recklessly engages in conduct that places another in imminent danger of serious bodily injury.

(b) A person commits an offense if he knowingly discharges a firearm at or in the direction of:

(1) one or more individuals; or

(2) a habitation, building, or vehicle and is reckless as to whether the habitation, building, or vehicle is occupied.

(c) Recklessness and danger are presumed if the actor knowingly pointed a firearm at or in the direction of another whether or not the actor believed the firearm to be loaded.

(d) For purposes of this section, "building," "habitation," and "vehicle" have the meanings assigned those terms by Section 30.01.

(e) An offense under Subsection (a) is a Class A misdemeanor. An offense under Subsection (b) is a felony of the third degree.

The second incident occurred during the scoring of my team by Larry Degal, the official scorekeeper on the opposing team. Degal intentionally violated numerous ATA (Amateur Trapshooting Association) rules and procedures governing a trap competition. A detailed list of the ATA rules Degal intentionally violated is cited in a subsequent chapter. ATA rules, which, according to the ECSC Board of Directors, July 12, 2018, board meeting minutes, governed their trap leagues.

The official scorekeeper, Larry Degal, positioned himself approximately fifty (50) measured feet out of position. Degal was outside the trap field, behind and to the left of the first firing position. Per the ATA rules and procedures, the proper position for the official scorekeeper is three yards behind the five shooters on the firing line.

As my squad leader, Shawn asked official scorer Larry Degal to move to an appropriate position on the trap field for scoring. Official scorer Larry Degal refused. When Shawn asked him to take a proper scoring position a second time, official scorer Larry Degal arrogantly refused, stating, "I'll score from wherever I want." As squad leader, Shawn informed Larry Degal that any mistakes in scoring were on the scorekeeper and not the shooters.

When official scorer Larry Degal took a position completely off the trap field, Degal was accompanied by two other competitors from the opposing team, Barbara Parks and Susie Thompson. Throughout the match, Degal, Parks, and Thompson laughed and talked.

Their disruptive and unsportsmanlike conduct was another violation of ATA rules and procedures. No one is to talk to the official scorekeeper during the match. The official scorekeeper is responsible for watching the competitor break the shot and accurately record the score. The official scorekeeper is responsible for watching the competitors to ensure the safe handling of loaded shotguns on the firing line. This rule is an ATA safety precaution.

According to ATA rules and procedures, as the official scorekeeper, Larry Degal was responsible for calling the lost shots. There is no co-scoring. Instead, Degal's co-scorekeeper, Barbara Parks, screaming to make herself heard, called the lost shots while official scorer Larry Degal wrote the scores on the scoresheet in his lap. All the while, the three misbehaving competitors continued to talk and laugh.

After the first relay, I discovered my score was incorrect. When I walked off the firing line, I knew I had missed three targets for a score of twenty-two. The misbehaving official scorekeeper, Larry Degal, had recorded my score as twenty-one. An adult guest also scored the match and recorded a twenty-two for my score.

After the second relay, both my and Shawn's scores were wrong. Shawn simply pointed out his incorrect score to the official scorer, Larry Degal. Degal voluntarily corrected one target for Shawn.

I missed five targets for a score of twenty, though Degal scored nineteen, indicating I missed six targets. Again, I checked the guest's scorecard. My score was a twenty, not a nineteen, as recorded by the misbehaving scorekeeper, Larry Degal.

Fed up with the opposing team's unsportsmanlike, dangerous conduct and Degal's botched scoring, I immediately headed to the clubhouse to find shoot management, leagues manager Dan Hunt.

In every local, state, regional, provisional, and national competition in the U.S. and Canada in which I have competed, and in every competition rule book I have read, a competitor has a right to file a protest. I followed proper ATA rules and procedures when I filed my protest with shoot management, leagues manager Dan Hunt.

Dan Hunt, also the ECSC cook, was in the kitchen getting the food set up for the award banquet, an event held on the final night of the league. I explained the scoring violations by the misbehaving co-scorekeepers Larry Degal and Barbara Parks, resulting in two errors in my scores. I also informed Hunt that a guest had scored the match, and the scores did not correspond to what Larry Degal recorded. Shoot management, leagues manager Dan Hunt said to note the two errors in the margin of the scoresheet, and he would take care of it.

As shoot management for the trap league, leagues manager Dan Hunt was responsible for investigating the unsportsmanlike conduct of the misbehaving opposing team that resulted in the scoring errors, then rendering a decision based on ATA rules and procedures.

Shawn, my team's squad leader, made one final attempt to resolve the issue with Larry Degal. Larry Degal was seated inside the clubhouse. Shawn walked over to him, squatted down and politely asked if they could discuss the scoring errors. Degal said, "I don't want to talk to you, change the scores to whatever you want." Shawn stood up and walked away. The conversation took place in a minute or less.

As my squad leader, Shawn followed Hunt's instructions, noted the two errors in the margin of the scoresheet and left the scoresheet on a table along with the scoresheets from the other teams. Shawn never spoke to shoot management Dan Hunt regarding my valid ATA protest or Hunt's instructions. The club's security camera system would have recorded Shawn's actions. We then left the property, long before the awards ceremony took place.

Let me be very clear on one point. At no time did any team member or I change the official scores on the scoresheet as recorded by the misbehaving official scorekeeper, Larry Degal. I was willing to abide by shoot management, leagues manager Dan Hunt's decision. For a knowledgeable, qualified leagues manager, it was a simple protest of the disruptive, unsafe conduct of the opposing team and the errors by an out-of-position, intentionally misbehaving official scorekeeper.

Unfortunately, I failed to consider that I was dealing with an incompetent, unqualified leagues manager who didn't have a clue about ATA rules and procedures, as I had already observed in Dan

Hunt's management of the leagues. I also failed to consider how the consumption of alcoholic beverages that night could exacerbate the actions of the remaining competitors.

My first clue came in the form of an email Dan Hunt issued on June 29, 2018, the day after the conclusion of the trap league, regarding the suspension of the league scores. On par with Hunt's incompetency, he sent his trap league email to the skeet league competitors. Since I didn't shoot the skeet leagues, my email address was not on the list. I didn't know about Hunt's email until it was forwarded to me by a skeet shooter.

From: Ellis County Sportsmans Club Leagues <ecscleagues@gmail.com>
Date: Fri, Jun 29, 2018 at 8:47 AM
Subject: League results

I am suspending the week 8 results pending investigation. Some of the scoring for the final night is under dispute. The awards that have been issued will not be reduced regardless of the findings so no issues there. The award(s) in dispute are being held until a finding has been reached regarding the scoring and the final results.

Upon closure of the league, the results can no longer be used. As a result, I will have to input the league scores for 8 weeks to determine the impact of the findings once they are reached. I will do my best to reach a conclusion by Monday evening.

Thanks,

D

To say I was stunned would be an understatement. What dispute? I had not discussed the scoring issue with the other competitors, so I had no idea what Hunt was talking about. I had done nothing except file a protest according to ATA rules and procedures. There shouldn't have been any dispute if shoot management Dan Hunt had followed ATA rules for the proper scoring of a match. The only person Shawn spoke to about the scoring errors was the official scorekeeper, Larry Degal, whose misbehaving antics caused the problem. Shawn never talked to Dan Hunt about my valid ATA protest.

On Saturday, June 30, 2018, I contacted ECSC leagues manager Dan Hunt to find out if he needed additional information. I was attempting to help. As soon as I identified myself and why I was calling, Hunt shouted he had over "half the damn league" complaining about the scores and threatening not to shoot the league again if he allowed Shawn to shoot.

Forty individuals had shot the league. When we left the property, many other competitors had also left. As Hunt proclaimed, "over half the damn league" would be twenty-plus individuals complaining.

I had the call on speakerphone since Shawn was also present. Shawn asked for the names of the individuals who complained. When Dan Hunt said he'd give us the names, Shawn told him to wait until he could get a paper and pen. Hunt then backtracked, stating he couldn't remember who complained.

Shawn and my attempts to get a straight answer from Dan Hunt about what caused all the ruckus or how a valid protest had escalated into a full-blown production only increased Hunt's hostility.

Dan Hunt accused us of making his job harder because he had to refigure and re-enter the scores into the software program. At the time, I had no idea Hunt had ruled in my favor. Dan Hunt had changed Degal's official scores, giving me credit for my two contested points in the computer program. If Hunt, as shoot management, had competently rendered a decision according to ATA rules and stood by his decision, he wouldn't have had a problem. As events played out, shoot management Dan Hunt's incompetence caused the problem.

Hunt's response was typical of what I had observed of his conduct. On another occasion, Hunt complained about difficulties with the skeet shooters because some teams refused to shoot with other teams. Hunt was irritated because he said he had to juggle the squadding of the skeet teams to pacify the skeet league competitors.

The trap league scores weren't Dan Hunt's only complaint during the phone call. Hunt falsely accused Shawn of mistreating a falsely alleged "helpless" new shooter in the first week of the league.

You have to understand Shawn is five-ten and weighs approximately 185 pounds. The new shooter, a mountain of a man from the rough and tough oil business, Hunt falsely referred to as "helpless," was approximately six-foot-three, weighing around 275 pounds. What's wrong with this picture?

Dan Hunt wasn't present on field zero on opening night of the Spring trap league, where this event allegedly occurred. As I would later discover, the complaint likely came from Laura McGee, the competitor in charge of the opposing team for the match. After their first relay, I tried to correct the mishandling of their weapons by Laura McGee and some of her teammates, not the new guy. It was McGee who was pissed off, not Hunt's some six-foot-three, 275-pound, falsely alleged "helpless" new shooter on McGee's team.

In another angry outburst, Dan Hunt told Shawn he couldn't shoot any more of his (Dan Hunt's) leagues. I asked if I was included. Dan Hunt told us no, just Shawn. Fed up with Dan Hunt's false accusations, Shawn said goodbye to Hunt, ending the call to keep the conversation from further deteriorating.

When I discovered my team had won the overall championship for the league, it began to make sense. When Hunt changed my scores, giving me credit for my two contested targets, it pissed someone off. If my team hadn't won, no one would have given diddly about my scores.

It wasn't until some nine months later I learned Dan Hunt's accusation, "over half the damn league," was, in reality, six people. In my subsequent dealings with Dan Hunt, I discovered Hunt didn't hesitate to embellish when it served his purpose. For a law enforcement officer, this was a bad trait. I've often wondered how many people may have been wrongfully convicted because of exaggerations and outright false statements by this vindictive Duncanville narcotics detective—testilying, as it's known.

Director David McDaniel and Tommy Nations, two mid-level ATA registered shooters on the second-place team, had complained. McDaniel and Nations did not witness nor have first-hand knowledge of the events surrounding my legitimate ATA protest. The other four complainers were members of the misbehaving opposing team, Larry Degal, Director Sherrie Lewis, Susie Thompson, and Jeff Gregory. In my valid ATA protest filed with shoot management, leagues manager Dan Hunt, I included the disruptive misbehavior of Larry Degal, Barbara Parks, and Susie Thompson, resulting in the two errors in my scores.

As it turned out, my two contested points didn't affect the overall standings. It didn't make one iota of difference to my team's score whether I got credit for my two contested points or not. My team still won the league. On July 1, 2018, Dan Hunt issued another email.

Ellis County Sportsmans Club Leagues <ecscleagues@gmail.com>
Jul 1, 2018 at 3:35 PM

I recreated the league and reviewed the impact of two disputed targets by comparing the scores and the standings did not change regardless of the following ruling(s) by league management. The score sheet in question was reviewed by the original scorekeeper for accuracy. The scorekeeper reported that the two targets in question were correctly recorded as lost targets. The targets remain lost. The scorekeeper reported a target that was changed, by the scorekeeper, from a lost target to a hit target at the request of the shooter. The scorekeeper confirmed that the target was correctly recorded as a lost target but was changed to avoid confrontation. This target was scored lost and the results adjusted accordingly.

Thanks,

D

This was the total of shoot management, leagues manager Dan Hunt's so-called investigation for why Hunt reversed his initial ruling. All this alleged trained investigator did was take the word of the individual who caused the whole mess in the first place. Not once did

ECSC shoot management, leagues manager Dan Hunt refer to ATA rules and procedures for properly scoring a match. According to the ATA rules and procedures, official scorer Larry Degal intentionally failed to score the match by the rules. As a veteran police officer, I would ask, were Dan Hunt's police investigations as one-sided and slipshod as this?

Dan Hunt initially ruled in my favor, giving me credit for my two contested targets when he entered the league scores into myskeet.com to obtain the league's results. Hunt then changed my scores a second time. This time, Dan Hunt re-entered the unchanged scores Larry Degal had recorded on the scoresheet.

Within shoot management, leagues manager Dan Hunt's email, Hunt never informed league competitors I filed a valid ATA protest according to ATA rules and procedures. Hunt never informed league competitors my protest was based on the intentional, disruptive, and unsportsmanlike conduct of the misbehaving, out-of-position co-scorekeepers Larry Degal and Barbara Parks, along with the antics of Susie Thompson. Hunt never informed league competitors that he instructed me to note my two contested targets in the margin of the scoresheet or that I followed his instructions. Dan Hunt never informed the league competitors that he ruled in my favor, changing my scores when he entered them into myskeet.com. My scores, as recorded by Larry Degal, have not been changed on the scoresheet.

Instead, Dan Hunt made Shawn the culprit with Hunt's nasty reference to *avoid confrontation*. Was Larry Degal trying to excuse his misbehavior? Degal certainly wasn't concerned about avoiding a confrontation when he arrogantly refused to score from a proper position on the trap field, telling Shawn, "I'll score from wherever I want." Or, considering Dan Hunt's subsequent conduct and propensity for embellishment, was this *avoid confrontation* another of Dan Hunt's false statements? As events played out, I was never afforded an opportunity to question Larry Degal.

Disturbed by Hunt's email, along with Dan Hunt's abrasive outburst, false accusations, and throwing Shawn out of the league during the phone call, our best option was to take the issue before the Board of Directors. The concerns Shawn had earlier expressed to ECSC Treasurer Rusty Porter about Hunt's deliberate and continuous misconduct with a loaded firearm in front of parents and children had been intentionally ignored. Now, there was a second incident of Hunt's misconduct with a weapon. In addition, there were other gun safety infractions by members we observed and reported to Rusty Porter, which appeared to have been ignored. We felt it was time to bring these gun safety issues, including Dan Hunt's misconduct with firearms and the dangers of mixing guns, alcohol, and children before the Board.

After contacting Rusty Porter, he said to call Charlie Beard to get on the schedule. Upon contacting Beard, he agreed to my request to address the board at their July 2, 2018, monthly meeting. Beard advised we would be first on the agenda. Shawn contacted Rusty Porter again to ask Dan Hunt be summoned to the meeting.

When we arrived at the ECSC clubhouse, President Charles E. Beard, Waxahachie, Texas, Treasurer Russell Alvin (Rusty) Porter, Jr., Ovilla, Texas, Directors Sherrie A. Lewis, Dallas Safari Club Life Member, and DIVA WOW instructor, formerly of Cedar Hill, now of Gatesville, Texas, Jerry Jay Gage, ATA registered shooter of Ovilla, Texas, Raymond Tab Haley, III, ATA registered shooter, now of Daingerfield, Texas, and Don R. Henslee, ATA registered shooter, Waxahachie, Texas, had already arrived. ECSC leagues manager Danny Garth Hunt, Waxahachie, Texas, now of Tuscola, Texas, was absent.

We entered the conference room approximately fifteen minutes before the meeting without the target rifle. Shawn asked Charlie Beard for permission to bring the target rifle into the meeting as an exhibit in his presentation concerning Dan Hunt's misconduct. Shawn clearly explained to Beard and Rusty Porter, who was listening, the need for the presence of the target rifle.

Shawn planned to impress upon the Board of Directors the improper and unsafe handling of said target rifle by their unqualified, unknowledgeable leagues manager, along with Dan Hunt's other inappropriate handling of and continuous clown-like misconduct with a loaded shotgun in front of parents and children, and the gun safety issues within the trap league. Beard discussed Shawn's request with Rusty Porter and then the other board members. No board member objected, especially Sherrie Lewis.

Once given permission, Shawn left the room, obtained his highly evolved competition target rifle, and placed it on the conference room table, careful not to scratch the Formica tabletop or, more especially, damage the expensive micrometer sights on the target rifle. Shawn's competition target rifle, weighing approximately 14.6 pounds, was unloaded, the bolt was open, a bright yellow plastic safety flag was inserted into its empty chamber extending approximately eight inches into the breech end of the bore, and its safety was engaged.

There was no magazine nor ammunition in the room, nor even on the property. For all intents and purposes, the 14.6-pound competition target rifle was inert evidence against shoot management, leagues manager Dan Hunt. This all took place before the meeting ever began.

The long conference table seats several people on each side. A door at each end of the west wall leads to the hallway. Shawn and I sat on the east side of the room with the table between us and the open doors. Charlie Beard was seated at the south end of the table. I sat to Beard's immediate right. To my right was Shawn, then Sherrie Lewis. To the left of Beard, on the west side of the table, sat Jerry Jay Gage, Rusty Porter, Don Henslee, and Tab Haley.

When President Beard called the meeting to order, Dan Hunt had not arrived. We were first on the agenda. Shawn asked Beard to delay any discussion of the Dan Hunt issue, saying, "What I have to say, I will say to Dan's face." Beard agreed to table the discussion until Dan Hunt arrived, then had Rusty Porter continue with the business portion of the meeting.

Sometime after the official agenda of the meeting began, I saw Dan Hunt walk by the south door of the conference room. As time passed, and Hunt didn't enter the room or walk back past the door, I figured he was hiding in the hallway, listening. Once the business portion of the meeting closed, as if on cue, Hunt finally entered the room. Hunt sat against the south wall, behind and just left of Charlie Beard, facing the security camera at the room's north end.

As a police officer, I learned to read body language. When Dan Hunt finally entered the meeting room, he was incensed. Danny Garth Hunt, a Duncanville narcotics detective, never commented on or objected to the target rifle that lay inert on the table in front of him. Even someone as unknowledgeable of firearms as Dan Hunt had to know it was the same target rifle he mishandled five days earlier. The large, bold, **bright red** toy sticker was clearly visible on the buttstock. So was the **bright yellow** NRA chamber safety flag stuck in its breech. The bolt was open, and it obviously had no magazine in it. Dan Hunt had to know it was not an assault rifle because he had been educated on it five days earlier in Shawn's short tutorial to him. The only way this inert piece of evidence was going to hurt Danny Garth Hunt was if he dropped it on his toe.

I won't even get into the firearms prowess of Dallas Safari Club Life Member Sherrie Lewis except to say Sherrie Lewis would spread a rumor that Shawn brought an assault rifle to the meeting, slamming it down on the table to intimidate the board members. Dan Hunt would ultimately jump on the bandwagon and include a false accusation of assault rifle intimidation in his future filings to the 443rd Ellis County District Court and the Court of Appeals, Tenth District of Texas.

We were concerned about keeping any comments confidential after Dan Hunt's antagonistic outburst and false accusations during his phone call and his inept handling of my proper ATA protest. We wanted to ensure neither the club nor any individual's reputation would be damaged. We didn't want to create rancor within the membership. We wanted to ensure what was said in the meeting would not be spread throughout the membership. Everyone, including Dan Hunt and Sherrie Lewis, agreed to abide by a confidentiality agreement.

During this discussion, Shawn asked about the security camera system. In the business portion of the meeting, Treasurer Rusty Porter mentioned the security camera system in his report on the installation of the new front gate, stating the camera system operated on a thirty-day cycle. In response to Shawn's question, Porter motioned to the security camera in the corner of the room near the ceiling. Porter informed everyone the camera system did not record audio.

Shawn started by asking Dan Hunt to explain why he had banned him from the leagues. Dan Hunt angrily responded, "I don't have to tell you a damn thing."

Since Hunt bowed up, refusing to talk, I started with my short presentation. I addressed my concerns about Hunt's management of the trap leagues and what led to my filing an ATA protest, which included the infractions by the opposing team and Dan Hunt's instructions regarding the scoresheet.

Once I finished, Shawn began his presentation. When Shawn attempted to describe Hunt's misbehavior with firearms, President Beard stopped Shawn's presentation. Like Porter, Charlie Beard didn't want to hear it. Instead, Beard told us that we had to file a complaint at a future meeting if we wanted to talk about firearms safety and other issues. I promptly told Beard I would file a formal complaint at the August monthly board meeting to air our concerns.

When the subject of the Hunt phone call came up, that's when it turned ugly. After Dan Hunt denied statements he made during the June 30, 2018, phone call, Shawn had heard enough and called Dan Hunt a liar to his face.

Hunt exploded from his chair, lunged to the table's edge between Charlie Beard and Jerry Jay Gage, then threatened Shawn, stating, "Nobody calls me a liar and gets away with it."

Dan Hunt, a police officer who was likely armed, had just threatened Shawn. Shawn never reacted, stayed calmly seated, never made any aggressive moves, nor retaliated in any fashion.

The fact their leagues manager, Dan Hunt, had aggressively threatened Shawn didn't seem to bother the ECSC Board of Directors. Hunt eventually retreated to his seat behind and just left of Charlie Beard. Throughout this tense episode, Dan Hunt faced the security camera. Hunt's aggressive behavior toward Shawn, his threat to Shawn, and Shawn's lack of reaction were caught on tape.

Not satisfied with threatening Shawn, Dan Hunt falsely accused him of "browbeating his scorer," Larry Degal. To justify this false accusation, Hunt told the Board that Shawn browbeat a "helpless" competitor during the first week of the league, some eight weeks earlier. Once again, it was the same, approximately six-foot-three, 275-pound, falsely alleged, "helpless" individual Hunt falsely accused Shawn of mistreating during our June 30, 2018, phone call. Dan Hunt's falsely alleged mistreatment of a new competitor had now become "browbeating" of the competitor. Hunt tried to prove his false accusation about Shawn "browbeating" Degal with another Dan Hunt false accusation. Dan Hunt falsely described acts of an event he did not witness.

Shawn challenged Hunt, stating, "Here's the man's phone number. I triple dog dare you to call him on your cell speaker phone and let him tell the board what really happened."

After stuttering for a moment, ECSC leagues manager Dan Hunt refused to make the call. Even when Shawn challenged him a second time to call, Hunt still refused. Dan Hunt was left with his foot in his mouth. Unbelievably, Dan Hunt had not finished making a fool of himself.

In a final outburst, Dan Hunt loudly proclaimed, "If you (Shawn) want to shoot the trap league, you can run it yourself." Big mistake. ECSC leagues manager Danny Garth Hunt, a vindictive, out-of-control Duncanville cop, had just stuck his other foot in his mouth.

Shawn had decades of small arms training and around twenty-five years of competitive shooting experience in local, state, regional, provisional, and national competitions. He had shot in ten states, on approximately a dozen U.S. military bases, on two foreign military installations, in one province and two countries. Shawn had overseen mid-range (500, 600-yard) competitions, Palma (800, 900, 1000-yard) competitions, and short-range, 300-meter prone competitions for years.

Shawn created the course of fire and conducted the Precision Rifle Course (300, 500, 600 yards) at the request of Dallas SWAT for the Texas Tactical Police Officers Association (TTPOA) annual convention in Dallas. Furthermore, he created the course of fire and managed a Police Precision Rifle Course (200, 300, 500, 600 yards) attended by police precision marksmen from a five-state area, a course sponsored and sanctioned by the Fort Worth Police Department. Shawn had attended the U.S. Army range control course at Ft. McClellan, Alabama. Lastly, being a knowledgeable, experienced, safety-conscious match director and high-level competitor, Shawn had actually studied the ATA rules and Trap Line Training Manual.

Shawn would have been more than qualified to replace leagues manager Dan Hunt, who, in my opinion, didn't have a clue about ATA rules and procedures. I have no doubt Shawn could easily manage a 16-yard trap league, safely and competently, by the rules. Though alcohol consumption would have been forbidden at any live-fire competition Shawn managed. Furthermore, competitors' unsafe handling of weapons during the trap leagues would have been properly addressed. Dan Hunt's grandstanding, acting like a laughing buffoon while continuously hip-shooting a loaded shotgun in front of parents and children in a trap league, would never have been tolerated.

Shawn promptly accepted ECSC leagues manager Dan Hunt's offer to let him run the trap league. When Dan Hunt didn't respond, Shawn repeated his acceptance of Hunt's offer, clearly stating, "I accept your offer to let me run the trap league." Hunt never responded. Instead, Dan Hunt, infuriated, stormed from the room.

Dan Hunt wasn't the only one who became abusive during the meeting. Earlier, before Dan Hunt left, Director Jerry Jay Gage, in a protracted tirade, shouted at me I had no right to file a protest. Gage's arms waved in the air as he wildly gesticulated in anger. Gage ranted for several minutes before informing everyone in the room, as he referred to a volatile Dan Hunt, "This man is God. What he says is the law."

I listened but never responded. What could you say to an elected director of a gun club and registered ATA shooter who obviously had never read a rule book and believed his misbehaving leagues manager was the deity?

Worse, no ECSC board member spoke up to stop Dan Hunt's aggression or his threat toward Shawn, or the ugly, abusive, unwarranted tirade to which I was subjected by an out-of-control, wildly gesticulating ECSC Director.

Before ending the meeting, President Beard told Rusty Porter and Don Henslee to look into the matter. By this time, I was visibly upset over Jerry Jay Gage's unwarranted, abusive attack. President Beard told me, "Don't worry about it. We deal with this all the time."

****

So where did Dan Hunt get the false story he told the ECSC Board about Shawn browbeating this so-called "helpless" competitor in the first week of the 2018 Spring trap league?

At the time, I suspected it was Laura McGee. It wasn't until after I filed my lawsuit that my suspicions were confirmed when I received *Defendant Dan Hunt's Responses to Plaintiff's Request for Disclosure: Request 194.2(E): The name, address, telephone number of person's having knowledge of relevant facts, and a brief statement of each identified person's connection with the case.*

Dan Hunt listed fifteen names. Two were Shawn and me. Hunt listed himself. That left twelve. Of those twelve, ten were identified as ECSC board members on their nine-member board. None of whom were present on field zero on the opening night of the trap league. That left two. One of them was the intentionally misbehaving scorekeeper, Larry Degal, who wasn't present on field zero on opening night. Lastly, Hunt listed Laura McGee as a *Former member of Defendant Desoto Gun Club with knowledge relating to Plaintiff and Shawn George's behavior towards other competitors at Desoto Gun Club.* Of the fifteen listed names, Laura McGee, Shawn, and I were the only individuals on field zero on the league's opening night.

It should be noted, there was a significant omission from Hunt's answer. It was the name of Dan Hunt's approximately six-foot-three, 275-pound, falsely alleged, "helpless" individual Hunt falsely accused Shawn of browbeating on field zero on opening night. Surely if this nefarious event had truly occurred as Dan Hunt described, then why didn't Hunt include this individual as a person *having knowledge of relevant facts, and a brief statement of each identified person's connection with the case?*

So, who is Laura McGee? What might Laura McGee have against Shawn and me, and what was her role in all of this?

On the opening night of the 2018 Spring trap league, Laura McGee was a member of the opposing team, Pink Alligators. That night, Laura McGee shot a combined score of 27 clay birds hit out of 50, averaging 54%. Laura McGee's average for the eight-week league was 51% or 204 clay birds out of 400 possible.

While scoring for the Pink Alligators, and per the ATA rules and procedures governing the scoring of a trap league, Shawn stood behind the firing line in a proper scoring position, clearly and distinctly calling the lost birds (missed targets). During Shawn's scoring duties, Laura

McGee became irritated from hearing "lost" called so often. She was visibly upset and demanded Shawn stop calling lost birds. For the night, Pink Alligators hit 143 of 250 birds for an average of 57%. Removing their best shooter, Dan Hunt's near six-foot-three, some 275-pound, falsely alleged browbeaten, "helpless" new guy and his 42 birds hit, Pink Alligators averaged just over 50% clay birds hit.

After firing ceased, an irritated Laura McGee, while picking up her hulls, constantly ran her mouth with her Wireless Canterbury Voice Release (CVR) still turned on. Laura McGee launched clay bird, after clay bird, after clay bird. In my opinion, a pissed-off Laura McGee with her head down and her heinie in the air may have broken more clay birds running her mouth than with fifty rounds of ammo and her shotgun.

During her relay, Laura McGee and some of her regular teammates danced around on the firing line doing the ECSC Two-Step described in a subsequent chapter, covering others with their shotguns. After the first relay, I told McGee that she and some of her teammates needed to be careful about where they were waving their shotguns. Laura McGee was already pissed off at Shawn for properly scoring the match. Now she was pissed off at me. Laura McGee told me to mind my own business and stomped off.

Learning nothing, Laura McGee and some of her teammates did it again during their second relay, covering others with their shotguns.

After the match, I attempted to locate Dan Hunt to inform him what had occurred. Shoot management, leagues manager Dan Hunt wasn't to be found. Wyatt Hunt, Dan Hunt's son, was a member of my team. I asked Wyatt to let his dad know what happened and to please send out an email telling competitors not to point their shotguns toward other competitors. Dan Hunt sent out an email and never mentioned any of the rules of gun safety. Instead, Dan Hunt focused on placating shooters, making them welcome. The social environment at the ECSC was far more important to shoot management Dan Hunt than correcting the dangerous misbehavior of competitors with weapons.

In my opinion, Laura McGee was representative of the gun safety issues within the trap leagues and the apathetic attitude of shoot management, leagues manager Dan Hunt. From what I observed, Laura McGee never demonstrated a knowledge of the rules under which she was competing, the proper handling of a shotgun or shooting range etiquette. Like many others at the ECSC, Laura McGee appeared to be trained through the ECSC osmosis method, the unknowledgeable leading the unknowledgeable. This was the Ellis County Sportsmans Club, in my opinion, the Wild West of the clay shooting sports.

As for Hunt's false accusation of browbeating a competitor during the opening night of the trap leagues, Shawn and I had each fired two practice rounds before the first match. Our once-fired AA hulls were in a small plastic container, saved to be reloaded later. On the side of the small, approximately three-gallon container was written, HULLS A.D./S.G. While we waited for the match to begin, we were sitting on the tailgate of our pickup parked at the edge of the staging area where other competitors milled around. Our gear, container of once-fired AA hulls, and guns were over by the trap field.

A large fellow, approximately six-foot-three, a nearly 275-pound mountain of a man, walked up. With an apologetic look, he informed us, "I just threw your hulls away." He apologized, saying he would dig our hulls out of the trash. Shawn asked why he threw them away. The new guy said he thought the hulls were trash and was trying to help by cleaning up the area.

Hull diving in the ECSC trash barrels, a money-saving activity used by some reloaders, was unlike at other gun clubs. At the ECSC, anything in the trash barrels was subject to beer cans and spilled beer. Shawn told the man, a man he'd never seen before, not to worry about it. No one was browbeaten or mistreated. There was no heated argument.

We were still sitting on our tailgate when the man returned with two or three new boxes of AA unfired shells. The man asked Shawn to accept them as restitution for the hulls he mistakenly had thrown away.

Shawn thanked the man, telling him he didn't want his shotgun shells. Shawn told him the hulls weren't worth much anyway.

From this non-event two months earlier, Dan Hunt fabricated his accusation that Shawn browbeat a "helpless" new shooter. Hunt's falsely alleged "helpless" new shooter, approximately six-foot-three, some 275 pounds, had been browbeaten by a five-foot-ten, 185-pound man sitting on the tailgate of his pickup truck. What's wrong with Hunt's fabrication? Like Hunt's accusation that Shawn browbeat Larry Degal, it never happened.

On the first night, Wyatt Hunt, Dan Hunt's son, was late getting to the club. As I recall, Wyatt Hunt said he was being fitted for a prom tux. The approximately six-foot-three, some 275-pound, Hunt's falsely alleged browbeaten, "helpless" new guy, the best shooter by far on the Pink Alligators, asked Shawn, our squad leader, if he could shoot on our team since Wyatt hadn't arrived. Shawn told him we would wait for Wyatt.

A point to consider. Why would Hunt's falsely alleged mistreated, "helpless" new shooter want to shoot on Shawn's team if he had been "browbeaten," as Hunt claimed? It was just another false accusation by Dan Hunt in what would become a long list of false accusations.

Dan Hunt made a full-blown production out of this non-event before the Board. Yet, some seven months later, in his court-ordered response, Dan Hunt did not list the name of his falsely alleged, "browbeaten," "helpless" new shooter as a witness. This falsely alleged browbeating of Hunt's falsely alleged "helpless" new guy, just like with the misbehaving scorekeeper Larry Degal, never happened.

By the way, the new guy averaged a very commendable 75% clay birds hit during the league. Laura McGee averaged 51%. I would point out Hunt's falsely alleged "helpless" new guy wasn't covering anyone with the muzzle of his shotgun. He should have been the squad leader, not Laura McGee, who only showed her ignorance of the rules and shooting etiquette with her disruptive, dangerous, wasteful behavior. What can I say? It's the Ellis County Sportsmans Club.

****

During the July 2, 2018, board meeting, Dan Hunt threatened Shawn saying, "Nobody calls me a liar and gets away with it." Later that night, I was on my computer and received an alert of an incoming email with a lengthy list of recipients. I read it in disbelief.

From: Ellis County Sportsmans Club Leagues <ecscleagues@gmail.com>
Sent: Monday, July 2, 2018, 11:26:07 PM CDT
Subject: Immediate resignation

On 7/2/18 I responded to a short notice request to speak before the ECSC board regarding grievances brought forth by Shawn George and Anita Dickason as a result of alleged conduct during the 2018 Spring trap league. These grievances stemmed from my volunteer service as the manager of the skeet and trap leagues at ECSC. During this board meeting I was directly accused by Shawn George of being a "liar" and to endangering STCP, 4H, and club shooters. The dispute was directed and intended solely as a character assault. In addition, Shawn George repeatedly invoked the name of my son as an involved party. The basis of these accusations are wholly and completely unfounded. However, I have no reason that I can determine, that would lead me to withstand such ridiculous abuse at the hands of such individuals.

I have attempted to instill a high level of quality enjoyment with accountability for all of those participating in the leagues that I have directed. That has been my main focus and direction while performing this volunteer function. I can no longer justify continued volunteer service, to my family or myself, while enduring ridicule, slanderous allegations, and outright misconduct allegations through no fault of my own.

I have participated in the last few leagues simply to fill teams or to assist other shooters who were new to the sport or who needed guidance. This has been met with biased attacks on my own credibility and has placed my family in a position of discomfort.

This sport allowed me an opportunity to relax and to enjoy good company after intense and severe exposures at work. Since that is no longer the case, I feel no need to continue with the leagues. I hereby resign any responsibilities or commitments related to the ECSC leagues that I have previously committed to. This includes any past, present, or future events. I cannot justify participation in these events to the detriment of my well being or the well being of my family. Any monies or data possessed by me will be transferred to the board as soon as possible. I apologize for any discomfort or inconvenience.

Having said that, any and all false allegations or slanderous events will be met with legal action.

Thank you and shoot well,

Dan Hunt

Following Dan Hunt's July 2, 2018, near midnight, adamant, no bones about it, I quit, I'm done, kaput, you can take it to the bank, I'm resigning from everything, … *past, present, or future events,* … to nearly one hundred club members, guests, and even children—on Thursday, August 16, 2018, at 11:55 A.M. CDT, less than two months later, Danny Garth Hunt, as leagues manager, sent out the very next ECSC trap league match bulletin to ninety-four openly listed recipients.

In the famous words of a movie character:

"HELLO BOYS! I'M BAAAACK!"

Cry Me A River!

Chapter Two

On July 2, 2018, we were at the ECSC monthly board meeting to discuss Dan Hunt's unwarranted actions against Shawn, who had done nothing to justify Hunt throwing him out of the league, as well as Hunt's misconduct before and during his trap leagues, and other issues we believed could affect the safety of the membership, guests, and children using the ECSC facility. Before making our presentations, Shawn required everyone in the meeting to consent to a confidentiality agreement, to which everyone agreed, including Dan Hunt.

Approximately three hours following the meeting, Duncanville narcotics detective and ECSC leagues manager Dan Hunt sent a libelous, malicious email, *Immediate resignation*, to nearly one hundred unsuspecting club members, guests, and even children, violating the confidentiality agreement Dan Hunt had agreed to. Within his libelous email, Dan Hunt declared to club members, guests, and even children that Shawn had called him a liar.

Within this book, Danny Garth Hunt's own words and conduct speak to his character and misconduct. After reading the facts, others can decide whether Danny Garth Hunt is what he told nearly one hundred people he was called. Mind you, this was a statement made directly to his face during a meeting in which Danny Garth Hunt agreed to keep confidential.

In Dan Hunt's near-midnight email, he maliciously attacked our reputations. Dan Hunt told nearly one hundred unsuspecting club members, guests, and children that Shawn and I abused him and harmed his family. I was appalled by such a vicious, cowardly act. I knew Dan Hunt's false accusations would extend far and wide beyond the nearly one hundred recipients who received his libelous email.

Worse still, in his official capacity as leagues manager, Dan Hunt used the club's official email address and list of members, guests, and even children, ensuring people would open and read his malicious, libelous email. If Dan Hunt had sent a similar defamatory email using an official Duncanville Police Department email address, he most likely would have been officially reprimanded, suspended, or fired.

Dan Hunt's contemptible behavior was unbelievable. Why would a supposed rational law enforcement officer send such a malicious email? For that matter, why would anyone of sound mind send a vicious, libelous email to nearly one hundred unsuspecting men, women, and even children nearing midnight?

Would any parent want their child receiving such a vicious diatribe from a Duncanville cop, possibly their own child's shooting coach, at nearly midnight? How could anyone construe this behavior as the act of a rational individual? How could a law enforcement officer consider this libelous act as appropriate behavior? Perhaps for Duncanville narcotics detective Danny Garth Hunt, it was normal.

Dan Hunt's *Immediate resignation* email was what I perceived as a dangerous pattern in Duncanville narcotics detective and ECSC leagues manager Dan Hunt's conduct and words. A pattern, I believe, displayed Hunt's mental instability, which was a genuine concern since Dan Hunt was an armed police officer.

After Shawn exposed Hunt's false accusations of browbeating during the board meeting, Dan Hunt attempted to make himself a victim. Hunt had gone from falsely accusing Shawn of browbeating Larry Degal and another competitor, to now, Shawn abusing Dan Hunt. Plus, Hunt added me to his hit list. Little did I know Hunt's malicious, libelous attack with his vicious email was only the beginning.

Dan Hunt's contemptible diatribe, a compilation of vindictive, false accusations, grew out of a meeting a few hours earlier in which Dan Hunt consented to a confidentiality agreement. If anyone should understand the importance of "confidentiality," it is a police officer. Yet, Danny Garth Hunt, a vindictive Duncanville cop and ECSC leagues manager, had just accomplished what Shawn and I attempted to avoid, creating rancor within the membership.

What a cowardly act. Dan Hunt didn't have the backbone to confront us face to face. Instead, Hunt lashed out, hiding behind his position as ECSC leagues manager to do his dirty work and stir up trouble.

At the start of the July 2nd meeting, Dan Hunt wasn't present. Upon being asked by President Beard to make his presentation, Shawn responded, "What I have to say, I will say to Dan's face." We didn't go behind Dan Hunt's back, talking to club members about Hunt's unwarranted behavior or gun safety concerns we had observed. We didn't send out malicious emails attacking Hunt. Instead, we took the issue to the Board of Directors, which we believed was the proper procedure, and specifically requested Dan Hunt be present.

We were giving Dan Hunt the courtesy and opportunity to discuss the issues we planned to raise. We were not there to attack anyone. Yet, ECSC leagues manager Dan Hunt turned the meeting into an ongoing confrontation with his false accusations, false exaggerations, and a threat. Hunt's vindictiveness didn't stop there.

Dan Hunt was enraged when he left the meeting. Less than three hours after the meeting ended, just before midnight, at 11:26 p.m., in his official capacity as ECSC leagues manager, Dan Hunt launched his vicious, cowardly attack against us, sending his *Immediate resignation,* what I view as Hunt's whining pity email.

It should be noted that up to this point, Duncanville narcotics detective and ECSC leagues manager Dan Hunt's vindictiveness had focused on Shawn. Hunt didn't like Shawn correcting him when Hunt pointed a target rifle toward the staging area, where trap league competitors were gathering. During the meeting, Shawn made a fool of Dan Hunt twice in front of the board.

During my phone call to Dan Hunt on June 30, 2018, in one of his angry outbursts, Hunt kicked Shawn out of the league. I asked if I was included. Hunt said no, just Shawn. In the meeting, there had been no confrontation between Dan Hunt and me. In fact, Dan Hunt ignored me and what I told the Board. Hunt never once accused me of any wrongdoing. Instead, Dan Hunt focused on Shawn with his false accusations, just as Hunt had focused on Shawn in our phone call and July 1, 2018, email. It was all about Shawn, not me.

However, Hunt now included me in his malicious, false, defamatory accusations. I was accused of abusing this mistreated Duncanville PD narcotics detective and ECSC leagues manager, causing harm to his family.

I have zero tolerance for a cop who lies, embellishes, or has a short fuse. To me, Dan Hunt hit all the marks. If this was how Duncanville narcotics detective Danny Garth Hunt conducted his personal life, what was he doing in his dealings with the public, his arrest reports, offense reports, and testimony on a witness stand? To me, a scary thought.

Duncanville narcotics detective and ECSC leagues manager Dan Hunt's appalling misconduct would reach far beyond his whining pity email, *Immediate resignation*. My lawsuit would result from Dan Hunt's libelous, false accusations and vindictiveness.

Dan Hunt would continue making malicious, false accusations for nearly five years. Dan Hunt did so to the Board of Directors. Dan Hunt did so in his filings with the 443rd Ellis County District Court. In two hearings, Dan Hunt's attorney regurgitated Hunt's malicious, false accusations before the Court. Dan Hunt would ultimately spread his malicious, false accusations in his filing to the Court of Appeals, Tenth District of Texas. Yes, Duncanville narcotics detective and ECSC leagues manager Danny Garth Hunt would fabricate statements to the Court of Appeals, Tenth District of Texas.

Dan Hunt's *Immediate resignation,* his whining pity email, was riddled with malicious, false statements and accusations, including his resignation. At thirty-four minutes preceding midnight on July 2, 2018, Dan Hunt wrote; *I hereby resign any responsibilities or commitments related to the ECSC leagues that I have previously committed to. This includes any past, present, or future events. I cannot justify participation in these events to the detriment of my well being or the well being of my family.* The nearly one hundred individuals who received Hunt's resignation notification included several board members.

At the time, a skeet league was underway in which Dan Hunt was leagues manager and a participant. On the day following his vicious, whining pity email, less than twenty hours after Hunt proclaimed he was resigning from *any past, present, or future events,* Dan Hunt was back at the ECSC, shooting in the skeet league and several weeks later was running the next trap league. In my opinion, Dan Hunt never intended to resign.

Dan Hunt's whining pity email was what I viewed as nothing more than grandstanding, a proclamation to promote dissension and ill will toward Shawn and me while garnering undeserved sympathy for himself. Hunt couldn't do that unless he went back to the ECSC. I believe Hunt's participation in the skeet league the following evening gave Hunt an opportunity to further spread his rancor and malicious, false, slanderous accusations. Dan Hunt's participation allowed him to suck up the pity I think he desperately craved. I believe Dan Hunt wanted to be begged to return. Someone did, considering Hunt was back in charge of the next trap league. It was likely the individual who ran the club, Treasurer Rusty Porter. If I had to characterize Porter's influence and power, I would describe Porter as His Excellency, the Grand Poobah of the ECSC.

Had Duncanville narcotics detective and ECSC leagues manager

Dan Hunt truly wanted to quit, all it would have taken was an email or a phone call to a board member. It was unnecessary to whine at thirty-four minutes before midnight to nearly one hundred unsuspecting fellow club members, guests, and children. Remember, during the meeting a few hours earlier, Dan Hunt had already resigned when Shawn twice accepted Hunt's offer to let Shawn run the trap leagues. There wasn't a valid reason for Hunt to quit a second time with a malicious, defamatory, whining pity email unless it was for revenge and pity. Hours earlier, during the board meeting, Hunt had threatened Shawn. "Nobody calls me a liar and gets away with it."

As Dan Hunt's whining pity email, *Immediate resignation,* is lengthy, I've separated it into sections, starting with the first paragraph. As a reminder, the basis for Hunt's vicious email was a meeting a few hours earlier that evening. A meeting during which Hunt agreed to a confidentiality agreement.

Excerpt: Dan Hunt's *Immediate resignation,*

On 7/2/18 I responded to a short notice request to speak before the ECSC board regarding grievances brought forth by Shawn George and Anita Dickason as a result of alleged conduct during the 2018 Spring trap league. These grievances stemmed from my volunteer service as the manager of the skeet and trap leagues at ECSC.

Dan Hunt's *alleged conduct,* what he viewed as *grievances,* were issues grounded in fact. As ECSC leagues manager, Dan Hunt was responsible for the proper management and safe operation of the trap leagues involving up to forty individuals, including children, all armed with loaded shotguns. Hunt was accountable. He was the person in charge, and if a participant were killed or injured, Dan Hunt would have to account for why it happened.

Sound gun safety procedures, policies, and education are paramount in reducing the liabilities of a gun club and ensuring the safety and well-being of all individuals using the club's facilities. It starts with the elected officers' administration of club activities, then their appointing a mentally stable, knowledgeable, qualified leagues manager.

Unfortunately, an irresponsible attitude existed within ECSC leadership and leagues manager Dan Hunt's administration of the trap leagues. "We're just volunteers" was a phrase I repeatedly heard, even in subsequent court documents. As if being a volunteer negated the responsibility and accountability to ensure the safety and well-being of club members, family members, guests, and the many children using the facility. Whether an individual was paid or a volunteer was a moot point. It's the individual's actions that are relevant. In this case, Dan Hunt's administration and behavior in his trap leagues.

This wasn't soccer night at the local schoolyard. No one was kicking a ball around. Loaded guns were involved, and live fire competitions were held. Mistakes with guns can lead to injury or death. ECSC leagues manager Dan Hunt was responsible and accountable for his behavior along with the behavior of the many armed participants in his trap leagues. Whether Hunt was a volunteer or a paid employee didn't change his accountability and responsibility. The ECSC Board allowed Dan Hunt to manage club-sponsored live-fire trap leagues for which people paid money, and ECSC profited. Yet, Dan Hunt attempted to disavow his responsibility and accountability as the ECSC leagues manager just because he was a volunteer.

Excerpt: Dan Hunt's *Immediate resignation,*

During this board meeting I was directly accused by Shawn George of being a "Liar" and to endangering STCP, 4H, and club shooters. The dispute was directed and intended solely as a character assault.

It's not the *STCP*. Coach Dan couldn't even get that right. It is SCTP, Scholastic Clay Target Program.

No character assault on Dan Hunt was planned or intended on the evening of July 2, 2018. It was quite the opposite. Shawn told the Board of Directors and Dan Hunt, "I want to thank Dan for his efforts in running the leagues. I've told him in person before, and I meant it. It's a thankless job most times. That's why I've mowed the trap fields, pavilion and around the clubhouse on non-mowing weeks and tried to load the trap houses afterward when time permitted on Thursdays. Anything to help out and make Dan's job easier."

Our going before the Board wasn't about Dan Hunt's character. It was about Dan Hunt throwing Shawn out of the league, Hunt's administration of the trap leagues, and gun safety issues. It was about Dan Hunt's actions, not his character. It wasn't until Dan Hunt denied statements he'd made during the phone call on Saturday, June 30, 2018, that Shawn called Dan Hunt a liar to his face. It should also be noted that Dan Hunt never actually denied he lied. Hunt's words and documents detailed in this book demonstrate Hunt didn't hesitate to fabricate or embellish when it served his purpose.

While we didn't raise the issue of Dan Hunt's character, Hunt did in his whining pity email. What did it say about Hunt's character, when questioned about his actions, Hunt responded with arrogance, hostility, false accusations, and threats. How could Hunt say his character wasn't questionable when Hunt, an off-duty law enforcement officer, verbally and aggressively threatened an elderly competitor?

How could Hunt say his character wasn't questionable when he couldn't control his temper in a small meeting room with eight other people?

How could Dan Hunt defend his character when he blatantly violated a confidentiality agreement by launching a cowardly, malicious, vicious attack with his libelous, whining pity email, *Immediate resignation* at thirty-four minutes before midnight? How could Dan Hunt defend his character when his false, defamatory accusations destroyed the reputation and credibility of two individuals who did him no harm?

How could Dan Hunt defend his character when he wrongly used his son and family to justify his false accusations? Not only were we accused of abusing this vindictive Duncanville narcotics detective, but also his family. Dan Hunt's whining pity email was cowardly, vicious, inexcusable, and unwarranted. In my opinion, what it said about Dan Hunt's character and mental makeup was extremely disturbing for an individual who was a sworn, armed law enforcement officer in the Duncanville Police Department.

I observed that Dan Hunt had a short fuse, and nowhere was it more apparent than during the July 2, 2018, ECSC board meeting. Judging by Dan Hunt's body language when entering the conference room, he was angry. When Shawn asked Hunt why he kicked him out of the league, Hunt arrogantly proclaimed, "I don't have to tell you a damn thing." Throughout the meeting, Hunt was confrontational and belligerent. At one point, unable to control his temper, Dan Hunt exploded from his chair, lunging toward the table while threatening Shawn, stating, "Nobody calls me a liar and gets away with it."

In my professional opinion, Dan Hunt's behavior was unwarranted and dangerous. It's one thing to indulge in an angry verbal outburst. When a police officer, most likely armed, explodes from his chair, lunging toward another person while verbally threatening the individual, it ramps the severity of the threat to a new level. Hunt eventually stormed from the conference room after repeatedly making a fool of himself.

From my observations, Dan Hunt is a hothead, unable to control his temper, and some three hours later, I believe Hunt was still out of control. Dan Hunt lashed out with his cowardly attack, hiding behind his malicious, defamatory, whining email. Dan Hunt wanted revenge and didn't care who he used to get it, including his family and nearly one hundred unsuspecting men, women, and children.

I believe Hunt's unstable behavior, during and after the meeting, certainly raised a question about his character. It also raised a question about how Dan Hunt reacted in performing his duties as a police officer. Did Dan Hunt lash out in anger when challenged? Had Dan Hunt covered up inappropriate or abusive actions by manipulating his police reports in the past with false statements and exaggerations, just as he did in his whining pity email? As a veteran police officer, it was a disturbing thought and, in my professional opinion, a valid question.

Excerpt: Dan Hunt's *Immediate resignation,*

In addition, Shawn George repeatedly invoked the name of my son as an involved party.

I never understood what Dan Hunt meant by *an involved party. An involved party* to what? Let's get something clear. Shawn never said a derogatory word about Wyatt Hunt.

Let's look at the truth. What did Shawn say? Shawn told the Board that on the first evening of the trap league, Wyatt was late getting to the club. As squad leader, Shawn was asked by a new shooter on the opposing team if he could also shoot on our team since Wyatt had not arrived. Shawn told the new shooter he would wait for Wyatt. This was the falsely alleged "helpless" new shooter Dan Hunt falsely accused Shawn of browbeating. That was all Shawn said about Wyatt Hunt.

There was no end to what this vindictive Duncanville cop and leagues manager would make up. Dan Hunt certainly made it sound ominous when he referred to his son. It was another fabrication by Dan Hunt of what transpired in the meeting. The fact Hunt added his son to justify his malicious, false statements was inexcusable. It demonstrated the depths to which Dan Hunt stooped to obtain club members' and guests' sympathy and support. I found a father's use of his teenage son a defining example of Danny Garth Hunt's character.

Excerpt: Dan Hunt's *Immediate resignation,*

The basis of these accusations are wholly and completely unfounded. However, I have no reason that I can determine, that would lead me to withstand such ridiculous abuse at the hands of such individuals.

The truth was, Dan Hunt did the accusing. Dan Hunt made false statements during the meeting and got caught. We didn't abuse anyone. We didn't explode out of our chairs, lunge toward the table, raise our voices, or verbally threaten Dan Hunt. No, that was Dan Hunt doing the threatening. Not once did Shawn nor I verbally abuse Dan Hunt. No, that was Dan Hunt with his false accusations of browbeating. No one went after Dan Hunt with a wildly gesticulating, abusive tirade. No, that was Director Jerry Jay Gage shouting at me. In actuality, the abuse and false accusations came from Duncanville narcotics detective and ECSC leagues manager Dan Hunt and ECSC Director Jerry Jay Gage.

I didn't leave the meeting and send an email about Director Jerry Jay Gage's abusive, wildly gesticulating, verbal attack to which I was subjected. Shawn didn't send an email concerning Hunt's aggressive threat and false allegations during the meeting. No, this was all about Dan Hunt and his vindictiveness. It was about a Duncanville narcotics detective and ECSC leagues manager Dan Hunt, airing his malicious, libelous comments to the club membership, guests and even children. It was about Dan Hunt making good his antagonistic threat. "Nobody calls me a liar and gets away with it."

Excerpt: Dan Hunt's *Immediate resignation,*

I have attempted to instill a high level of quality enjoyment with accountability for all of those participating in the leagues that I have directed. That has been my main focus and direction while performing this volunteer function. I can no longer justify continued volunteer service, to my family or myself, while enduring ridicule, slanderous allegations, and outright misconduct allegations through no fault of my own.

Note Hunt's words, *through no fault of my own.* Let's look at the facts.

- ✓ Shawn didn't cause Dan Hunt's mishandling of the target rifle. Dan Hunt did.
- ✓ We didn't make Dan Hunt continuously act like a buffoon firing from the hip with a loaded shotgun in a trap match. Dan Hunt did.
- ✓ We didn't ignore the gun safety infractions in Dan Hunt's trap leagues. Dan Hunt did.

- ✓ We weren't responsible for Dan Hunt not being able to man-up after his original ruling on my valid ATA protest. That was Dan Hunt.
- ✓ We didn't make false accusations during the meeting. Dan Hunt did.
- ✓ We followed the ATA rules. Dan Hunt didn't.
- ✓ We didn't threaten anyone. Dan Hunt did.
- ✓ We didn't violate a confidentiality agreement. Dan Hunt did.
- ✓ We didn't send out a whining pity email to nearly one hundred unsuspecting men, women, and children. Dan Hunt did.
- ✓ We didn't tell nearly one hundred people that Dan Hunt was called a liar in the meeting. Dan Hunt did.
- ✓ We had no contact with Danny Garth Hunt's family after the meeting. Dan Hunt did.

So, whose fault was it, if not Dan Hunt's?

In my extensive experience in shooting competitions, I never experienced the lack of rules, supervision, sportsmanship, and fair play that I found during the trap leagues managed by ECSC leagues manager Dan Hunt. There was no accountability for the participants, or especially for shoot management Dan Hunt's clown-like, buffoonish behavior with a loaded weapon in front of parents and children. In twenty-plus years of NRA competitions, I never saw anyone managing a shooting competition misbehave with a loaded gun, as did Dan Hunt.

What's not in Hunt's whining pity email is any concern for the safety of his participants. Instead, Hunt referred to *quality enjoyment,* the social atmosphere. From what I observed, when it came to safety, Hunt was oblivious. To me, the lack of gun safety, rules, and accountability was quite evident. Hunt's reaction to my concern about McGee and some of her team members haphazardly waving their shotguns resulted in Hunt's email, where he stressed the importance of making shooters welcome. Yet, as usual, Hunt never mentioned safety with firearms.

Once again, there is the word *volunteer.* I question whether Dan Hunt ever recognized he was responsible and accountable for his *volunteer services.* Hunt would be held liable. Dan Hunt oversaw a live-fire shooting competition with up to forty armed participants, some with little to no experience, no guidance or supervision. Dan Hunt was the individual that ECSC leadership placed in charge of a live-fire shooting competition.

Shoot management Dan Hunt never held Larry Degal, Barbara Parks, or Susie Thompson accountable for their disruptive, dangerous behavior by ignoring ATA rules and procedures for the safe, proper scoring of a match. In my observations, Hunt's so-called investigation was as incompetent as his administration of the trap league, which raised another concern about Dan Hunt's investigative abilities as a police officer. Was this how Dan Hunt handled a police investigation?

In actuality, what Dan Hunt described was his own misconduct during the meeting. Dan Hunt threatened Shawn. Dan Hunt falsely accused Shawn of numerous bad acts. Shawn then dared Hunt to back up his false statements and phone the fellow club member. Hunt refused to make the call even after Shawn gave him the man's phone number. All Hunt had to do was put his "helpless" new shooter on his speakerphone. Hunt refused.

Excerpt: Dan Hunt's *Immediate resignation,*

I have participated in the last few leagues simply to fill teams or to assist other shooters who were new to the sport or who needed guidance.

What a self-serving statement. I never viewed Dan Hunt helping anyone. In reality, Hunt's actions were quite the opposite. The problem with new or novice shooters was ongoing. As ECSC leagues manager, I never observed Dan Hunt take the initiative to address gun safety issues, ATA rules and procedures, safety briefings, or range etiquette.

According to Treasurer Rusty Porter, the ECSC did not require league managers, such as Dan Hunt, to be qualified. That was their problem. In my professional opinion, the ECSC Board of Directors allowed an unqualified, questionably unstable individual to oversee live-fire shooting competitions as their designated leagues manager.

Dan Hunt's concept of managing a live-fire competition with some forty-armed individuals was to set out the scoresheets and disable the debit card readers. Upon conclusion of the match, Hunt entered the scores into a software program. As the ECSC cook, Hunt served a meal on the final night of his league and handed out awards.

After years of participation in NRA competitions managed by qualified individuals, it appeared to me that Hunt ran his trap leagues by the seat of his britches, and sometimes, his britches weren't even on the property. As shoot management, the individual in charge of up to forty armed competitors, Hunt would leave once his league started. Imagine for a moment what would have happened had a competitor or child been shot or killed during Hunt's league. As the ECSC representative in charge of the event, Dan Hunt would have to account for his whereabouts at the time of the incident.

Was Dan Hunt's concept of *who needed guidance* his justification to continuously and laughingly show off with a loaded shotgun in front of children? During one of his trap leagues, Dan Hunt shot from the hip rather than placing his shotgun correctly against his shoulder. This type of clown-like grandstanding, acting like a buffoon while laughing at his own, look at me, look at my unsafe misbehavior, certainly wasn't sanctioned by the ATA. I don't believe Hunt's misconduct with a loaded weapon defines *needed guidance* for young shooters.

If anybody believed they could get away with continuously misbehaving like a jackass firing a shotgun in front of parents and children, it was Porter's unqualified leagues manager and shoot management Dan Hunt, Coach Dan as he was known. Hunt was the adult running the league, the adult in charge. The adult setting the example. Hunt's conduct wasn't the type of message for the safe handling and proper behavior with a loaded weapon to the children at the event. Remember, according to Dan Hunt, he was just a volunteer. According to

Rusty Porter, Dan Hunt didn't have to be qualified. From my observations, if anyone *needed guidance* in the proper handling of firearms, especially in front of children, it was ECSC leagues manager Dan Hunt.

Excerpt: Dan Hunt's *Immediate resignation,*

This has been met with biased attacks on my own credibility and has placed my family in a position of discomfort.

Dan Hunt's egregious statement was even more disturbing than Hunt's accusation we abused him. According to Dan Hunt, his *Immediate resignation* email resulted from the board meeting a few hours earlier. His falsely alleged grievances and *biased attacks* stemmed from that meeting. Why would Hunt's family be *in a position of discomfort* from something Hunt claimed happened in a small meeting with eight other people a few hours earlier? I believe it is a valid question. Who had contact with Hunt's family after the meeting besides Dan Hunt? We certainly didn't. Quite frankly, whatever happened to put Dan Hunt's family *in a position of discomfort* was most likely due to Dan Hunt himself. When Dan Hunt stormed from the meeting, he was livid. It's my belief, that some three hours later, Dan Hunt was still out of control when he sent his vindictive, libelous, whining pity email.

Excerpt: Dan Hunt's *Immediate resignation,*

This sport allowed me an opportunity to relax and to enjoy good company after intense and severe exposures at work.

If there was ever a statement expressly designed to suck up pity, Duncanville narcotics detective Danny Garth Hunt's statement, *after intense and severe exposures at work,* was it. What pray tell, could Shawn or I, or a board meeting, have to do with Dan Hunt's admitted psychological problems at work? Absolutely nothing. Much like Dan Hunt's cowardly use of his son, then his family, Hunt used his admitted work-related problems to garner more sympathy. There was simply no end to the whining and self-pity Dan Hunt displayed.

The more overriding question was whether Dan Hunt experienced severe mental trauma from his admitted pressures associated with his duties as a Duncanville police officer. Was Dan Hunt, an armed individual, under severe mental duress? So much so that Dan Hunt had to rely on a gun club's activities and his position as leagues manager for therapy. What can be garnered from Hunt's whining pity email, and subsequent conduct of ECSC leadership is, in their infinite wisdom, Porter and his cronies put an admittedly overstressed, suffering from mental whatever, hothead Duncanville cop back in charge of forty individuals with loaded weapons, where the consumption of alcoholic beverages was allowed on the property. Furthermore, Dan Hunt, their overstressed, suffering from mental whatever *after intense and severe exposures at work* leagues manager, appeared to me the most likely person who placed the Danny Garth Hunt family *in a position of discomfort.*

Why did a Duncanville narcotics detective and ECSC leagues manager feel it necessary to send out an email about his perceived injuries and psychological problems to teenagers, especially at thirty-four minutes before midnight, or to anyone for that matter?

What parent wants an admitted, psychologically overstressed cop informing their child of his mental or personal problems at thirty-four minutes before midnight?

Did Danny Garth Hunt want everyone to feel sorry for him because he needed his activities at the ECSC to cope? Could anyone believe this was rational behavior for an armed police officer? I didn't and still don't.

Based on what I observed in Dan Hunt's demeanor, it was a troubling question about Duncanville narcotics detective Dan Hunt's emotional stability. Especially in light of Dan Hunt's comment regarding discomfort to his family and his threatening, aggressive behavior toward Shawn some three hours before Hunt issued his whining pity email to nearly one hundred unsuspecting men, women, and children.

Excerpt: Dan Hunt's *Immediate resignation,*

Since that is no longer the case, I feel no need to continue with the leagues. I hereby resign any responsibilities or commitments related to the ECSC leagues that I have previously committed to. This includes any past, present, or future events. I cannot justify participation in these events to the detriment of my well being or the well being of my family. Any monies or data possessed by me will be transferred to the board as soon as possible. I apologize for any discomfort or inconvenience.

Less than twenty hours after Dan Hunt issued his above non-participation proclamation, Hunt was back at the ECSC to participate in the skeet league. Hunt's statement did raise another troubling question. Hunt claimed he resigned because *I cannot justify participation in these events to the detriment of my well being or the well being of my family.*

What happened to his *well-being,* or more importantly, the *well being of my family?* Did the *detriment* miraculously disappear so Dan Hunt could return to the club the next day to shoot in the skeet league? Or was this just Danny Garth Hunt once again attempting to suck up more pity. More importantly, what was the detriment to the Hunt family? Was it an out-of-control Danny Garth Hunt himself?

Excerpt: Dan Hunt's *Immediate resignation,*

Having said that, any and all false allegations or slanderous events will be met with legal action.

Within approximately four hours, a hothead Duncanville narcotics detective and ECSC leagues manager threatened a senior citizen, and somehow, after Hunt stormed from the meeting livid, within those four hours, his family, according to none other than Danny Garth Hunt, had also been *placed in a position of discomfort.*

Dan Hunt clearly stated his intentions regarding *legal action.* So why did Dan Hunt **not** take legal action against us based on what he accused us of in his email? Why did Dan Hunt **not** sue us if what he claimed in his email was true? It's a simple, obvious answer. To sue us meant Dan Hunt would have to prove his false, malicious accusations in a court of law.

Within ten days, instead of suing us, what did Dan Hunt do? This vindictive Duncanville narcotics detective and ECSC leagues manager launched a second, cowardly, vicious attack behind our backs, resulting in a bogus cheating scandal. Dan Hunt made false statements to the ECSC Board of Directors about my legitimate ATA protest. Dan Hunt willfully and with malicious intent destroyed the reputations of two innocent individuals. Dan Hunt's malicious, false accusations within his vicious, whining pity email, *Immediate resignation,* and Hunt's malicious false statements to the ECSC Board of Directors would expose Dan Hunt and the ECSC to a lawsuit. From my observations, Dan Hunt's malicious misconduct and his own words clearly define the character of this Duncanville Police Department narcotics detective and ECSC leagues manager.

Dan Hunt's whining pity email, *Immediate resignation,* and none of Hunt's malicious accusations were referenced in Dan Hunt's three future court filings. None of the malicious, false accusations within Hunt's pity email, or even the email itself, were brought up in two court hearings by his attorney. Why? Because Danny Garth Hunt's whining pity email, *Immediate resignation* was a compilation of false statements and accusations by an admittedly overstressed, suffering from mental whatever, vindictive Duncanville cop and ECSC unqualified leagues manager.

Gathering of Roos

Chapter Three

Merriam-Webster defines a kangaroo court as a mock court in which the principles of law and justice are disregarded or perverted. Roos are defined as kangaroos, idiots, or fools. A gathering of roos is called a mob, troop, or court. No mention is made as to whether roos gather only in secret. It probably has a lot to do with the integrity of the roos.

I fully expected the Board of Directors to be as appalled over Duncanville narcotics detective and ECSC leagues manager Dan Hunt's defamatory, malicious, whining pity email, *Immediate resignation* as we were. Acting in his official capacity as leagues manager, Dan Hunt used the ECSC email address and list of nearly one hundred unsuspecting ECSC members, guests, and children to ensure the recipients would open and read it. A vicious, vindictive email sent thirty-four minutes before midnight by a Duncanville cop, ECSC leagues manager Dan Hunt, wasn't what I considered a rational act by a mentally stable individual.

Before contacting President Charlie Beard again, we decided to wait and see what action the Board of Directors would take in response to Dan Hunt's use of the club's official email address and list of members and guests for his vicious, libelous, vindictive attack.

To my utter dismay, I found out on Sunday, July 15, 2018. At 2:51 p.m., Chris Rose called, leaving a voicemail to call him. Rose called again at 4:12 p.m. This time, Rose didn't leave a message. At 4:19 p.m., I returned Rose's call, leaving him a voicemail. Rose called at 4:36 p.m.

Christopher Lyons Rose was an ECSC member and former president. Shawn and I had shot with him a few times. Rose is a highly educated individual, having graduated from one of the most prestigious schools of veterinary medicine. I could not think of any reason Rose would repeatedly call me. Suspicious, especially after Dan Hunt's behavior during his phone call, what transpired in the meeting and Hunt's vicious email, I hit record when I answered Rose's phone call.

Excerpt: Transcript of DVM Chris Rose's phone call,

I answered, "Hi Chris."

DVM Chris Rose: "Hello. The reason I'm calling is the board met on Thursday night concerning the scoring controversy and all the stuff that went on in the trap league."

I responded, "Okay."

DVM Chris Rose: "And the ruling was made that with all the stuff that went down the board is to support the guy running the league and that, uh, you and Shawn would not be able to participate in the trap league for two years."

I said, "So we've been kicked out for two years as well?"

DVM Chris Rose: "No, just the trap league. You just, you can go out and do all the other things you just can't play in the trap league."

I felt as if I had been sucker punched. I didn't know what to say.

After several seconds, DVM Chris Rose, rushing through his words, said, "So I wanted to let you know straight up it's really not my job, but it turned out it was my job. But uh uh how I call (garbled) send you an email (garbled). So I just wanted to call straight up. Uh Rusty'll follow it up with an email so you can get something you know kind of officials thing so it's just not my word and all that kind of stuff that what the board did. So I just wanted to let you all know."

I had the call on speakerphone. Shawn was listening and asked, "For what reason?"

I repeated Shawn's question. "For what reason?"

DVM Chris Rose: "Uh, changing scoresheets without you know

talking to anybody and all the stuff that went on with it from what I understand and what was reported to the board."

I protested: "But ah, Chris, we didn't change any score, scoresheets. All we did was follow what Dan told us to do, and that was to note the scores onto the outer edge of the scoresheet. We didn't actually change any scores."

DVM Chris Rose: "Well, that's you know not how it was reported. So like I said that's the action that's been taken, and uh we can't argue about it right now. So, they'll send you an email."

By the time the call ended, I was physically sick. None of what Rose said made any sense. Shawn and I had been thrown out of the league on a bogus charge of cheating. Rose even implied I was lying about following Dan Hunt's instructions. "Well, that's you know not how it was reported."

Were the board members so ignorant they didn't know what would happen to our reputations, the irreparable damage from their bogus charge of cheating and throwing us out of the trap league? Or did they just not give a damn. As subsequent events played out, I learned the arrogance of ECSC leadership had no boundaries. Texas laws, a signed contract, and First Amendment Rights would have no meaning to the elected leadership of the ECSC.

I had filed a valid ATA protest with shoot management Dan Hunt. I followed Hunt's instructions. It was what I told the Board during their July 2, 2018, monthly board meeting. How did my legitimate ATA protest become a bogus accusation of cheating? As Chris Rose said, "Uh, changing scoresheets without you know talking to anybody." This was asinine. All Rose or the Board had to do was look at the scoresheet. It was the proof the accusation of cheating was bogus.

Yet, Chris Rose said, "The board is to support the guy running the league," and "Well, that's you know not how it was reported."

The guy running the league was none other than their vindictive leagues manager, Dan Hunt. The guy doing the reporting was their vindictive leagues manager, Dan Hunt. The same, admittedly overstressed Duncanville cop who threatened Shawn in the meeting, saying, "Nobody calls me a liar and gets away with it."

Dan Hunt had already spread his malicious, false accusations about Shawn and me to nearly one hundred unsuspecting club members, guests, and children. What other false accusations about us had Hunt told the Board that resulted in a bogus cheating charge? I wouldn't learn the answer until some nine months later. It took a lawsuit and thousands of dollars to discover a vindictive Duncanville narcotics detective and ECSC leagues manager Dan Hunt lied to the Board. More on this in a subsequent chapter.

Here is another point to consider. On July 2, 2018, Dan Hunt adamantly declared in his whining, pity email, *Immediate resignation*, to nearly one hundred unsuspecting men, women, and children; *I hereby resign any responsibilities or commitments related to the ECSC leagues that I have previously committed to. This includes any past, present, or future events.*

How could the Board "support the guy running the league," when the guy running the league had officially resigned in his official notification ten days earlier, to multiple board members?

What wasn't in doubt was the 2018 ECSC Board of Directors condoned Dan Hunt's malicious misbehavior, Hunt's use of the club's official email address and competitors list, to viciously attack a fellow club member. How could such an inexcusable mentality exist within the Board of Directors to condone Hunt's vicious, irrational behavior?

How could such an inexcusable mentality exist within the Board of Directors to intentionally and maliciously destroy the reputations and credibility of two individuals with a bogus charge of cheating?

It wasn't until after I filed my lawsuit that I discovered the stench that permeated ECSC leadership. In March 2019, I learned the ECSC Board of Directors' July 12, 2018, meeting was titled *Board Meeting-Emergency Meeting*. During their clandestine *Board Meeting-Emergency*

Meeting, the Board of Directors suspended my paid membership rights to participate in club sponsored events without allowing me to defend myself. Even worse, I didn't know I had been accused of anything.

Along with the minutes I received, I also obtained a copy of the ECSC Constitution and Bylaws. What I discovered certainly raised a serious concern over the 2018 ECSC Board of Directors' behavior and motivation. I came to view their clandestine *Board Meeting-Emergency Meeting* as a kangaroo court. The ECSC roos had gathered, behind our backs.

DVM Chris Rose of Cedar Hill, Texas, was Vice President when he called me on July 15, 2018. On July 12, 2018, Vice President DVM Chris Rose chaired their clandestine *Board Meeting-Emergency Meeting,* kangaroo court.

As for the phone call from former council member and past mayor of Cedar Hill, Texas, ECSC Vice President DVM Chris Rose, several facts could be garnered from Rose's words concerning what I believe was his unprincipled conduct.

Rose didn't think he should be the one to make the call to inform me of the Board's actions, but it turned out he was. Rose stated, "So I wanted to let you know straight up, it's really not my job, but it turned out it was my job." Vice President DVM Christopher Lyons Rose led the clandestine, behind my back, attack. The former Cedar Hill mayor was in charge of their secret meeting. Yet, Rose felt he shouldn't be required to notify his innocent victim.

It appeared that Chris Rose wanted to remain incognito concerning his participation during his clandestine *Board Meeting-Emergency Meeting,* kangaroo court. Rose never informed me that he was the Vice President and presided over the meeting. Yet, the former council member and past mayor of Cedar Hill, Texas, Vice President DVM Christopher Lyons Rose, believed he was a "straight-up" kind of guy, so much so that Rose mentioned "straight-up" twice in his phone call.

As of the July 2, 2018, monthly board meeting, I had not been accused of any wrongdoing. I had not been suspended from the trap league. Yet, within ten days, I was falsely accused, secretly judged, wrongly convicted, and punished for a bogus charge of cheating. To make matters worse, I was never afforded an opportunity to defend myself.

As the highest-ranking elected official at his clandestine, kangaroo court, this admitted "straight-up" guy, Vice President DVM Chris Rose, denied me knowledge of the false accusations against me, denied me rebuttal testimony to the false charges, denied me the opportunity to produce witnesses and evidence on my behalf, never divulged the names of my secret accusers, and even denied me the opportunity to be present at my trial. Lastly, Christopher Lyons Rose, the former mayor of Cedar Hill, Texas, that self-professed "straight-up" kind of guy, didn't have the decency to notify me beforehand I was even on trial.

Vice President DVM Chris Rose wasn't present at the July 2, 2018, board meeting. To quote Rose, "From what I understand and what was reported to the board." Evidently, Rose just followed along with whatever he was told.

At the end of the July 2, 2018, board meeting, President Charlie Beard told two board members, Porter and Henslee, to look into the matter. Through their future court filings, I learned their findings were based on one person. Their investigation, just as Dan Hunt had done, ignored the willful and intentional misbehavior of the scoring team and the ATA rules and procedures governing the safety of the shooters and proper scoring of the match. Want to guess who Rusty Porter named as the one and only person interviewed for the Porter/Henslee investigation? It was Larry Degal, the intentionally misbehaving scorekeeper.

That's right, one person. Believe it or not, Porter and Henslee only interviewed the original culprit, Hunt's misbehaving, falsely alleged browbeaten scorekeeper, whose intentional disregard for the ATA rules caused the initial problems. Of course, as the accused, I was never allowed to question Larry Degal, who, like their security camera tapes, conveniently disappeared. It was all kept hush-hush. If you have a clandestine kangaroo court, why not a clandestine Porter/Henslee kangaroo investigation?

This is what I would ask the "straight-up" former mayor of Cedar Hill, Texas. After years of education at one of the most prestigious universities in the state, did it ever occur to you to question what you had been told?

Vice President DVM Chris Rose was one of nearly one hundred club members, guests, and children receiving Dan Hunt's near-midnight, vicious, whining pity email. Did it not occur to Rose there was something seriously wrong with a Duncanville police officer's late-night, irrational, disturbing behavior? Did Rose have admittedly overstressed cops on his watch in Cedar Hill, sending malicious emails, using the Cedar Hill PD or his City's official email address?

Did it not occur to Vice President DVM Chris Rose to go into the next room, view the security camera tapes for the night of June 28, the final night of the trap league, or the July 2, 2018, board meeting that was the subject of Hunt's vicious, vindictive email? Did it not occur to Rose to ask to see the scoresheet before he wrongly convicted me of changing it? Vice President DVM Chris Rose was about to vote on something that would have far-reaching, life-altering impact and financial consequences for an innocent club member.

Was Vice President DVM Chris Rose just plain ignorant, or was Rose so gullible he willingly swallowed what his vindictive leagues manager Dan Hunt and Porter fed him? That's what the former council member and past mayor of Cedar Hill, Texas, Vice President DVM Christopher Lyons Rose did. To quote Rose's words, "... from what I understand and what was reported to the board." Though let's not forget, Christopher Lyons Rose is an admitted "straight-up" guy.

There was nothing "straight-up" about Vice President DVM Chris Rose's phone call. Rose talked as if he'd been forced to contact me, wanting to separate himself from what had happened. Rose's manner was that of a messenger boy only—give me the bad news and get off the phone. I asked about sending Rose a letter. To quote ECSC Vice President DVM Chris Rose, "No. I really don't want to get in the middle of it." Seriously! Did Rose have any conscience at all?

The former council member and past mayor of Cedar Hill, Texas, ECSC Vice President DVM Chris Rose, actually had the unmitigated gall to say, "No. I really don't want to get in the middle of it." Rose wasn't just in the middle of it. Rose was at the head of it, the individual in charge, the leader. Rose presided over their clandestine *Board Meeting-Emergency Meeting*, kangaroo court.

If Vice President DVM Chris Rose didn't want to "get in the middle of it," why didn't "straight-up" Rose recuse himself from the meeting? Was it because "straight-up" Rose didn't mind being in the middle of it, as long as it was behind my back? Did Rose believe his unprincipled behavior was acceptable if it took place in secret? Maybe this was why "straight-up" Rose clearly didn't want to make that phone call. Rose preferred to hide and not have to account for his underhanded, clandestine conduct behind an innocent woman's back.

While I didn't believe it could get much worse, the next attack was Rose's promised email from Treasurer Rusty Porter.

Scoring issue

From:	*Russell Porter (rustyporter@mindspring.com)*
To:	*dickasonwx@sbcglobal.net;*
Date:	*Monday, July 16, 2018 7:10 AM*

The Ellis County Sportsmans Club Board of Directors has decided to uphold and enforce the ruling made by the Spring 2018 Trap League Manager on this subject.

Therefore you, or any family members, will not be permitted to participate in, observe, or score any league competition for a two year period starting on July 12, 2017. At the end of that time period assuming there are no additional controversies, you will be allowed to participate in our league competitions.

    Sincerely

    The Board of Directors

Upon reading Porter's email, I first noted the starting date, *July 12, 2017*. According to Treasurer Rusty Porter, his two-year edict was already half over. Porter, the guy responsible for managing ECSC finances, couldn't get the date right, not unlike his unqualified, incompetent, vindictive leagues manager Dan Hunt.

Several other glaring discrepancies were evident. There was a distinct difference between what the presiding officer, Vice President DVM Chris Rose said during his recorded phone call and what Treasurer Rusty Porter put in his email. Why would there be a difference? Why would Chris Rose lie? He's a "straight-up" kind of guy. Just ask him.

In Porter's email, he informed me I was barred from *any league competition,* not "just the trap league," as Vice President DVM Chris Rose clearly stated. When I questioned Rose, he was most emphatic that it only applied to the trap league. To quote Rose, "No, just the trap league. You just, you can go out and do all the other things you just can't play in the trap league."

ECSC Vice President DVM Chris Rose's use of the term "play" was certainly indicative of the lackadaisical and irresponsible attitude I observed at the ECSC. You play baseball, football, soccer, ping-pong, and card games. You don't "play" loaded guns. From my observation, the disregard displayed by ECSC leadership concerning gun safety and the consumption of alcoholic beverages on club property was never-ending. In my opinion, these people just didn't get it, or they didn't care.

Rusty Porter's email added other restrictions Vice President DVM

Chris Rose never mentioned. I could not observe or score. It was certainly an oxymoron comment. It's hard to score if you are prohibited from watching the match. In my opinion, Porter's snide comment about scoring was just a cheap shot to emphasize I would falsify the scores.

The stipulation I couldn't watch a match raised red flags. Was it to keep me from documenting further evidence of the lack of gun safety and the dangers of mixing guns, alcohol, and children at the ECSC? It certainly made sense when Porter added his last stipulation, a threat.

If there were *additional controversies*, my two-year suspension would be extended. What controversies? I wasn't aware I had caused any controversies. All I did was file a valid ATA protest, then attempt to tell them the truth about Hunt and the problems on their property in a closed meeting under a confidentiality agreement.

What does Porter do? Porter slaps me with a gag order. Keep my mouth shut, or the two years would be extended. Another way to ensure I didn't talk about the dangers of mixing guns, alcohol, and children at the Desoto Gun Club d/b/a Ellis County Sportsmans Club.

Nearly nine months later, when I finally obtained their unsigned, legal minutes of the July 12, 2018, clandestine *Board Meeting-Emergency Meeting*, kangaroo court, I discovered His Excellency, the Grand Poobah, Treasurer Rusty Porter, exceeded his authority. Porter barred me from all leagues, said I couldn't watch or score, and if I opened my mouth, my two-year suspension would be extended. The Board of Directors never approved Porter's additional stipulations in his email. Porter ignored a vote of the Board.

The behavior of Dan Hunt, Grand Poobah Porter, and the former mayor of Cedar Hill, Texas, Chris Rose was appalling. They had one set of rules for themselves and another set for everyone else.

The ECSC had a hothead, vindictive, unqualified leagues manager in Duncanville narcotics detective Danny Garth Hunt. Hunt had continuously and intentionally misbehaved with a loaded firearm, acting a clown-like buffoon in front of parents and children. I never observed Hunt display any knowledge of ATA rules and procedures governing a trap league. This was acceptable behavior to the Board.

Dan Hunt maliciously sent a vicious email to nearly one hundred unsuspecting men, women, and even children at thirty-four minutes before midnight, in which Hunt falsely accused us of abusing him, then placing his family *in a position of discomfort.* On the late evening of July 2, 2018, Dan Hunt was most likely the person who placed his family *in a position of discomfort.* It certainly wasn't Shawn and me. Within the same self-serving, whining pity email, Duncanville narcotics detective Danny Garth Hunt admitted to suffering from mental whatever *after intense and severe exposures at work,* needing his gun club activities to help him cope. This was acceptable behavior to the Board.

The ECSC had a treasurer, Rusty Porter, the guy holding their purse strings, who didn't know what year it was. Porter sat kowtowed next to Director Jerry Jay Gage as he wildly gesticulated and verbally abused a female club member for an extended period. Director Jerry Jay Gage's verbal abuse was okay with Porter. If, however, I opened my mouth about legitimate concerns regarding the safety of club members and the policy to allow the consumption of alcoholic beverages on club property, the Grand Poobah threatened to extend my cockamamie, trumped-up suspension. This was acceptable behavior to the Board.

Next was the former mayor of Cedar Hill, Texas, Vice President DVM Chris Rose, who believed he was a "straight-up" kind of guy after presiding over his clandestine *Board Meeting-Emergency Meeting,* kangaroo court. Behind my back, Rose sanctioned a vote suspending my paid membership rights to participate in club sponsored events. Then, adding to his appalling behavior, Rose stated in his phone call, "No. I really don't want to get in the middle of it." Christopher Lyons Rose, what a "straight-up" guy. This was acceptable behavior to the Board.

So, what did Porter and his cronies do? In their infinite wisdom, they awarded gesticulating, woman berating Director Jerry Jay Gage, the individual stating Danny Garth Hunt was the deity, their Honorary Lifetime Award, presented by Director Don R. Henslee. So what was their award to a wildly gesticulating Director Jerry Jay Gage? They presented him with a large-bladed weapon.

To view Henslee's presentation of said large-bladed weapon, there is a photo #4 on the carousel dated October 19, 2019, on the club's Facebook page. Jerry Jay Gage is wearing a black cowboy hat.

To further identify these ECSC leaders, in photo #3 on the same date at the head table, Treasurer Rusty Porter is in burnt orange, Director Sherrie Lewis in black and white check, President Mike Lee in yellow, and Director Don Henslee, standing, in dark blue.

For me, all I did was walk into the clubhouse and file a valid ATA protest with shoot management about the numerous violations of ATA rules and procedures by the opposing team that affected the proper scoring of the match, and errors to my scores. I get kicked out of the leagues on a bogus charge of cheating. All because Dan Hunt, a vindictive Duncanville narcotics detective and incompetent, unqualified ECSC leagues manager, lied to the Board. When I attempted to defend myself, asking for club records, I was stonewalled. Because they wrongly destroyed my reputation, I was forced to file a lawsuit to obtain the evidence to clear my name. Blaming me for the lawsuit, I get thrown out of the club. As if that weren't enough, they later intentionally lied to me and stole my money.

What Rose, Porter, Hunt, and their cronies never considered was that some women do not take kindly to being kicked. I didn't. I also didn't take kindly to Porter telling me to shut up or else. Not when it comes to the dangers associated with mixing guns, alcohol, and children at a live-fire shooting range, the Ellis County Sportsmans Club, Waxahachie, Texas.

Stonewalled

Chapter Four

A few days before I received Vice President DVM Chris Rose's phone call, we had gone to the club to shoot a few rounds of trap. Upon arriving, we found over a hundred solid orange clay targets littering the ground to the side and back of the trap house. These were not clay targets the machine had thrown. These were deliberately and wastefully tossed out of the trap house because a few registered trap shooters wanted to use only the black-banded clay targets on field zero as they did in registered competitions.

There were no written rules anywhere, no posted signs prohibiting the use of solid orange clay targets on field zero like they used on all the other fields, and no emails to the membership. The storage shed next to field zero was even filled with solid orange clay targets. The only way to know this group's private rule was through the ECSC osmosis system.

As the damage represented a financial loss to the club, I took pictures with my cellphone, then attached them to a text to Rusty Porter, explaining what we'd found. Over the next several days, Porter didn't answer my phone calls, nor did he acknowledge my text messages.

When I asked Vice President DVM Chris Rose if I could send him a letter, Rose refused, saying, "No. I really don't want to get in the middle of it." After Rose presided over his clandestine kangaroo court, he now wanted to disclaim any responsibility.

Following Rose's phone call, I again attempted to contact Rusty Porter. I sent a text message asking Porter for his and President Beard's mailing address. Porter never responded. I was intentionally being stonewalled. Grand Poobah Porter and former Cedar Hill mayor, Vice President DVM Chris Rose had gone underground.

Adding to my dilemma was the way the Board of Directors operated in secret. What I referred to as the ECSC Duck & Cover, their way of avoiding accountability. Unlike other gun clubs, there was no transparency. The Board of Directors had a history of hiding their management of the club's activities. Club events or monthly meetings were seldom posted on their website event calendar. One day we arrived at the club to shoot, only to find all the trap fields in operation with an unscheduled event. I asked Director Don Henslee why it wasn't on the calendar. Henslee told me the Board didn't post the events because they didn't want to hear complaints from the membership.

The identity of their elected officers wasn't on their website. Neither were the Bylaws, the rules governing the operation of a non-profit corporation, such as Desoto Gun Club d/b/a Ellis County Sportsmans Club.

During the monthly board meeting on July 2, 2018, a discussion ensued over the camera security system and the link to the new gate, which a card reader would activate. Treasurer Rusty Porter stated the security tapes from the camera system operated on a thirty-day cycle.

Since the camera footage for June 28, 2018, would be destroyed after thirty days, I had less than thirty days to obtain part of the evidence that would clear my name.

The security camera tapes for June 28th would have shown ECSC leagues manager Dan Hunt's mishandling of the target rifle before the start of the trap league. The tapes would have shown the clubhouse activity, including my walking inside to talk with ECSC leagues manager Dan Hunt when I filed my valid ATA protest. The tapes would have shown Shawn's brief attempt to speak with the misbehaving scorekeeper. Also recorded would have been Shawn's actions with the scoresheet when he followed Dan Hunt's instructions. Lastly, the tapes would have shown who was present for the award ceremony and who was drinking beer or hard liquor.

The security camera tape for July 2nd would have shown us entering the conference room, Shawn speaking to Beard and Porter about the target rifle before being given permission to go out and bring the target rifle into the room. The tape would have shown Shawn carefully laying the target rifle on the table before the monthly board meeting began. The tape would have shown Director Sherrie Lewis fabricated her malicious accusation that Shawn brought an assault rifle to the meeting and slammed it down on the table to intimidate board members. The tape would have shown Dan Hunt's accusations within his future filings to the 443rd Ellis County District Court and Court of Appeals, Tenth District of Texas, about assault rifle intimidation were blatantly false. The tape would clearly have shown Dan Hunt didn't enter the conference room until long after the meeting was underway, and the evidence, the target rifle, not an assault rifle was already on the table. The tape would have shown there was no intimidation by Shawn during the meeting.

The security camera tape would have shown Rusty Porter pointing to the camera during the discussion of the confidentiality agreement. The tape would have shown ECSC leagues manager Dan Hunt's aggressive misconduct when he exploded out of his chair, lunged to the table's edge, and threatened Shawn. The tape would have shown Director Jerry Jay Gage's abusive, lengthy, wildly gesticulating tirade directed towards me.

The tape for their July 12th, clandestine *Board Meeting-Emergency Meeting* would have shown who attended their kangaroo court.

My only option to obtain this critical evidence was to contact an attorney for assistance, which also became an issue. The clock was ticking. I had little time.

During my search for an attorney, another problem arose that would haunt me throughout the judicial proceedings. Shawn once talked with Porter about the numerous safety infractions he observed at the club. He asked Porter if the club was adequately insured should someone be negligently shot or killed. Shawn also asked Porter if anyone had ever been shot at the club. Porter told him that years ago, a man was murdered on club property, and they had law enforcement crawling all over the place. Porter never commented on Shawn's question concerning their liability insurance. Instead, Porter described how the club held money-raising events for the Ellis County District Attorney, and many attorneys in the Ellis County legal community were either members of or were guests at the club. Because of this, Porter believed the club was basically sue-proof in Ellis County.

Porter was right regarding the association with local attorneys. Upon calling an attorney, my first question was whether the attorney was a club member. Ultimately, I hired an attorney in Tarrant County.

My attorney recommended contacting the ECSC in an attempt to obtain their cooperation. My attorney called Treasurer Rusty Porter. Porter refused to speak with her. My attorney then contacted Clay Hinds, a local Waxahachie attorney I knew had provided the club with legal services. Hinds refused to return her phone calls. If Rusty Porter or Clay Hinds had the courtesy to speak to my attorney, I believe the subsequent events over nearly five years might have been avoided.

After my attorney was stonewalled, our only option was a *Litigation Hold* notification. Their continued refusal to speak with my attorney or me didn't leave me a choice. I had to attempt to preserve the evidence I needed to clear my name. On July 24, 2018, three days before the security tape for June 28th would be destroyed, my attorney served the ECSC Board of Directors with a *Notice of Representation of Anita Dickason and Litigation Hold*, identifying the documents and records ECSC was lawfully required to preserve.

Excerpt: *Notice of Representation of Anita Dickason and Litigation Hold,*

As you are undoubtedly aware, on June 28, 2018, a scoring dispute with Ms. Dickason's team arose on the final night of an eight-week Spring shotgun trap league organized by the Ellis County Sportsman's Club. Ms. Dickason notified the match director, Dan Hunt, of the scoring dispute, and was specifically told to write the disputed scores on the outer edge of the team's score sheet and then return the score sheet to him. Ms. Dickason informed the team squad leader, Shawn George, who complied with Mr. Hunt's instructions. At no time, did Ms. Dickason or Mr. George change the scores recorded by the scorer Larry Degel. During a phone call on June 30, 2018, Mr. Hunt informed Ms. Dickason and Mr. George that Mr. George was suspended from any further participation in the Club's leagues due to complaints from unnamed participants. Following a board meeting of the Ellis County Sportsman's Club on July 2, 2018 to discuss Mr. Hunt's actions, Mr. Hunt, as the representative of the Ellis County Sportsman's Club Leagues, by and through the Ellis County Sportsman's Club Leagues' designated e-mail address, published to nearly 100 League members an email accusing Ms. Dickason and Mr. George of making "wholly and completely unfounded" accusations, of "ridiculous abuse," and "slanderous allegations.

On July 15, 2018, former club president Chris Rose, at the direction of the board, contacted Ms. Dickason to inform her the board had met on Thursday, July 12, 2018. He further stated that Ms. Dickason and Mr. George would be banned from participation in the club leagues for two years. When Ms. Dickason questioned the reason why, Mr. Rose stated, "changing score sheets without talking to anybody." This ban was confirmed in a follow-up email from Rusty Porter, on July 16, 2018.

It is the hope of my client that this matter can be resolved amicably. It should be noted that Ms. Dickason has made every attempt to protect the club's reputation, the reputation of Mr. Hunt, and her reputation in dealing with Mr. Hunt's accusations and actions. Unfortunately, she was not afforded the same courtesy. After Ms. Dickason received an email confirmation from the Club President, Charlie Beard, that she would be granted time to address the board at the July 2, 2018 meeting, Rusty Porter was contacted to request that Dan Hunt be present. Mr. Porter *advised that Mr. Hunt had already been contacted. When Mr. Hunt failed to arrive on time, Ms. Dickason and Mr. George requested the discussion be deferred until Mr. Hunt was present. Even after Mr. Hunt's arrival, Ms. Dickason and Mr. George refused to continue until they ascertained whether the meeting was being recorded by any electronic device. Mr. George referenced the inadvisability of "airing the club's dirty laundry on the internet." It was agreed by all parties present, to include Dan Hunt, that what was said would not go beyond the participants at the meeting. Approximately three hours after the conclusion of the meeting, Dan Hunt, as the representative of the Ellis County Sportsman's Club Leagues, by and through the Ellis County Sportsman's Club Leagues' designated e-mail address, violated this agreement with his defamatory and malicious email.*

As a 22-year veteran of the Dallas Police Department, Ms. Dickason has an impeccable reputation that is backed by numerous awards and commendations. She is an accomplished markswoman and has shot competitively for close to thirty years. Safety on a shooting range is always her first concern, most specifically where there are new or inexperienced shooters and children. She hopes incidents of safety violations that she has observed at the Ellis County Sportsman's Club and her subsequent intervention to correct the violation has not unduly influenced the testimony of the individuals interviewed as part of the Board's investigation.

My client takes matters of truth and integrity very seriously, and despite being a 74-year old woman, will not hesitate to take the necessary steps to clear her name and restore her reputation in the community. She will vigorously defend against any continuation of defamatory attacks or actions that will further impugn her good character and reputation.

After receiving my notification, Vice President DVM Chris Rose, Rusty Porter and their cronies had to know they had a serious problem. The *Litigation Hold* notification spelled out the inexcusable actions of their vindictive leagues manager, Dan Hunt, in sending his malicious, vicious, whining pity email, *Immediate resignation* to nearly one hundred unsuspecting men, women, and even children.

I would think Vice President DVM Chris Rose had to know he had wrongly convicted me of cheating. "Uh, changing scoresheets without you know talking to anybody." All Rose had to do was look at the scoresheet. Rose had to know what he had been told was a false accusation. "From what I understand and what was reported to the board." "Well, that's you know not how it was reported." I had to wonder if Rose truly believed he wasn't responsible or wouldn't be held accountable just because he didn't want to "get in the middle of it."

Not a single person on the 2018 ECSC Board of Directors had the ethics, integrity, or guts to step forward and remedy the damage they'd done. Instead, Vice President DVM Chris Rose, Rusty Porter and their cronies took stonewalling to a new level.

My attorney had identified the Desoto Gun Club d/b/a Ellis County Sportsmans Club as a registered nonprofit corporation with the Texas Secretary of State. As such, the ECSC is governed by Texas law, the *Business Organizations Code* (BOC). A copy of such can be found on the Texas Secretary of State's website.

The BOC stipulates the regulations for the formation of a not-for-profit corporation, the election of a board of directors, bylaws to regulate and manage the corporation, monthly and annual meetings, membership rights, the conduct and termination of directors and officers, and even the dissolution of the corporation. The Texas Attorney General has the authority to investigate not-for-profit corporations and can assess criminal and civil sanctions.

In compliance with Texas law, the *Business Organizations Code*, my attorney also requested numerous club records, including the ECSC Bylaws, a copy of the contested scoresheet, minutes of club meetings, along with copies of the entire security camera footage for June 28, July 2, and July 12, 2018, within the *Litigation Hold* notification.

The ECSC Board of Directors never acknowledged the *Litigation*

Hold nor produced the requested club records. Their refusal violated two *Texas Business Organizations Code* sections: *Sec. 3.153. Right Of Examination By Owner or Member,* and *Sec. 22.351. Member's Right to Inspect Books and Records.* It would take filing a lawsuit, an official court request, and thousands of dollars to force the ECSC leadership to produce the club records.

Instead of stepping forward, taking responsibility, and correcting the damage they had done to my reputation, the Board pulled their typical stunt, the ECSC Duck & Cover. ECSC leadership ignored a lawful request by an attorney on behalf of a paying club member for copies of club records, to which I was entitled by Texas law.

Did Porter and his cronies truly believe they could blatantly kick me, and I would somehow just go away? Well, I didn't. I didn't roll over and play dead as Porter and his cronies obviously expected. I stood my ground and demanded answers. I wondered how many other ECSC club members they had done this to. As a reminder, at the end of the July 2nd monthly board meeting, President Beard told me, "Don't worry about it. We deal with this all the time."

It took a lawsuit and thousands of dollars to obtain the evidence proving Rose's "Uh, changing scoresheets without you know talking to anybody" was bogus. It wasn't until March 2019, I finally received the Bylaws, scoresheet, minutes of meetings, and other club records I had legally requested in July of 2018. I had the evidence to expose their false accusations, revealing how deep the stench went within the Desoto Gun Club d/b/a Ellis County Sportsmans Club.

What I didn't receive were copies of the security camera tapes. The visual evidence of Dan Hunt's misconduct with a target rifle, his physical aggression and threat toward Shawn in the meeting, Jerry Jay Gage's wildly gesticulating, verbally abusive tirade upon me, and the clear proof Sherrie Lewis and Dan Hunt made false accusations about assault rifle intimidation, never saw the light of day.

In addition to the *Litigation Hold* notification, ECSC leagues manager Dan Hunt was served with a *Cease and Desist* notification.

Excerpt: Cease and Desist Notification,

Since the scoring dispute of June 28, 2018, you have purposefully and maliciously made and publicized defamatory statements that have impugned Ms. Dickason's honesty and integrity and caused injury to Ms. Dickason's reputation. In an email dated, July 2, 2018, to nearly 100 Club members and/or participants of the Club league events, you implied that Ms. Dickason was a liar by indicating that she had been making "wholly and completely unfounded" accusations, that she has committed "ridiculous abuse," and that she herself had made slanderous allegations, and was responsible for causing discomfort to your family. You have also stated, explicitly or implicitly, that my client was a cheater by indicating to members of the Ellis County Sportsman's Club board that Ms. Dickason purposefully attempted to change the scores on her team's scoring sheet. As a result of your wrongful and unlawful conduct, Ms. Dickason and her family have been banned from league play with the Ellis County Sportsman's Club for a period of two years. She has suffered tremendous embarrassment and loss of social standing in the Club and in her community.

Ms. Dickason is a 74-year-old-woman who is a highly decorated 22-year veteran of the Dallas Police Department and an accomplished markswoman. Honesty, integrity, and a respect for rules and law are of the utmost importance to her. Your actions have caused physical and mental stress and stigmatized her good character and reputation.

This letter hereby demands that you <u>immediately cease and desist</u> from making any false, misleading, or defamatory statement to any person, club, or organization about Ms. Dickason, and that you <u>immediately cease and desist</u> from contacting Ms. Dickason, her family, and her colleagues, or anyone else in her community regarding this incident.

<u>Further, pursuant to Texas Civil Practices and Remedies Code 73.055, the Texas Defamation Mitigation Act, Ms. Dickason hereby demands that you correct, clarify, and retract your defamatory statements described</u>

above within thirty (30) days of the receipt of this request.

If you fail to heed these demands, my client will be forced to exercise any and all legal remedies available. This may include obtaining a permanent injunction to prohibit you from the activities complained of in this demand and filing suit to recover my client's actual damages incurred as a result of your defamatory statements, as well as exemplary damages, court costs, and attorney fees.

Duncanville narcotics detective and ECSC leagues manager Dan Hunt ignored my lawful demands. Hunt never responded. Likewise, Dan Hunt never initiated any legal action for the charges I stipulated in the *Cease and Desist Notification*, as Hunt clearly threatened in the last sentence of his whining pity email, *Immediate resignation.* Dan Hunt wrote; *Any and all false allegations or slanderous events will be met with legal action.* Dan Hunt was a no-show when it came time to make good his threat of *legal action.* Perhaps it was all too much for Danny Garth Hunt following his admitted mental whatever *after intense and severe exposures at work.*

Just as Shawn told President Beard in the July 2, 2018, meeting, "What I have to say I will say to Dan's face," I was upfront with Dan Hunt and ECSC leadership. In the *Cease and Desist* notification, I legally warned Duncanville narcotics detective and ECSC leagues manager Dan Hunt what would happen if he refused to retract his malicious, false accusations. I also informed the Board in my *Notice of Representation of Anita Dickason and Litigation Hold.*

Dan Hunt's malicious, libelous, whining pity email, his false accusations to the Board of Directors, the unprincipled conduct of Vice President DVM Chris Rose, Treasurer Rusty Porter, and their cronies, and their continued refusal to remedy the damage to my reputation forced me to take further legal action.

On December 10, 2018, I filed a lawsuit for Defamation, Breach of Contract and Conversion against Dan Hunt and the Desoto Gun Club d/b/a Ellis County Sportsmans Club.

The Secret 7

Chapter Five

It wasn't until after I filed my lawsuit that Porter and his cronies were finally forced to produce club records as part of the judicial proceedings. The documents I received in March 2019, included a copy of their Bylaws and minutes of club meetings. Within the minutes of their July 12, 2018, meeting, I discovered their clandestine kangaroo court had been titled *Board Meeting-Emergency Meeting*. I finally learned the identity and number of roos who gathered in secret, with what I believe a malicious intent to destroy the reputations and credibility of two individuals who never harmed anyone at the ECSC.

Seven elected officers, the ECSC Secret 7, Vice President DVM Chris Rose, Treasurer Rusty Porter, and Directors Sherrie Lewis, David McDaniel, Wayne Johnston, Jerry Jay Gage, and Don Henslee gathered for their clandestine kangaroo court. A meeting in which a vote was taken that I believe violated the Constitution and Bylaws of the club.

This secret meeting led to Rose's July 15, 2018, phone call to inform me I had been kicked out of the trap league for two years because of Hunt's bogus charge of cheating. This meeting led to Porter's email, adding more outrageous stipulations to their trumped-up suspension of my paid membership rights to participate in club-sponsored events. So, who called their *Board Meeting-Emergency Meeting?*

According to the ECSC Bylaws, the President was the only person who could call a *special meeting* of the Board. It's interesting their clandestine meeting minutes were titled *Emergency*, not *Special*. If this meeting was so urgent, an *Emergency,* why wasn't their President, Charlie Beard, presiding over the *Board Meeting-Emergency Meeting* he supposedly called? Ten days earlier, at the end of the July 2nd monthly board meeting, Beard told me, "Don't worry about it. We deal with this all the time."

President Beard's absence left Vice President DVM Chris Rose to preside. A responsibility Rose tried to disavow in his infamous, recorded phone call. "So I wanted to let you know straight up it's really not my job, but it turned out it was my job." Later in the call, Rose still acted as if he hadn't been involved when I asked if I could send him a letter. "No. I really don't want to get in the middle of it." Rose presented himself as the messenger boy, not the officer in charge.

Who did Rose think should have called me? Was it Rusty Porter? From my observations, Porter appeared to be a master at avoiding accountability. Or was it Charlie Beard, their missing president? I wonder exactly when the light came on, and Rose figured out he'd been hung out to dry. Perhaps at the February 4, 2019, board meeting, when Rose resigned as the new ECSC President and then walked out.

If Beard didn't call the *Emergency* meeting, who did? It's my belief it was likely the Grand Poobah, Rusty Porter. Porter would ultimately ignore the vote of the Secret 7, adding additional stipulations to my suspension. Would a clause in the Bylaws regarding the authorization to call *special meetings* be a deterrent to the Grand Poobah?

If you hold a *Board Meeting-Emergency Meeting,* one would think you would have an actual *Emergency.* What was the Secret 7's *Emergency?* What was so critical that the Secret 7 had to rush to hold their *Board Meeting-Emergency Meeting?*

If they only wanted to keep me from participating in the trap league, why the urgency to hold their clandestine kangaroo court? They could have waited since the next trap league wouldn't start until after the August 6, 2018, monthly board meeting. Why the bogus charge of cheating, Porter's gag order, and the need to keep Shawn and me away from the leagues? I believe the answer was in the ECSC Bylaws and what transpired during the July 2, 2018, monthly board meeting.

During the July 2nd meeting, Shawn and I attempted to address gun safety, alcohol consumption, Hunt's misconduct with firearms, and Hunt's incompetency in overseeing the trap leagues. President Charlie Beard refused to allow us to proceed. Instead, President Beard told us to file a complaint at a future meeting if we wanted to talk about gun safety and other issues. I immediately informed President Beard I would file a formal complaint at the next monthly meeting, which would have been held on August 6, 2018.

Ten days after my declaration to the ECSC Board, the Secret 7 rushed to hold their clandestine kangaroo court, *Board Meeting-Emergency Meeting.*

Until I filed my lawsuit, Porter and his cronies had refused to give me a copy of their Bylaws or minutes of the meeting. As a paying member, I was entitled to their Bylaws and other club records, according to none other than Texas law. Within the Bylaws was a provision that only members in good standing could file charges at a board meeting.

Once the Secret 7 voted to suspend my paid membership rights to participate in club-sponsored events, I believe they planned to argue I was not a member in good standing. Such a determination would block me, not only from filing a formal complaint at the August 6, 2018, monthly board meeting, but also the next two years.

I believe their use of Hunt's vindictive, bogus charge of cheating was a malicious intent to destroy not only my reputation but also my credibility within the shooting community, if I spoke out about the gun safety issues I observed, and my concerns regarding the dangers of the consumption of alcoholic beverages on club property.

Porter, the Grand Poobah, went even further to ensure my silence. In writing, Porter threatened to extend my suspension beyond the two years if I caused any more *controversies.* Porter's stipulation was nothing but a gag order. Porter added another condition to my suspension. I couldn't watch a match. I believe this was Porter's way of keeping me from documenting further evidence of gun safety liability in their leagues. As I will show in a subsequent chapter, Porter exceeded his authority with his additional stipulations not voted on by the Secret 7. Porter just kept kicking me.

On July 12, 2018, seven ECSC elected officers and directors gathered secretly to suspend my paid membership rights for two years. They would take my money while denying me the privileges for which I had paid. They hid behind their vindictive leagues manager Dan Hunt's bogus accusation of cheating, Rose's phone call and Grand Poobah Porter's email. The Secret 7 intentionally destroyed the reputations and credibility of two knowledgeable, professionally trained, highly experienced individuals with their bogus charge of cheating, for what I came to believe, to simply silence us.

Guns! Alcohol! Children!

Chapter Six

During my tenure with the Dallas Police Department, the procedures for safely handling and firing weapons were a repetitive topic in every training activity involving firearms.

I competed in rifle matches across the U.S. and Canada for over twenty years. I earned an NRA High Master certification in mid-range (300, 500, 600 yards) and long-range (800, 900, 1000 yards), iron sight only competitions. Gun safety dominated NRA competitions. When Shawn and I joined the Ellis County Sportsmans Club, we expected to find a similar attitude and dedication to gun safety and the well-being of participants. We didn't.

I observed numerous incidents of inappropriate and dangerous handling of shotguns by purported instructors, members, and guests during their casual use of the ECSC facilities and within the ECSC sponsored trap leagues. I soon learned ECSC's promotion of gun safety was nonexistent. Don't upset the members and guests with rules or regulations.

On many occasions, Shawn and I spoke out about the infractions of gun safety we saw, either in the operation of ECSC's sponsored trap leagues or the general use of the facility. While we brought many of the incidents to the attention of Rusty Porter, in my observations, nothing was ever done.

Increasingly, new members had little to no experience with weapons or the use of the facility. The new clubhouse increased the number of club-sponsored events, including competitive events and the clubhouse rental for parties. Many of the sponsored events were for youth groups. The inherent liability from the unsafe handling of firearms and alcohol consumption could not be ignored.

I spoke out about the lack of gun safety education and the consumption of alcoholic beverages on club property. The club's continued failure to recognize and implement sound gun safety procedures and address the issue of alcohol consumption was tantamount to a recipe for disaster. I think the only reason it hadn't already happened was the club was just lucky.

The ECSC's lackadaisical attitude about gun safety and alcohol, especially in the presence of children, was alarming. From what I viewed, leagues manager Dan Hunt and ECSC leadership's primary concern wasn't about sound gun safety rules and regulations, but instead the club's social atmosphere and how much money they made from the events they sponsored, especially those involving youth groups.

Treasurer Rusty Porter and ECSC leagues manager Dan Hunt made it clear they didn't want any comments about gun safety issues. *Fostering good fellowship* to keep club members and guests happy was more important than correcting improper behavior with loaded weapons that could affect the well-being of members, guests, and children. I found their attitude irresponsible, as reflected in their website.

ECSC *Home* page: *STRENGTHENING THE SPORT OF SHOOTING THROUGH SAFTEY AND EDUCATION.*

ECSC *About Us* page: *WE BELIEVE IN FUN, SAFTEY, AND EDUCATION.*

The word **SAFTEY,** prominently displayed on ECSC's two website pages, is not a misprint. An internet search of the ECSC immediately brings up *saftey* before you even get to their website. The correct spelling is **SAFETY.**

Since we joined in 2015, this was how a gun club spelled safety on its website. I think such a lack of attention to detail was an ominous warning about ECSC leadership's failure to promote gun safety and other safety issues on ECSC property and during ECSC-sponsored events.

Their *About Us* page was a clear indication of the ECSC's priorities. The social atmosphere, *FUN*, takes precedence over safety and education.

This wasn't the only place where the social atmosphere was emphasized. The *About Us* page lists their seven (7) *Safety Requirements*. The Desoto Gun Club d/b/a Ellis County Sportsmans Club, a Texas gun club's first rule isn't about the safe handling of a weapon, but their alcohol consumption policy.

1. *Never drink beer or alcohol before or while shooting.*
2. *Always load your gun only when on station and ready to shoot.*
3. *Always point your gun in a safe direction.*
4. *Always keep your gun broken or the action open when not shooting.*
5. *Never load more than (2) shells at one time.*
6. *Never shoot larger than 7-1/2 shot.*
7. *Any shooter under the age of 18 must be accompanied by a responsible adult.*

At the edge of the trap and skeet fields were benches, wooden racks for shotguns, and large trash cans. The trash containers were attached to the wooden gun racks. Shooters could throw their hulls into the trash cans instead of walking across the parking lot to the large dumpsters.

Not long after joining the ECSC, we were getting ready to shoot on one of the trap fields, and I saw beer cans in the trash container attached to the gun rack. Nothing had been said about the use of alcohol during their brief new member orientation. Upon querying another member, I learned the club allowed the consumption of alcoholic beverages on their property.

Throughout my law enforcement career and decades of competitive shooting, alcohol on a gun range was an absolute no-no. To say I was shocked was an understatement. Not only because of the club's policy but also the proximity of the beer cans to the trap and skeet fields. Were members drinking beer while shooting?

As I discovered, the consumption of alcoholic beverages was a common occurrence during the general use of the facility and league matches. For approximately eighteen years with the Dallas Police Department, I was a certified instructor in field sobriety testing for DWI offenses and the Drug Recognition Expert (DRE) program (procedures to identify drivers under the influence of drugs). I was certified by the Dallas Police Department, the U.S. Department of Transportation, and the International Association of Police Chiefs. As such, I trained officers in law enforcement agencies across the state. I was an adjunct instructor for Texas A&M University and Sam Houston State University. I know how alcohol affects judgment, physical abilities, and exacerbates disputes.

I was very aware of the inherent danger of mixing alcohol and loaded firearms, especially with the inordinate number of children using the ECSC facility. Seated behind the trap fields, league participants openly drank beer before the competition ended. In my professional opinion, seeing members drinking alcoholic beverages didn't set a good example for the children who were present.

The unsupervised consumption of alcoholic beverages at the ECSC facility depended solely on an individual's judgment. The loss of judgment is one of the first levels of impairment. It starts as low as a .02 BAC (Blood Alcohol Content), which, depending on gender and body weight, can be one can of beer.

Once alcohol consumption begins, rational thinking fades. If a drunk can't figure out not to drive, how can anyone believe he or she won't decide to load his or her shotgun and start shooting? Mixing alcohol and firearms just isn't rational, especially with so many kids using their facility.

As a long-time, experienced, competitive shooter, field sobriety instructor, and concerned observer at the ECSC, I found the combination of guns, alcohol, and children irresponsible, if not negligent, by ECSC leadership. The consumption of alcoholic beverages at the ECSC shooting facility exacerbated the risk of gun accidents. As I said, the ECSC has been lucky for years, and the longer their luck runs, the closer they get to the day it runs out.

In my professional opinion, and that of other individuals who operate gun ranges, alcohol consumption should never be allowed at a shooting facility. This was how the Grand Poobah and his cronies ran the club. From what I observed, the ECSC Board of Directors was more concerned with their happy-go-lucky social environment for club members than the danger of mixing guns, alcohol, and children.

On the ECSC website, their first *Safety Requirement* addressed alcohol consumption, sending a strong message about the priorities of the ECSC, social atmosphere first, gun safety second.

The consumption of alcoholic beverages in a competitive environment, such as that in ECSC's sponsored leagues, increased the potential for arguments and altercations. The dinner and award ceremony on the final night of league competitions included beer and hard liquor consumption. On the ECSC's Facebook page are pictures of the award banquet for the June 22, 2017, Spring/Summer Trap League and the December 18, 2018, award banquet for the Winter Skeet League. The alcoholic beverages are clearly visible in the pictures. In the December/2018 pictures, bottles of Exotico Tequila Reposado and Di Amore Amaretto are on the counter dividing the kitchen and large conference room.

On the night of June 28, 2018, I saw competitors drinking beer before we left the property. I believe alcohol played a role in what happened after we left.

During the discovery phase of my lawsuit, my attorney requested the rules for the consumption of alcoholic beverages at the ECSC. Defendant ECSC provided two documents. The first was a photo of their ECSC Texas Sales and Tax Permit attached to a bulletin board.

Underneath the tax permit was typed: *Drinking and Shooting Don't Mix. If you plan to shoot-Don't drink. If you drink-You can't shoot. A shooting facility insured under the NSSA/NSCA liability insurance program will be canceled if this policy is not strictly enforced.*

Their typed statement on a bulletin board in the clubhouse was the only place on seventy-eight-plus acres where their alcohol policy was posted—a clubhouse you didn't even have to enter to shoot. To me, this appeared merely a way to cover their backside with their liability insurance carrier. Their purported *strictly enforced* alcohol policy relied on the possibly impaired judgment of a club member or guest.

The second document was their *2010 Rules **Polices** & Operating Guidelines.* Please note the word **Polices** is not a misprint on my part. It was how the ECSC spelled policies. Under *Shooting Safety & Regulations* is written: *No beer or alcohol beverages are to be taken onto any shooting range. If you are shooting or plan to shoot don't drink.* This document was not available to members or guests. I had to sue the ECSC, spending thousands of dollars to obtain a copy.

When I joined the club, paying for a round of clays was on the honor system. After shooting, members were trusted to leave cash or a check on a clipboard in the clubhouse to pay for the number of rounds they shot. The problem was that the ECSC honor system didn't work and cost the club a lot of money. Following years of financial bleeding, the club was forced to install an expensive card reader system. To activate the clay-throwing machines, club members had to use their ECSC club-issued debit card loaded with money from a charge to the member's credit card. For years, members ignored the honor system to pay for their rounds of targets. Yet, ECSC leadership believed members would honor a policy about not drinking and shooting.

As a law enforcement officer, Dan Hunt should have known the danger of mixing alcohol and guns. Yet he condoned the consumption of alcoholic beverages during his leagues. Once a competitor finished firing, they were allowed to consume alcoholic beverages even though the event was ongoing. In my opinion, it wasn't a rational decision by a law enforcement officer running the event. Allowing the consumption of beer and liquor only increased leagues manager Dan Hunt's liability if someone was hurt or killed. This lack of concern for the safety of the participants was what I observed as typical of the way Dan Hunt ran his trap leagues.

****

Safety briefings reinforce the mechanics of properly handling firearms, whether you are a new or experienced shooter. Mistakes with guns can lead to injury or death. With one exception, I never saw a safety briefing on ECSC property.

I shot with a group of DIVA WOW women during my first ECSC trap league competition. On the first night, Sherrie Lewis and Barbara Parks handed out the team assignments. There was no safety briefing, yet many of the women had little experience with the loaded weapon they were about to use. A live-fire shooting competition isn't the place to learn how to handle firearms safely. It needs to be addressed before you start shooting.

During the competition, shooting was suspended due to a problem with the trap machine. Shotguns had to be removed from the firing line before anyone could go downrange to get into the trap house.

An inexperienced competitor on the firing line had already loaded a round into her shotgun in preparation for her turn to fire. The woman did not unload her gun when the shooters were told to remove their shotguns from the firing line. Instead, she turned to walk off the firing line, pointing her loaded shotgun at other competitors standing at the back of the trap field. I immediately headed toward her. I told her to turn around, return to the firing line, face downrange, and unload her shotgun.

After the match's conclusion, I recommended to Sherrie Lewis and Barbara Parks a safety briefing be held before the start of the following week's match. The next day, April 10, 2015, I received an email from

Barbara Parks in which she wrote; *Also, next week we will have a safety talk before hand, our main aim is to keep everyone safe, and there were a couple of things that happened last night that were uncomfortable.* This led to the only time I saw a safety briefing conducted at the ECSC during the trap leagues I competed in. It only applied to the DIVA WOW women and no one else.

This incident didn't endear me to Sherrie Lewis. Her attitude toward me changed, bordering on hostility. Sherrie Lewis subsequently became one of the main instigators in the events surrounding my valid ATA protest. This wasn't Sherrie Lewis' first involvement in a controversy. During another trap league, shoot management Dan Hunt bragged about kicking a competitor out of his league. Hunt said he was tired of complaints from the other team members, including Sherrie Lewis. It was disturbing how often Sherrie Lewis kept popping up whenever there was a conflict. Dan Hunt's actions were a point I made at the July 2, 2018, ECSC monthly board meeting. I told the Board that Hunt's way to handle an issue was to kick someone out of the league rather than trying to fix the problem.

The trap leagues were open to non-members. An individual with no firearms experience could buy two boxes of shotgun shells and a shotgun, pay to join Hunt's league and start shooting.

As shoot management and leagues manager, Dan Hunt was responsible for the safety and competent management of the trap league, involving up to forty-armed club members, guests, and children. Yet, I never observed any guidance, supervision, or even a semblance of a safety briefing before his trap leagues to ensure the well-being of all competitors.

I cannot imagine the Duncanville Police Department was this apathetic about gun safety or didn't conduct safety briefings during their firearms training sessions. Dan Hunt also conducted license to carry classes at the ECSC. Hunt certified persons to carry a handgun. Another scary thought. I never saw Dan Hunt apply a single standard of gun safety to ECSC sponsored trap leagues for which he was responsible.

What I never saw within approximately two and a half pages of Dan Hunt's match bulletins were the words, RULES, ATA RULES, ECSC RULES AND PROCEDURES, SAFETY, SAFETY RULES, ALCOHOL CONSUMPTION, ATA TRAP LINE TRAINING MANUAL, OR RANGE ETIQUETTE. Instead of safety, Hunt refers to handicaps, wagering, trash clean-up, fees, and collection of money.

In response to my attorney's question regarding qualifications for league managers in *Plaintiff's First Set of Interrogatories*, Treasurer Russell Porter answered: *There are no qualifications for the position. League managers are tasked with ensuring the club's rules, policies, and bylaws are followed.*

It's no wonder Dan Hunt was incompetent and his trap leagues poorly managed when Porter admits there were no qualifications for the position. I never witnessed Hunt demonstrate any knowledge of ATA rules and procedures in his administration of the trap leagues.

How could ECSC leadership expect a club member or especially a guest to follow *the club's rules, policies, and bylaws* when even shoot management didn't have a clue? How could ECSC leadership expect a member or guest to follow *the club's rules, policies, and bylaws* when the documents were unavailable? They weren't to be found. They weren't on the ECSC website. I never saw them in the ECSC clubhouse or ECSC leagues manager Dan Hunt's match bulletins. It's hard to abide by *rules, policies, and bylaws* you've never seen. I had to file a lawsuit and spend thousands of dollars to obtain *the club rules, policies, and bylaws* because the ECSC Board of Directors refused to provide them in response to a lawful request from my attorney.

At the ECSC, up to forty individuals of far varying skill, knowledge, and experience with loaded guns did things the way they assumed they should be done. Everybody had an opinion, and no one wanted to be corrected. From what I observed, the ECSC was the Wild West of the clay shooting sports. And the most irresponsible, misbehaving competitor, acting like a buffoon with a loaded gun, was ECSC shoot management and LTC instructor Danny Garth Hunt.

What was also noticeably missing from Porter's answer to my interrogatory regarding qualifications was any requirement of knowledge or expertise with firearms or training in range safety. I obtained a copy of the insurance application for the ECSC insurance provider. One of the questions dealt with range officers' qualifications and range safety. I've often wondered how the Board of Directors answered this question.

I'm sure some would argue a police officer is a qualified individual to oversee events involving live-fire competitions. Nothing could be further from the truth. Unfortunately, the assumption a police officer has more than rudimentary knowledge of guns and range safety is a common myth.

It's hard to argue otherwise when Dan Hunt, a Duncanville narcotics detective, ECSC shooting leagues manager, Texas license to carry (LTC) instructor, and children's shooting coach, picked up a target rifle and pointed it in the direction of other competitors—a criminal act per the *Texas Penal Code.*

It's hard to argue otherwise when Dan Hunt, a Duncanville narcotics detective, ECSC shooting leagues manager, and children's shooting coach acted like a buffoon in front of parents and children during his trap league, laughing while he repeatedly fired from his hip. An action that violated the very rules Porter claimed league managers were *tasked* to follow. According to the *2010 Rules **Polices** & Operating Guidelines of Desoto Gun Club; Exhibition shooting of any kind is prohibited.* Was this another example of Dan Hunt not knowing the rules he was *tasked* to follow or simply ignoring the rules to show off?

It's hard to argue otherwise when Dan Hunt, a Duncanville narcotics detective and ECSC shooting leagues manager, allowed infractions of the proper handling of weapons by competitors in his league. Being a police officer does not automatically qualify an individual to supervise or direct the activities of individuals using loaded firearms.

There is a video on YouTube of a DEA Special Agent wearing a police shirt giving a talk on gun safety to a classroom full of grade school children and adults. With the slide on his weapon locked back, he showed the room full of children and adults his pistol, which according to him, was clearly unloaded. The agent then intentionally released the slide on his weapon, loading a round from the magazine into the chamber while clearly stating to the children, "I am the only one in this room professional enough to handle this Glock 40. I am the only one …" POW! He fired a round into his leg. Luckily, no children or other attendees were injured. Being a police officer doesn't automatically confer competency with firearms. It's one of the reasons Federal and State laws require officers to qualify each year with their weapons. Shawn knows of three individuals who have negligently shot themselves. All were in law enforcement.

As I said earlier, leagues manager Dan Hunt disabled the card readers, set out the scoresheets, collected them from a pile in the clubhouse at the end of the match, entered the scores into a computer program, and then posted the results. On several occasions, Hunt would show up, disable the card readers, put out the clipboards, then leave. A competent Plaintiff's attorney would have a field day if someone were hurt or killed. Who was in charge at the ECSC? The answer—no one.

I never observed any supervision over the matches or guidance to new shooters. It was the ECSC osmosis method, new shooters relying on what other unknowledgeable competitors told them. You're on your own at the ECSC with up to forty differing opinions about the rules. Nothing out of the ordinary, just the usual live-fire shooting trap league at the ECSC. The ECSC collected its $4000 in entry fees. Oh, and by the way, beer and hard liquor were permitted once you finish shooting. It meant a competitor, having finished firing, could start drinking alcoholic beverages while the league was still ongoing and other teams were still shooting.

What a way to run a live-fire shooting competition. No safety rules, no rules, no safety briefing, loaded guns, new shooters, some who were clueless, children, alcohol, and no qualified on-site supervision. Yep, it's opening night at the ECSC sponsored trap league. As I said, in my opinion, the Wild West of the clay shooting sports.

Dan Hunt's downright incompetence was never, in my opinion, more evident than in his paperwork. As a law enforcement officer charged with incarcerating alleged criminals with truthful, concise facts and evidence, one would expect ECSC leagues manager Dan Hunt's paperwork, as it applied to the proper and safe oversite of his live-fire shooting trap leagues be professionally prepared. Straightforward and concise, containing all necessary information required to conduct a safe, enjoyable live-fire event for children and adults alike, no matter the experience level of any one competitor.

The first fact needed to run a live-fire shooting event would be the date it takes place. One cannot conduct a shooting event without telling the participants when it will occur. It seems simple enough, especially for a professional report writer and testimony giver such as Duncanville narcotics detective Danny Garth Hunt. In Dan Hunt's profession, it's hard to charge and convict someone of a crime without the correct date on which it occurred. Yet, repeatedly, ECSC leagues manager Dan Hunt couldn't even get something as simple as the dates of the league competitions correct.

ECSC shoot management, leagues manager Dan Hunt's documents for the 2017 fall trap league indicated his league commenced on 9/7/17 and ended on 12/22/17, three days before Christmas. That's four months for a two-month league. In actuality, the league ended on 10/26/17. This was the trap league where Hunt bragged about throwing a competitor out of the league because of complaints from the man's fellow team member, Sherrie Lewis. The competitor was thrown out of the league following the third week of competition.

The title of Dan Hunt's match bulletin for the 2018 spring trap league listed the dates of 5/3/18 to 6/21/18. The correct date was 5/10/18 to 6/28/18. The document's first sentence was even wrong. *The trap league will begin on Thursday, 5/3/18.*

Hunt's scoring reports after each week's competition often had the wrong dates. Not only did leagues manager Dan Hunt not know when his trap leagues began or ended, but neither did any of the participants.

It was the same error for the next league, the 2018 summer trap league, the first league after Hunt's so-called resignation in his vicious, whining pity email, *Immediate resignation.* The 2018 summer trap league started on September 6, 2018, as indicated in the first sentence of the document. Yet, in the summer trap league match bulletin title, Dan Hunt used the same incorrect dates he used for his spring trap league, 5/3/18-6/21/18. Sloppy, sloppy, sloppy, and inexcusable for a law enforcement officer. Did Hunt have the same problem in his police reports? Hunt's errors also raised another issue, his lack of attention to details. A critical element for an individual the Duncanville Police Department allowed to arrest, incarcerate, and write reports to support Hunt's enforcement.

****

I can't overstate that mistakes with guns can lead to injury or death. Even though keeping the shotgun pointed in a safe direction was the third *Safety Requirement* on the ECSC website, muzzle awareness was never enforced or emphasized. At the ECSC, covering others with a shotgun was a disturbing recurrence. The typical response to the infraction—"It's not loaded." How many people have been hurt or killed because of a belief the weapon was empty? Most individuals don't know it is a criminal offense in Texas to point a weapon *at or in the direction of another*, irrespective of whether the individual believes the weapon is unloaded.

Late one afternoon, we had finished firing. Shawn began reloading the machine in the trap house, and I headed inside the clubhouse. A group of kids had arrived and planned to use the trap field once we finished. When I exited the clubhouse, I saw kids holding shotguns on the firing line. Shawn was still downrange, loading the trap house. Yet, the so-called *responsible adult* in charge of this group had sent five kids to the firing line with their shotguns. Shawn asked the so-called *responsible adult* why he sent the kids to stand on the firing line with their shotguns while he was still downrange. The so-called *responsible adult* responded, "Their guns aren't loaded." It was an egregious safety infraction, one that sent the wrong message regarding the safe handling of weapons to the kids.

On another day, I was practicing with a group of members. As there were more than five of us, we took turns shooting. While I was watching the firing group, one of the men had a problem with his shotgun. The loaded round in his gun failed to fire, a misfire. The shooter turned his shotgun so the receiver ejection port faced up. He then began to yank on the bolt's charging handle, attempting to extract the live round. The only problem was that as he yanked on the charging handle, he kept pulling the barrel to his right, pointing the muzzle at the competitor next to him. I walked up and told him to turn and point the shotgun downrange, not at his fellow competitors. Of course, he didn't react well to my intervention. In my opinion, it's better to piss off an unknowledgeable competitor than to ignore a dangerous situation that could result in injury or death.

Another incident occurred when a group of children (maybe a dozen or more whose ages ranged from around 8 to 15) were being instructed by an alleged instructor at the back of the skeet field next to us. As we stood next to the gun rack at the back of our trap field and watched, the instructor demonstrated how to shoulder the shotgun and track the clay target. Instead of keeping his shotgun barrel pointed downrange, he swung it toward us. The instructor then swung the muzzle of his shotgun over the parents observing from behind the trap field, past the clubhouse, then back toward us as he demonstrated the movement to shoot a clay target. At the ECSC, children were learning it was okay to point a gun in the direction of others.

Another day, two teenagers and a man were on the trap field next to where I had been shooting. I watched from a nearby bench. The young girl stepped to the firing line and loaded three rounds into her shotgun. This violated one of the seven *Safety Requirements* posted on the ECSC website. No more than two rounds were to be loaded. She broke one shot. The *responsible adult* standing behind her, stopped her. When she turned to speak to him, her loaded shotgun swung as her body twisted. Her loaded shotgun now covered the other teenager a few feet away. The *responsible adult* never corrected her nor made her point the shotgun downrange. I headed toward her, telling her to point the loaded shotgun downrange.

We reported these incidents to ECSC Treasurer Rusty Porter. To my knowledge, nothing was ever done to mitigate this type of behavior. Rusty Porter's stock answer; "We're just volunteers."

During a trap league, as Hunt's team was shooting, shoot management Dan Hunt, instead of raising his shotgun to a proper firing position in his shoulder, chose to shoot like he was *The Rifleman,* an old TV western series. Dan Hunt repeatedly fired from his hip, indiscriminately firing into the air. With parents and children watching, ECSC shoot management Dan Hunt behaved like a circus clown with a loaded gun as he laughed about his continuous, reckless, dangerous misconduct with a loaded shotgun. There was absolutely nothing funny about what Hunt was doing. Shawn reported the incident to ECSC Treasurer Rusty Porter, who wasn't interested.

After this incident, Shawn checked the ATA rulebook and found no rule against ECSC leagues manager Hunt's misconduct. Shawn then called the ATA office to ask if hip shooting was an acceptable firing position in trap shooting. Shawn was told they didn't have a rule against it because no one would be dumb enough to do it.

Another incident occurred before the start of one of Hunt's trap leagues. A man was mowing the downrange area in front of the trap and skeet fields. Competitors practicing on field zero before the start of the league never stopped firing as the tractor passed back and forth in front of them. Yet, another egregious safety infraction I reported to Rusty Porter.

During the first week of the trap league, Laura McGee and some of her regular teammates danced around on the firing line doing the ECSC Two-Step, covering others with their shotguns. I told McGee that she and some of her teammates needed to be careful about where they were waving their shotguns, only to be told to mind my own business. I have news for Laura McGee. It is the responsibility of all participants to ensure the safe handling of weapons. Something Laura McGee had obviously never learned.

There was the incident on the final night of the 2018 spring trap league. The same night I filed my legitimate ATA protest. ECSC leagues manager, Duncanville narcotics detective, and licensed to carry instructor Dan Hunt shouldered Shawn's competition target rifle, pointing it in the direction of competitors forming in the staging area behind the trap fields, then put his finger on the trigger.

If ECSC shoot management, leagues manager Dan Hunt could act like a buffoon while continuously firing a loaded shotgun from his hip in his own trap league, then why couldn't the participants, especially the kids, do the same? If a children's instructor could cover others on adjoining fields, parents, and the clubhouse with his shotgun, why couldn't the kids he's teaching do the same? If adults competing in Hunt's trap leagues could haphazardly cover others with their shotgun, what message did such misconduct send to the many children on ECSC property?

****

Rule #7 of the ECSC *Safety Requirements* listed on their website addresses children using the facility. *Any shooter under the age of 18 must be accompanied by a responsible adult.*

From the previous examples of gun safety infractions at the ECSC, one could garner from the actions and teachings of the *responsible adults* that *responsible* did not equate to qualified. In these examples, children were learning from purportedly *responsible adults*. The adults may have been responsible, but they weren't qualified to teach children and young teenagers how to handle firearms properly. Remember, this was the gun club where Treasurer Rusty Porter stated in a court document there were no qualifications for a leagues manager. I found this was certainly the case with Dan Hunt.

Another problem with Rule #7 is that it stipulated *accompanied*, not supervised. At the ECSC, *accompanied* could mean five young children or teenagers shooting while Mom or Dad, or whoever *accompanied* them, was in the clubhouse visiting with other parents, reading a book, or possibly even drinking alcoholic beverages.

The many clay-throwing machines are dangerous, even for adults. An experienced ATA registered shooter, ECSC Director David McDaniel, now of Shamrock, Texas, having nearly 12,000 registered targets to his name, suffered head and facial injuries while repairing one of the trap machines. At the ECSC, children were allowed to reload the machines unsupervised. A careless action, failure to turn the machines off, or de-cock the throwing arm could result in injury or death. If it could happen to an experienced ATA registered shooter like ECSC Director David McDaniel, how much easier would it be for a child to be injured by one of the clay-throwing machines? What parent wants to see their child with a face full of stitches, loss of an eye, head injury or worse?

****

Another egregious safety infraction was placing one's finger on the shotgun's trigger before the shotgun was in the proper position to fire. I saw this repeated over and over. ATA rules and procedures state the

ATA's safety outline is based on NRA guidelines. Per the ATA and the referenced NRA guidelines, the second rule of gun safety is; *Always keep your finger off the trigger until ready to shoot.* At the ECSC, the rule wasn't important enough to even make their list of seven *Safety Requirements,* beginning with alcohol use.

The ECSC Facebook page shows a picture of ECSC Director Sherrie Lewis. The eight-picture carousel is dated October 19, 2019. Lewis is the sixth picture with a date of October 21, 2019. Sherrie Lewis, a Life Member of the Dallas Safari Club, is holding a loaded shotgun, which is not pointed downrange. Instead, Lewis is turned toward the camera, grinning, with her finger on the trigger.

In 2018, Director Sherrie Lewis was listed under the *Shotgun Showcase* in the *Meet Your Tribe* section on the DIVA WOW website, an organization dedicated to introducing women to outdoor hunting and shooting sports. From my observation of Director Sherrie Lewis, much like my observation of Dan Hunt and Laura McGee, Lewis never demonstrated a rudimentary knowledge of gun safety rules or the proper handling of weapons.

Having one's finger on the trigger before assuming a proper firing position was a frequent occurrence at the club. As the shooter's hand gripped the stock to raise the shotgun, instead of extending the forefinger alongside the receiver until the gun was in the shoulder, the finger went on the trigger. It's how negligent discharges happen. Any distraction that creates a corresponding tension in the hand can result in the finger pulling the trigger. Considering how competitors were allowed to clown around on the firing line with a loaded shotgun, it was another recipe for disaster.

Competitors, especially new or novice shooters, had a bad habit shoot management, leagues manager Dan Hunt never corrected. It was what Shawn and I referred to as the ECSC Two-Step. Competitors would dance and joke while on the firing line. After breaking a shot, they would step back or to the side, twisting and shuffling to watch or joke with other shooters or competitors behind them, while haphazardly waving their shotguns. If a round had already been loaded into their shotgun, they were now waving a loaded firearm. I've already mentioned what occurred on the opening night of the 2018 spring trap league. When I attempted to correct Laura McGee's unsafe handling of her shotgun, and that of some of her team members, she became belligerent, telling me to mind my own business.

****

Talking while other competitors were shooting was an ongoing problem and a dangerous distraction in the trap leagues. Another situation, in all my years of rifle competition, I had not encountered. Unnecessary, unsportsmanlike chatter on or near the firing line can be highly distracting to a competitor with a loaded gun. The ATA rules and procedures stipulate the only individuals on an active trap field are the competitors and a scorekeeper. The only person talking is the scorekeeper to call lost for a missed target or the competitor to call for the bird. Not so at the ECSC. It's a party, with competitors gathering around the scorekeeper, laughing and chatting.

One of the competitors, Susie Thompson, had a bad habit of talking and laughing on her cell phone or carrying on with other competitors in a loud voice. Thompson's voice would overpower the scorekeeper, making it difficult to hear or concentrate. During one match, her voice was so loud I turned, pointed to her, and ran my finger over my lips. She marched off in a huff. Once the match was finished, I spoke to her, trying to soothe her ruffled feathers. I politely explained why her talking was an issue.

Unfortunately, her disrespect for fellow competitors and unsportsmanlike misbehavior didn't change. Her attitude and talking became an issue during the scoring dispute on the last night of the 2018 Spring trap league. Thompson was a competitor on the misbehaving opposing team that violated numerous ATA rules and procedures, resulting in scoring errors. Susie Thompson was seated alongside co-scorekeepers Larry Degal and Barbara Parks, and as usual, talking and laughing in a loud voice.

An article in *Field and Stream* titled the *Beginner's Guide to Trap Shooting* addresses talking. To quote the article, **Zip Your Trap.** *Keep quiet except when you call "pull." Save any razzing and conversation for after the round ends.* Not in Dan Hunt's trap leagues. It was a party, and then they started drinking.

https://www.fieldandstream.com/beginners-guide-to-trap-shooting

A gun club cannot rely on posting a few rules on its website. Would you want to stand beside a competitor or have your child stand beside a competitor who had never been told—don't inadvertently point your shotgun at people, or put your finger on the trigger until the shotgun is in the shoulder and safely pointed down range?

Gun safety must be reinforced over and over. People forget or don't know and make a mistake. I cannot overstate it. Mistakes with guns can lead to injury or death. It was though, the Ellis County Sportsmans Club. In my observation, the Wild West of the clay shooting sports.

Unlike what ECSC Vice President DVM Chris Rose told me in our recorded phone call, you don't play in the trap leagues. You don't play with loaded guns. Although fun, competitive shooting is a serious sport. The only thing to be thinking about when shooting is your shooting. Not some competitor loudly yacking on a phone or the disruptive behavior of two intentionally misbehaving, out-of-position, laughing tag team scorekeepers. A live-fire shooting competition is not the place to intentionally misbehave, especially at a gun club that allows alcohol consumption. At the ECSC, one never knew if such misbehavior with loaded firearms was because someone was impaired from the consumption of alcoholic beverages.

Yet, at the ECSC, the social atmosphere took precedence over the safety and well-being of members and guests. Let's not irritate anyone by correcting misconduct that could seriously injure or kill someone.

Game On! New Rules!

Chapter Seven

Once I filed my lawsuit, it was game on, new rules. The ECSC leadership could no longer hide. In March 2019, I received numerous ECSC documents, including several ECSC Board meeting minutes, Bylaws, and a copy of the contested scoresheet. To support the *Factual Allegations* in my lawsuit for defamation, breach of contract, and conversion, my attorney amended my lawsuit on April 16, 2019, adding the scoresheet, Bylaws, and *Anita Dickason's Notice of Representation and Litigation Hold.*

Within the meeting minutes, I discovered a second *Board Meeting-Emergency Meeting* was held on December 20, 2018. President Charlie Beard was again conspicuously absent. According to another ECSC document, Beard was identified as the 2018 ECSC President. Per their Bylaws, the president was the only person who could call a special board meeting. Once again, Vice President DVM Chris Rose presided. Why was President Beard calling meetings he wouldn't attend?

On December 21, 2018, I was served with a letter from Secretary Shannon Edwards informing me of a meeting to be held on January 14, 2019, to vote on terminating my membership. Treasurer Rusty Porter had filed a formal complaint, which was attached to the letter. Porter's complaint highlighted Porter's hypocrisy and ignorance of the corporation to which he held the purse strings.

I, Russell Porter, as a member of the Ellis County Sportsmans Club in good standing, refer charges to the Board of Directors regarding the member, Anita Dickason, and hereby request imposition of Article VII of the Bylaws to cancel her membership. In support thereof, I have attached a copy of the Citation and Plaintiff's Original Petition personally served on me as the alleged registered agent for service for ECSC. I intend to use a copy of this petition as an exhibit at any hearing regarding my request for the cancellation of Ms. Dickason's membership. I also serve as the ECSC Treasurer and as Treasurer I know this lawsuit will cost the club money and expose the club to a potential judgment for damages. In my opinion a member suing the club, costing the club money and taking action detrimental to the club's mission of fostering good fellowship among its members and guests constitutes grounds for cancellation of the membership. December 20, 2018. His Excellency, the Grand Poobah of the ECSC, had spoken.

Porter wrote he was the *alleged registered agent.* I've got news for him. Russell Porter was the Registered Agent of Record with the Texas Secretary of State. There's nothing alleged about it. On February 3, 2013, Russell Porter, Treasurer, signed the *Periodic Report of a NonProfit Corporation,* a report required by the Texas Secretary of State. Section B of said report required the identification of the Registered Agent. The individual listed was Russell Porter.

When Porter signed the document, he affirmed he was the Registered Agent. *The undersigned affirms that the person designated as registered agent has consented to the appointment. The undersigned signs this document subject to the penalties imposed by law for the submission of a materially false or fraudulent instrument and certifies under penalty of perjury that the undersigned is authorized under the provisions of law governing the entity to execute the filing instrument.*

Not only did Porter attempt to disclaim his responsibility as the corporation's registered agent, ECSC did the same in future court filings to the 443rd Ellis County District Court, Court of Appeals, Tenth District of Texas, and 40th Ellis County District Court. ECSC leadership attempted to negate their liability by falsely claiming the club was *not a corporation*—an assertion refuted by their Bylaws and other documents.

There was another significant detail. Porter wrote; *as a member of the Ellis County Sportsmans Club in good standing, refer charges to the Board of Directors regarding the member, Anita Dickason.* Porter emphasized his right to file charges as a member in *good standing.*

As I previously addressed, I believe the suspension of my paid membership rights to participate in club-sponsored events by the ECSC Secret 7 during their July 12, 2018, clandestine *Board Meeting-Emergency Meeting,* kangaroo court, meant I would no longer be a member in *good standing.* If I had been stripped of my rights as a member in good standing, I couldn't file a formal complaint at the next monthly board meeting, or the next two years about their leagues manager Dan Hunt's misbehavior with firearms, other gun safety issues and the dangers of mixing guns, alcohol, and children on club property.

Porter also wrote; *I know this lawsuit will cost the club money and expose the club to potential judgment for damages.*

I wasn't the one who exposed the club to the consequences of the lawsuit. Poobah Porter and attorney Clay Hinds had multiple opportunities to avoid a lawsuit. I tried. My attorney tried. Porter and Hinds intentionally ignored us. Porter had no one to blame but himself. Yet, Porter cried foul when I refused to roll over and play dead for him. After all, they couldn't have a woman defend herself against their malicious, false accusations and unprincipled conduct. Instead, I was blamed for; *costing the club money and taking action detrimental to the club's mission of fostering good fellowship.*

Using Porter's arguments, the individuals that should have been kicked out of the club for exposing the club to the consequences of a lawsuit were leagues manager Danny Garth Hunt and the Secret 7, Vice President DVM Christopher Lyons Rose, Treasurer Russell Alvin (Rusty) Porter Jr., and Directors Jerry Jay Gage, Don R. Henslee, Wayne Johnston, David C. McDaniel, and Sherrie A. Lewis.

As elected officers of the ECSC, I believe the Secret 7 intentionally ignored their fiduciary responsibilities. These arrogant, backstabbing individuals cost the club money by *taking action detrimental to the club's mission of fostering good fellowship*. I have already identified the 2018 ECSC Board of Directors violated two sections of Texas law, *Business Organization Code, Sec. 3.153, and Sec. 22.351,* when they refused to provide club records in response to my attorney's legal request, *Notice of Representation of Anita Dickason and Litigation Hold.*

Section 22.221: General Standards for Directors, and *Section 22.235: Officer Liability* of the *Business Organization Code,* governs the conduct of Directors and Officers. When such conduct can be proven not in the *corporation's best interests,* the elected officers and directors lose their immunity and can be held liable. No distinction is drawn as to whether the individual in question is a volunteer or paid.

Furthermore, I believe the vote to suspend my paid membership rights to participate in club sponsored events violated ECSC Bylaws. Rose, Porter and their cronies met in secret, then convicted me of something I clearly didn't do. Their misconduct resulted in the unwarranted destruction of my reputation and credibility. Then, they tried to cover themselves using ATA rules. Rules they apparently never read. In addition, Treasurer Rusty Porter ignored a vote of the board when he augmented my suspension.

The Board deliberately failed to take any action to avoid the consequences of a lawsuit. In my opinion, all this certainly qualified as *taking actions that are detrimental to the club's mission of fostering good fellowship,* and therefore detrimental to the *best interests of the corporation.* Poobah Porter should have been charging himself, the rest of his backstabbing, clandestine cronies, and his incompetent leagues manager, not me. I'm not the one who led them down this path. Danny Garth Hunt did.

In my dealings with the ECSC Board of Directors, I discovered a lack of responsibility and accountability to the membership. It's easy to make decisions that have a disastrous impact on a club member and ignore the consequences when such behavior doesn't affect you personally. It certainly appeared it was the board's attitude. No board member had their reputation destroyed.

I didn't use their underhanded, backstabbing, unprincipled tactics. I was clearly upfront about my intentions. I warned Dan Hunt and the Board of Directors in my *Notice of Representation of Anita Dickason and Litigation Hold* and the *Cease and Desist Letter*. I asked for their voluntary compliance to amicably resolve the issues. They ignored me.

I wasn't the one to be blamed for the lawsuit. I wasn't the one to be blamed for *costing the club money*. I wasn't the one to be blamed for *taking action detrimental to the club's mission of fostering good fellowship among its members and guests*. The responsibility and accountability for the lawsuit fell on the shoulders of a vindictive Duncanville cop, admittedly suffering from mental whatever *after intense and severe exposures at work*, ECSC leagues manager Danny Garth Hunt, and the ECSC Board of Directors, led by their "straight-up" Vice President DVM Christopher Lyons Rose and the Grand Poobah, Treasurer Russell Alvin (Rusty) Porter, Jr.

Another significant detail in Edwards' letter was, unlike their *Board Meeting-Emergency Meeting*, kangaroo court, I would be afforded a hearing at the January 14, 2019, board meeting. The thought of appearing before the Board, especially after what they had done to me during and after the July 2, 2018, monthly board meeting, was disturbing. I didn't know if Dan Hunt would be present. Another discussion in a club meeting triggered Hunt's aggressive, vicious attack on me with his whining pity email, *Immediate resignation,* some three hours after the meeting ended, and sent to nearly one hundred unsuspecting club members, guests, and children at thirty-four minutes to midnight. What would Hunt do now that he was a defendant in my lawsuit? Remember, even before I sued Hunt, he admitted to mental whatever *after intense and severe exposures at work*. Shawn had made a fool of him in the July 2nd meeting. Hunt had clearly threatened Shawn. Who other than an enraged Danny Garth Hunt could have possibly been responsible for placing the Danny Garth Hunt family in a *position of discomfort*? I didn't believe it was a good idea to be in a room with this admittedly overstressed, most likely armed, vindictive Duncanville cop.

There were other concerns. I didn't want to be subjected to another abusive, gesticulating tirade from Director Jerry Jay Gage, which I fully expected would occur. Then there was Sherrie Lewis, another troublemaker, who had twisted the July 2, 2018, monthly board meeting events into a malicious falsehood solely perpetrated to discredit Shawn. Lewis falsely claimed Shawn brought an assault rifle to the meeting and slammed it on the table to intimidate the board members. As I pointed out in Chapter One, nothing could have been further from the truth. Had instigator Sherrie Lewis spread other false accusations about us? It was certainly a valid concern. At the time, I was unaware Lewis had been an instigator in what happened after I left the property on June 28, 2018. Such knowledge would have reinforced my concerns about attending the meeting.

Considering what the ECSC Board and Dan Hunt had done to my reputation, I couldn't risk giving them another opportunity to spread more malicious, false accusations. That's why we stayed away from the ECSC facility. As I recall, after July 2018, the only time we had been on the property was in December 2018. We measured how far out of position the misbehaving co-scorekeepers had set up.

We also obtained the evidence to dispute Director Sherrie Lewis' false accusation about Shawn bringing an assault rifle to the meeting and slamming it on the table to intimidate the board members. We took pictures of the Formica tabletop in the conference room. There was no damage, nary a single scratch on the Formica tabletop.

Evidently, it never occurred to Sherrie Lewis that Shawn's target rifle, the falsely alleged assault rifle she falsely claimed Shawn slammed on the Formica tabletop, weighed approximately 14.6 pounds. The target rifle is nearly the combined weight of a ten-pound and five-pound sledgehammer slammed on a Formica tabletop. Such an action would have severely damaged the Formica tabletop.

We don't slam our expensive target rifles down on tabletops or anywhere else—especially custom-built, highly specialized 14.6-pound target rifles with expensive micrometer sights. The more you know about firearms, the more outrageous Dallas Safari Club Life Member Sherrie Lewis' false claim becomes.

My attorney agreed with my concerns and suggested the best response would be to send a letter to the club's attorney and request it be read at the meeting.

In my letter to the Board, I again pleaded with ECSC leadership to resolve the issues and avoid further court action. I wanted to clear my name of their bogus charge of cheating. As usual, Porter and his cronies ignored my request to work out a solution. Instead, they voted to terminate my membership.

A few days after the meeting, I received another letter from club secretary Shannon Edwards informing me of the Board's decision and the procedures to request a membership appeal meeting.

I didn't want to appeal. I told my attorney it was a bad idea. I knew Porter and his cronies would not provide a level playing field. My attorney was still concerned about ECSC's refusal to produce a copy of their Bylaws. I didn't have the falsely alleged changed scoresheet, meeting minutes, or other documents I legally requested. I would be defending myself unarmed. I fully expected Porter, Rose and their cronies would continue with their underhanded, unprincipled conduct to ensure I would lose my appeal.

My attorney overrode my concerns. She believed I needed to request the membership appeal meeting to demonstrate to the Court that I had taken every possible step to resolve the issues with the club.

As I was to find out, my prediction became painfully true. I was right. I walked into an ambush.

Ambushed

Chapter Eight

In a letter prepared by my attorney and submitted to the Board, I requested a 30-day written notice of the membership appeal meeting date to allow ample time to prepare my presentation and witness testimony. I requested one and one-half hours for my presentation and that of my witnesses, a copy of the agenda, and the names and positions of the board members. I asked if the meeting would be conducted under *Robert's Rules of Order,* and if the board members would be available for questioning.

On February 13, 2019, I received a letter from ECSC Secretary Shannon Edwards advising the meeting would be on March 2, 2019. The Board gave me sixteen days to prepare instead of the thirty days I requested. Their response was on par with the Board's previous unprincipled conduct.

Once my attorney received Secretary Shannon Edwards' letter, in which all of my requests were ignored, my attorney advised it would be best to hold my discussion to a short, prepared statement. We still didn't have a copy of the club's Bylaws, which was of concern. They wouldn't even tell me if the meeting would be conducted according to *Roberts Rules of Order* or identify the board members.

Then mediation entered the picture. On Friday, February 22, 2019, my attorney held a conference call with Defendants' attorney to discuss the mediation procedures. My attorney requested the appeal meeting be canceled until after the mediation. My attorney was concerned the membership appeal meeting would inflame tensions on both sides and be counterproductive to any settlement discussion. ECSC's attorney agreed, stating he would contact his client.

The membership appeal meeting had been posted on the event calendar on the club's website. This was highly unusual as board meetings were typically not posted—another way to keep a club member from showing up and complaining.

After my attorney's conversation with Defendants' attorney, I started watching the event calendar for a change to the scheduled meeting. I checked the website late on Tuesday, February 26, 2019. Nothing had changed on the notice for the meeting for the following Saturday, March 2, 2019.

On Wednesday morning, February 27, 2019, after I checked the club's website, I emailed my attorney. I told her the club was not going to cancel the meeting. They added a comment to the event calendar—breakfast would be served at the Saturday meeting.

Later that morning, I received confirmation from my attorney that the club had indeed refused to cancel the meeting. According to Defendants' attorney, the ECSC claimed, per their Bylaws, they couldn't cancel the meeting because of time restrictions to notify the membership. Without a copy of their Bylaws, we didn't know if this was the truth. It wasn't until after the appeal meeting that I obtained a copy of the Bylaws through the judicial proceeding and discovered there was no such restriction.

ARTICLE VI; C. Notice of all meetings shall be given in writing by mail to all members in good standing in writing not less than seven days prior to the date established for the meeting and stating the purpose of the meeting.

This stipulation only addressed the procedures to notify the membership of an upcoming meeting, not canceling one already scheduled. Any number of reasons could result in a meeting being canceled, including bad weather. Such a restriction would be highly impractical. As for informing the membership, the Board notified club members three days before the meeting that breakfast would be served to those attending. A bribe?

At the time, I had no doubt Poobah Porter and his board's goal was to humiliate me further. Still, I couldn't imagine the level of humiliation they had planned.

A covered porch runs the length of the side of the ECSC clubhouse that faces the trap and skeet fields. Next to the clubhouse is a large, covered pavilion for outdoor cooking, but it wasn't used on this Saturday. Instead, club members clustered around a grill in front of the double doors leading into the clubhouse.

I was appalled to see Dan Hunt behind the grill, cooking. Dan Hunt, their vindictive cop and leagues manager, had sent out a malicious, defamatory email to nearly one hundred unsuspecting members, guests and children, falsely accusing me of abusing him and causing harm to his family. Dan Hunt, the same vindictive cop and leagues manager who admitted to mental whatever *after intense and severe exposures at work*. Dan Hunt, the same vindictive cop and leagues manager who made false accusations to the Board. False accusations that resulted in a bogus charge of cheating, and according to Vice President DVM Chris Rose, the individual responsible for my suspension. Dan Hunt was a defendant in my lawsuit. Yet, there stood Danny Garth Hunt, cooking breakfast for and glad-handing club members at the front doors. These club members were about to vote on whether to overturn the board's decision to kick me out of the club.

It was another sucker punch to my gut. I considered it a deliberate act by ECSC leadership to humiliate me. Porter and his cronies knew I would have to walk past my lying accuser, Dan Hunt, to enter the clubhouse. In my opinion, it was equivalent to a victim making her way into the courtroom, causing her to walk past her assailant cooking breakfast for the jurors on her case.

From there, it never got any better. Until I walked into the clubhouse, filled with club members, I did not fully comprehend the damage the Board of Directors and Dan Hunt had done to me.

Even considering the Board had bribed them with breakfast, the number of members present was surprising. Most of them I didn't know. Why would they care whether the Board kicked me out of the club?

I was approached by an individual, introducing himself as Mike Lee. It wasn't until I obtained a copy of the February 4, 2019, board meeting minutes I learned self-proclaimed "straight-up" guy, the former mayor of Cedar Hill, Texas, DVM Chris Rose had resigned from his newly elected position as 2019 ECSC President. Was Rose's sudden departure because he would now have to face me? As President, Rose would have presided over my appeal meeting. He'd have to look me in the eye, the innocent woman he helped convict in secret over a bogus charge of cheating. Was this the ultimate cowardly ECSC Duck & Cover? Just quit and get the hell out of Dodge. But remember, Chris Rose is a "straight-up" guy.

In Rose's place, the Board appointed an Executive Vice President of a Waxahachie bank, Mike Lee, as their new President. Mike Lee directed me to a table facing rows of chairs on the opposite side of the room. Many club members turned their backs on me as I approached the table. As a Dallas police officer, I spent many hours working a beat. I encountered hostility on numerous levels while enforcing my duties as a police officer. I had never experienced a wave of hostility from a group of individuals as I did that day. The animosity I felt in the ECSC clubhouse emphasized the effectiveness of the Board of Directors and Dan Hunt's destruction of my reputation and credibility. Just as I had feared, the membership appeal meeting was a lost cause and only added to the physical and emotional stress I had already endured.

For some eight months, the only people doing the talking, spreading their false accusations, were the Board of Directors, Dan Hunt, and Sherrie Lewis. Still, what I encountered in the clubhouse was excessive and didn't make sense. It wasn't until later in the meeting I realized the reason.

I read a short speech covering the highlights of the scoring dispute. I also explained the bogus charge of cheating, wrongful suspension of my paid membership rights and the willful disregard of Texas law by the Board in refusing to produce club records to which I was entitled.

Once I finished, Mike Lee opened the meeting to questions. After everything that had already happened, I don't know why I should have been disturbed by the attitude of one of the members, a mid-level ATA registered shooter, Robert D. Fournerat of Irving, Texas.

Since joining the club, Shawn and I had shot with Fournerat numerous times. Several times, Fournerat had complained about how he'd been mistreated by the Board of Directors when he unsuccessfully ran for a director position. Fournerat emphasized how Porter and the board had blackballed him.

Robert Fournerat had always led me to believe he was my friend. In 2017, Robert Fournerat built a device to insert into the buttstock of a shotgun. Robert Fournerat wanted to market the device under a new company name. Knowing I was a graphics designer, my thought-to-be friend, Robert Fournerat, asked for my help in designing a logo for his company. Since Fournerat had no idea what he wanted, I created over thirty designs for Fournerat to choose from. In addition, I designed labels and recoil reduction charts for Fournerat's advertising. Over approximately four months, I estimate I spent around a hundred hours on Robert Fournerat's project. I didn't ask him to pay me for my time, wanting to help out a fellow competitor—someone I wrongly perceived as my friend. Ultimately, I accepted one of Fournerat's used, inexpensive prototypes for my shotgun. A small piece of metal about four inches long.

At the membership appeal meeting, Robert Fournerat showed no outrage over the bogus charge of cheating, the ATA rules violations and intentional misbehavior of the scoring team, or the unprincipled conduct of the Board of Directors. Instead, Robert Fournerat was incensed by the fact Shawn had brought a wrongly purported assault rifle to a meeting. Fournerat's comments echoed Director Sherrie Lewis' malicious false statement that Shawn had brought an assault rifle to a board meeting, slamming it on the Formica tabletop to intimidate the Board.

Fournerat overlooked ECSC Treasurer Rusty Porter, an individual who built AR-15 assault-style rifles at his home in Ovilla, Texas, had proudly brought his assault-style rifle to the club to show to club members. Fournerat overlooked the former mayor and council member of Cedar Hill, Texas, that "straight-up" kind of guy, Vice President DVM Christopher Lyons Rose, had proudly brought his Ruger 6.5 Creedmoor Precision (sniper-style) Rifle to the club. Rose even asked Shawn to teach him how to shoot it.

Robert Fournerat never expressed any outrage about perceived intimidation with assault-style rifles Rusty Porter built, or 6.5 Creedmoor sniper rifle intimidation on the part of the former mayor of Cedar Hill, Texas, DVM Chris Rose. What if a member witnessed the former mayor of Cedar Hill, Texas, with his 6.5 Creedmoor sniper-style rifle in his hands, or ECSC Treasurer Rusty Porter holding what appeared to be an M-16 assault rifle? They probably wouldn't give it a second thought. My point is—the ECSC is a GUN club. People bring guns to a gun club, even taking them into the clubhouse.

Shawn's 14.6-pound, across-the-course, specifically built target rifle was no more an assault rifle than Robert D. Fournerat's trap gun was a combat shotgun or entry weapon. All Robert D. Fournerat wanted to do was grill me about the wrongly purported assault rifle. A target rifle that, before the meeting ever began, President Charlie Beard and Treasurer Rusty Porter gave Shawn permission to bring into the meeting with no objections from any board member, including Sherrie Lewis.

Before answering questions, I stated that due to the ongoing lawsuit, there were issues I couldn't discuss. My attorney, who was present at the meeting, had been very emphatic that I could not address any details of the lawsuit. As the reason for the presence of the target rifle at the July 2, 2018, board meeting was part of the evidence in the lawsuit, I couldn't explain. Yet, there sat Robert D. Fournerat in the front row, directly in front of me. My thought-to-be friend, Robert D. Fournerat, the guy who accepted so much for so little, hammered me with unending questions as he regurgitated Sherrie Lewis' false statements. In nearly eight months, Robert D. Fournerat never gave me the courtesy of a phone call. My thought-to-be friend, Robert D. Fournerat, waited to ambush me during the membership appeal meeting. So much for my thought-to-be friend Robert D. Fournerat *fostering good fellowship*. After what I did for Robert D. Fournerat, I found his behavior toward me inexcusable. Robert D. Fournerat brought new meaning to an old saying. With friends like this, one doesn't need enemies.

I have no idea why Robert D. Fournerat believed Porter and his cronies blackballed him. Personally, I think Robert D. Fournerat would have fit in perfectly on Porter's Board of Directors.

Then, there was a question from a club member who wanted to know if mediation was involved and how to keep the facility from getting shut down. Suddenly, it all made sense, why so many club members had shown up. The reason for all the hostility toward me.

In my experience, I have learned people don't typically react to a situation until it personally affects them. Someone was telling the membership my lawsuit could shut the club down. While most of the club members could have cared less about what the Board of Directors did or didn't do or that the Board voted to throw me out of the club, this purported threat to shut down the ECSC affected them.

Nothing could have been further from the truth. The ECSC had an insurance policy under the Master Commercial General Liability Policy for the National Skeet Shooting Association & National Sporting Clays Association.

T.H.E. Insurance was a division of AXA, a massive insurance conglomerate headquartered in Paris, France. Total assets for the

French insurance conglomerate were a reported 830-plus billion dollars. That's right, close to a trillion dollars. To compare, the total assets for Exxon Mobil are 369 billion dollars. T.H.E. Insurance insured high-risk venues such as gun clubs. At the time, thirty-one (31) high-risk venues were listed on T.H.E.'s website. Curiously, gun clubs were not listed.

The 830-plus billion-dollar French insurance conglomerate hired a large, multi-state law firm in downtown Dallas to represent Dan Hunt and the ECSC. The French insurance conglomerate was paying the freight for the ECSC and Hunt's defense.

There was no threat of closure to the property, but evidently, that's not what the members were told. Even though their insurance company was paying for their downtown Dallas multi-state law firm, it didn't stop the Board from misleading the membership.

My lawsuit wouldn't bankrupt the club or shut it down, not with their 830-plus billion-dollar French insurance conglomerate picking up their tab. It was par for the course, the way Porter and his cronies ran the club. Let's keep the membership in the dark.

I hadn't been wrong in my concerns the deck would be stacked against me. I just had no idea the depths to which Porter and his cronies were willing to stoop with their false statements to ensure they had the support of club membership.

When the vote was taken, it turned into a Keystone Cops routine. It was apparent the procedures were poorly planned and executed. I had asked about *Robert's Rules of Order* in my appeal request to Secretary Shannon Edwards. Secretary Edwards refused to answer my simple question.

It wasn't until the Board was later forced to produce their Bylaws through the judicial proceedings that I discovered the Bylaws stipulated *Robert's Rules of Order* governed all meetings.

Waxahachie banker Mike Lee's actions certainly didn't demonstrate knowledge of *Robert's Rules of Order*. When a show of hands didn't work, Lee had members popping up and down, attempting to get a count. A few brave individuals voted for me, but the majority didn't. The vote was a foregone conclusion. I never had a chance.

The last issue dealt with my $48 balance on my ECSC debit card, money the club obtained from a charge to my credit card. The club had installed a card reader system to activate the clay target throwing machines. The reason was to stop the extensive theft by members not paying for their clay targets. Members were issued a debit card. Members loaded money to their debit card via a charge to the member's credit card to pay for rounds of clay targets.

According to their minutes of the January 14, 2019, board meeting, the Board voted to refund the balance on my debit card, which was $48. This was my money the club had obtained by a charge to my credit card. It didn't belong to the club. Furthermore, Secretary Shannon Edwards informed me in her January 15, 2019, letter that upon receipt of the debit card, the Board would refund the balance.

At the conclusion of the March 2nd ambush, otherwise known as the membership appeal meeting, I complied, returning my debit card, gate card, and club keys to Waxahachie banker and ECSC President Mike Lee. President Mike Lee promised to send me a check for the $48 balance on my club debit card. My attorney was present when this conversation took place. At the time of his promise, Mike Lee was a Vice President of a local Waxahachie bank where I had an account.

There is a line from a Bret Maverick episode, *Shady Deals at Sunny Acres*. "If you can't trust your banker, who can you trust?" As of the date of this book, some five-plus years after the membership appeal meeting, I still have not received my $48 as promised by Waxahachie banker Mike Lee. Instead, the ECSC Board of Directors intentionally stole it. Remember, "If you can't trust your banker, who can you trust?" As usual, it was Poobah Porter and his cronies *fostering good fellowship*.

Duck Died

Chapter Nine

Once I filed my lawsuit, Dan Hunt and the ECSC Board of Directors could no longer hide. As I said earlier, it was game on, new rules. Poobah Porter and his cronies could no longer stonewall me. They could no longer employ the ECSC Duck & Cover. Duck died.

It took a lawsuit and thousands of dollars to force ECSC leadership to produce documents I had lawfully requested on July 24, 2018, and per Texas law, should have been readily available to me as a paying member. Within their documents I received on March 20, 2019, I discovered the evidence of Hunt's and the ECSC's culpability.

I viewed these documents as a damning indictment of the unprincipled, malicious conduct of the 2018 ECSC Board of Directors and Dan Hunt, their unqualified, incompetent, vindictive, hothead leagues manager. Dan Hunt and the ECSC Board of Directors knowingly and maliciously destroyed the reputations and credibility of two innocent individuals who never harmed anyone at the ECSC.

Among the documents I finally received included the following:
- ECSC Bylaws
- ECSC Board of Directors Summary: 2015-2019
- Copy of the contested scoresheet
- ECSC board meeting minutes
- *2010 Rules, **Polices** & Operating Guidelines of Desoto Gun Club Operating as Ellis County Sportsmans Club*

Just as with **Saftey** on their website, the ECSC misspelled policies.

The Bylaws were an enlightening document that refuted numerous actions by the Board, as I have referenced in this and other chapters. Among these was the section, Article VII of the Bylaws, that Rusty Porter utilized to justify his formal complaint to the Board to terminate my membership. The section also stipulated the same conditions for suspension. According to this section of the Bylaws, no vote could be taken on suspending a member without a fifteen-day notice and a hearing for the accused. Not only was I not afforded a notice or hearing, I didn't even know I had been accused of any wrongdoing. This section was the reason my attorney amended my lawsuit to add their Bylaws.

****

Within the *ECSC Board of Directors Summary: 2015-2019*, I discovered what appeared to be a discrepancy with the elected directors. The ECSC Bylaws stipulate that the Board shall comprise nine (9) directors elected by a majority vote of the members. Per the Bylaws, the elected Board of Directors by the membership then elects *from their numbers a President, Vice-President, Secretary and Treasurer.*

The *ECSC Board of Directors Summary, 2015-2019*, listed their names and titles by year. In 2018, the Board of Directors consisted of the following:

> President—Charlie Beard
> Vice President—Chris Rose
> Treasurer—Rusty Porter
> Secretary—Shannon Edwards
> Directors—Wayne Johnston, Tab Haley, Jay Gage, Don Henslee, and David McDaniel

In total, nine board members. The list of officers and directors appeared straightforward until compared to the meeting minutes for July 2, 2018. The Board members present were Charlie Beard, Rusty Porter, Jay Gage, Don Henslee, Tab Haley, and Sherrie Lewis.

Whoa! Wait a minute. Back up. Where did Sherrie Lewis come from? The individual I perceived as an ECSC instigator was identified as a board member in the minutes of the July 2, 2018, July 12, 2018, and December 20, 2018, meetings. Yet, Sherrie Lewis was not elected to the 2018 Board of Directors as stipulated in the *ECSC Board of Directors Summary, 2015-2019*.

Had Sherrie Lewis been appointed to replace another director who had resigned? The missing board members at the July 2, 2018, meeting, Vice-President, DVM Chris Rose, Secretary Shannon Edwards, and Directors Wayne Johnston and David McDaniel, were still on the board. Had they shown up, there would have been ten (10) board members, not nine (9) as stipulated by the Bylaws.

Three of the four missing officers at the July 2nd meeting, Rose, McDaniel, and Johnston, showed up for the July 12, 2018, clandestine *Board Meeting-Emergency Meeting*, kangaroo court. Secretary Shannon Edwards was present at the meeting on December 20, 2018. This certainly raised another question regarding the 2018 Board of Directors' adherence to their Bylaws.

****

The 2010 Rules **Polices** & Operating Guidelines of Desoto Gun Club Operating as Ellis County Sportsmans Club, is what I refer to as their phantom manual. This was a document I had never seen.

In my July 24, 2018, *Notice of Representation of Anita Dickason and Litigation Hold*, I asked for a copy of the club's rules and regulations. It took suing the ECSC, spending thousands of dollars to obtain this document.

Not long after I joined the ECSC, I asked Rusty Porter about holding registered ATA matches at the club. Porter said they didn't hold registered matches because they didn't want the ATA telling them what to do. Maybe this was why the ECSC Bylaws, and their 2010 *Rules Polices & Operating Guidelines of Desoto Gun Club Operating as Ellis County Sportsmans Club* were kept secret, unavailable to the members or guests. The Grand Poobah and the rest of the ECSC leadership didn't want to play by their own rules. They didn't want to be held accountable for not following the club's bylaws or their *rules, policies and operating guidelines*. Yet, Treasurer Rusty Porter stated in response to an interrogatory, *"League managers are tasked with the responsibility of ensuring the club's rules, policies and bylaws are followed."*

Schedule and Operating Hours: *A Range Master will be present at the Club on Wednesday between 5:00 p.m. and 8:00 p.m. and on Saturday and Sunday between 12:00 noon and 6:00 p.m.*

I never saw or heard of such an individual during the years I was a member. Was this written for the benefit of their insurance carrier, the 830-plus billion-dollar French insurance conglomerate? I mentioned in a previous chapter that I obtained a copy of the insurance application. One of the questions dealt with range officers' qualifications and range safety. In that chapter, I speculated how the Board answered the question. Was this provision the answer? If you have a phantom manual, why not a phantom *Range Master*?

General Rules-Leagues*: Non-members will be expected to adhere to all club policies and procedures.*

Since I, as a member, had to sue the club to obtain a copy, how could a non-member be held responsible? Was this more verbiage for their insurance carrier? Here is another point to consider. How could the members be expected to *adhere to all club policies and procedures* or be held responsible for their guests when the members didn't know the rules? Talk about the blind leading the blind.

This was the osmosis system at the ECSC. The unknowledgeable leading the unknowledgeable. It was why there were problems in the administration of the trap leagues. It was what I told the Board during the July 2, 2018, monthly board meeting. There were no rules governing the proper scoring of matches in the trap leagues.

General Rules-Member Conduct*: Violation of any applicable federal, state, or local laws, ordinances or any Club rules or any behavior not in the best interests of the club or its membership will result in disciplinary action by the Board.*

This was truly an enlightening provision. Perhaps this was another reason why this document wasn't to be found. Dan Hunt, Poobah Porter, and their cronies were club members and should have been held to the same standards as any other club member.

Dan Hunt's malicious, libelous *behavior* in sending his whining pity email, *Immediate resignation* to nearly one hundred unsuspecting members and guests, and Hunt's false statements to the Board of Directors exposed the club to a lawsuit.

It would seem Hunt's malicious *behavior* wasn't in the *best interests of the club.* Hunt's *behavior* should have resulted in *disciplinary action* against Dan Hunt, not me.

Dan Hunt and the Secret 7 intentionally destroyed the reputation and credibility of two innocent individuals with a bogus charge of cheating. Their *behavior* exposed the club to a lawsuit that wasn't in the *best interests of the club.* Such *behavior* should have resulted in *disciplinary action* against Dan Hunt and the Secret 7.

The 2018 Board of Directors violated *state law* by refusing to provide club documents legally requested by my attorney. A *violation* that should have resulted in *disciplinary action* against the Board of Directors.

According to the stipulations within the *2010 Rules* **Polices &** *Operating Guidelines,* a vindictive leagues manager Dan Hunt, and the 2018 Board of Directors were subject to disciplinary actions. Of course, that wasn't going to happen. The 2018 Board of Directors were not about to discipline themselves. At the ECSC, a double standard existed, one for the members and one for the Grand Poobah and his cronies. Besides, as long as no one knew what they were up to, the Board had no qualms about their unprincipled *behavior not in the best interests of the club.*

Shooting Safety & Regulations*: All shooters, referees, and spectators shall wear safety glasses and hearing protection while on or near shooting ranges.*

Another rule that was never enforced. Nor was it mentioned in any of Dan Hunt's match bulletins I read. Was this just additional verbiage for their insurance carrier?

Shooting Safety & Regulations: *Exhibition shooting of any kind is prohibited unless approved in advance by the Board.*

So much for shoot management, leagues manager Dan Hunt, the individual *tasked with the responsibility of ensuring the club's rules, policies and bylaws are followed* when shoot management Dan Hunt enacted his extensive, clownlike antics, shooting trap from his hip like an armed buffoon in front of parents and children. Hunt's misbehavior with a loaded weapon should have resulted in disciplinary action per the provision under **General Rules-Member Conduct.** Yet, when Shawn notified Porter of Dan Hunt's misbehavior with a loaded weapon in front of parents and children, Porter wasn't interested. As I said, a double standard existed.

Shooting Safety & Regulations: *No beer or alcohol beverages are to be taken onto any shooting range. If you are shooting or plan to shoot don't drink alcohol.*

This one was a humdinger. In a previous chapter, I cited the issues with this policy. On many occasions, I'd see beer cans in the trash barrels at the edge of the trap and skeet fields. These barrels were in place so competitors could dispose of shotgun hulls without leaving the trap and skeet fields and walking to the dumpster in the parking lot. The trash barrels were attached to a wood rack where competitors placed their shotguns while waiting for their turn to shoot. The wood racks were near benches where competitors would sit. To me, the proximity of the beer cans to the trap and skeet fields certainly raised a question as to whether members and guests were drinking while shooting.

****

The most critical evidence I received was a copy of the contested scoresheet. I had proof that the charges of cheating were bogus. If you recall, according to the former mayor of Cedar Hill, Texas, that self-proclaimed "straight-up" guy, ECSC Vice President DVM Christopher Lyons Rose, I was thrown out of the trap leagues for, "Uh, changing scoresheets without you know talking to anybody." When I protested, telling Rose I had followed shoot management Dan Hunt's instructions to note the errors in the margin, Rose stated, "Well that's you know not how it was reported."

The scoresheet, along with their July 2, 2018, monthly board meeting minutes, showed Dan Hunt intentionally made false accusations to the Board of Directors. Dan Hunt was doing the reporting as referenced by Vice President DVM Chris Rose during his phone call. It didn't take a NASA engineer to know I didn't change my scores on the scoresheet, nor did any team member.

Scores are written in pencil. An altered score is clearly visible. Larry Degal, the misbehaving scorekeeper, entered zeros for my two contested points. To this day, there are still zeros indicating misses on the contested scoresheet. Did that "straight-up" former Cedar Hill mayor, Vice President DVM Christopher Lyons Rose even look at the scoresheet?

The scoresheet reflects Dan Hunt's instructions. My squad leader's notations for my two contested points are in the margin of the scoresheet. As my squad leader, Shawn did what Dan Hunt told me to do. It proves what I said to Vice President DVM Chris Rose during our recorded phone call was true.

What was also clearly evident on the scoresheet was Larry Degal erased a zero, "0," for a missed target and drew a line, "/," to show a hit target on the second relay for Shawn. It was confirmed by what Dan Hunt wrote in his July 1, 2018, email. *The scorekeeper reported a target that was changed, by the scorekeeper, from a lost target to a hit target at the request of the shooter.* In his email, Dan Hunt identified the only person who changed a score on the official scoresheet was the misbehaving scorekeeper Larry Degal.

The scoresheet and Hunt's email were proof that neither I nor any member of my team cheated. It was the evidence the Board, led by the former mayor of Cedar Hill, that "straight-up" kind of guy, Vice President DVM Chris Rose, ignored in their clandestine *Board Meeting-Emergency Meeting*, kangaroo court.

After I carefully examined the scoresheet, I made a surprising discovery. The misbehaving official scorekeeper, Larry Degal, changed two other scores. It was the first and twenty-third shot on the second relay for another team member, the fifth shooter in the rotation. Degal erased two zeros in the scores for the fifth shooter and entered lines, changing the scores from a miss to a hit. Shawn was the first shooter in the rotation, and I was the third shooter.

These two scores Degal changed were never referenced in Dan Hunt's so-called investigation. According to Dan Hunt's July 1, 2018, email, "*The scorekeeper reported a target that was changed, by the scorekeeper, from a lost target to a hit target at the request of the shooter.*

Larry Degal only admitted to changing one score, not three, as evidenced by the scoresheet. The official misbehaving scorekeeper Larry Degal obviously didn't want to admit he had made other mistakes. Such an admission would certainly cast doubt on Degal's credibility that he accurately recorded the contested targets for Shawn and me.

Larry Degal's mistakes were further evidence of Dan Hunt's incompetent, slipshod, one-sided, biased so-called investigation. Larry Degal's mistakes in the score for the fifth shooter on my team further emphasized Dan Hunt's malicious intent to make Shawn the culprit and ignore the blatant mistakes of the misbehaving scorekeeper.

I seriously doubt Larry Degal could attest to any of the scores or would know whether they were correct or not. The tag team of co-scorekeepers Larry Degal and Barbara Parks and a laughing, chatty Susie Thompson were seated some fifty measured feet from a proper scoring position.

Typically, clay targets are launched at forty-one to forty-three miles per hour, depending on the radar gun used. Shooting is fast. Once a shooter has fired, the next shooter is ready, calling for the next bird. The ATA stipulates that the correct scoring position is three yards behind the firing line. The three-yard proximity ensures the scorekeeper can see whether the shooter hit the clay bird and whether the guns are empty when "rotate" is called. It's pretty hard to do this some fifty feet out of position.

Dan Hunt had the scoresheet. Dan Hunt was shoot management. Dan Hunt is a purported, trained investigator. Dan Hunt knew that neither my teammates nor I changed my scores. Yet that was not what Dan Hunt told the Board, as recorded in the July 2, 2018, meeting minutes. The meeting minutes, discussed in a later chapter, will show Duncanville narcotics detective and ECSC leagues manager Dan Hunt lied to the Board. I don't believe Dan Hunt ever expected his false accusations to be exposed.

I would ask this of the Secret 7's presiding officer, ECSC Vice President DVM Chris Rose. When and where did I cheat? When I attempted to find out during Rose's phone call, Rose refused to tell me. This was what "straight-up" Rose said, "So like I said, that's the action that's been taken and uh we can't argue about it right now. So they'll send you an email." I asked if I could send him a letter. Rose replied, "No. I really don't want to get in the middle of it."

ECSC Vice President DVM Chris Rose presided over his clandestine kangaroo court that wrongly suspended my paid membership rights and denied me an opportunity to defend myself. I was wrongfully kicked out of the trap leagues. Rose and his cronies caused irrevocable damage to my reputation. Then Rose had the gall to tell me, "No. I really don't want to get in the middle of it." Doctor of Veterinary Medicine Christopher Lyons Rose, Dallas area noted clay shooter, the former council member and past mayor of Cedar Hill, Texas, what a "straight-up" kind of guy.

****

What I did not receive were security camera tapes for June 28, July 2, and July 12, 2018, which the ECSC had been ordered to preserve in the July 24, 2018, *Notice of Representation of Anita Dickason and Litigation Hold*. I also asked for a copy of the tapes. A request the Board ignored, along with other club records my attorney requested.

The Board's receipt of the *Litigation Hold* on July 24, 2018, was within the 30-day cycle for the security camera system referenced by Rusty Porter in the July 2, 2018, monthly board meeting. Porter's statement occurred during a discussion of the automated front gate installation and the security camera system.

Obtaining a copy of the tapes before their destruction date was why I rushed to get an attorney, prompting my attorney's quick action in sending the *Notice of Representation of Anita Dickason and Litigation Hold*. It was to preserve the evidence that would demonstrate the truthfulness of my statements before the security camera tapes were erased.

The reason ECSC cited for their failure to produce the tapes along with the other club records I received on March 20, 2019, was: *The club's security cameras contain an "auto delete" feature that deletes and records over footage every 14 days. By the time Defendant received notice of the lawsuit, the footage was gone.*

Porter's statement of a thirty-day cycle during the July 2, 2018, monthly board meeting was now *14 days*. For argument's sake, the security camera tapes should have been preserved for their July 12, 2018 meeting. Based on ECSC's alleged *14 days*, the security camera tape wasn't destroyed until July 26, 2018, two days after receiving my attorney's notification to preserve the tapes. The ECSC never notified my attorney of any issues in providing the tapes. Either way, *14 days* or 30 days, Porter and his cronies intentionally ignored a legal notification to preserve the security camera tapes.

In my opinion, Poobah Porter would never allow the security

camera tapes to see the light of day. The camera tapes were too damning for the ECSC Board, especially Danny Garth Hunt, Jerry Jay Gage, and Sherrie A. Lewis.

On June 28, 2018, the security camera tapes would have shown Duncanville narcotics detective, shoot management and leagues manager Dan Hunt pointing a competition target rifle in the direction of the staging area where people were gathering before the league started. The camera tapes would have provided visible evidence of what transpired in the clubhouse before and after I left the property.

The security camera tapes for the July 2, 2018, board meeting would have provided visual evidence of the actions of the meeting participants. The conference room camera tape would have shown Shawn carefully laying an inert competition target rifle on the table as evidence before the meeting began. This only took place after being given permission by both President Beard and Treasurer Rusty Porter to do so with no objection from any board member.

The camera tape would have shown Rusty Porter pointing to the camera during the discussion on the confidentiality agreement.

The camera tape would have shown Dan Hunt's aggressive behavior when he exploded from his chair, lunging toward the table as he threatened Shawn.

The camera tape would have shown ECSC Director Jay Gage's abusive, lengthy, wildly gesticulating tirade upon a female club member.

The camera tape would have shown that neither Shawn nor I exhibited any threatening gestures or misconduct.

The camera tape would have shown Hunt, Porter and his cronies in a true light.

Then consider Sherrie Lewis' malicious, false accusation about Shawn slamming a falsely alleged assault rifle onto the table. The camera tape would have shown Sherrie Lewis' malicious, defamatory story about assault rifle intimidation never took place. If Sherrie Lewis' falsely alleged assault rifle intimidation had indeed occurred, then consider these points.

- ✓ Why did Rusty Porter, nor anyone on the board, not immediately save the security camera tape to use against us?
- ✓ Why wasn't the meeting immediately suspended?
- ✓ Why did Duncanville narcotics detective Dan Hunt, a veteran police officer, not react to what Hunt and Lewis later falsely alleged was an act of intimidation with an assault rifle?
- ✓ Why was the Sherrie Lewis version not in the minutes of the meeting?
- ✓ Why was this falsely alleged intimidation with a falsely alleged assault rifle not mentioned in Dan Hunt's pity email, *Immediate resignation,* some three hours later?
- ✓ Why did the Board revert to a bogus two-point cheating scandal to get rid of us when, according to Lewis, they supposedly had Shawn intimidating the Board with an assault rifle?
- ✓ Why did Sherrie Lewis, who, according to their minutes, was alarmed by a small, plastic container clinking the table, not run out of the room after allegedly being intimidated by an assault rifle slammed on the table two feet in front of her?
- ✓ Why did Sherrie Lewis just sit there, never stirring from her chair during the lengthy meeting?
- ✓ Why was there no damage to the Formica tabletop from a target rifle weighing approximately that of a fifteen-pound sledgehammer slamming onto the tabletop? Nope, nary a scratch was on that table.

What's wrong with this picture? The answer is quite simple. It never happened. Director Sherrie Lewis maliciously made it up for one purpose—to falsely malign Shawn. Evidently, in Sherrie Lewis' zeal to falsely accuse Shawn, none of these contradictions ever occurred to her. I believe Sherrie Lewis was used to getting away with badmouthing others. According to Hunt, he kicked Lewis' fellow team member out of a trap league because of her complaints. To me, it appeared Porter condoned the misbehavior of Dan Hunt and Jerry Jay Gage. Porter did the same with Sherrie Lewis.

Lewis wasn't the only one to spread the false accusation about intimidation with an assault rifle. Dan Hunt jumped on the bandwagon when he lied in his filings to the 443rd Ellis County District Court. Furthermore, in Hunt's filing to the Court of Appeals, Tenth District of Texas, he embellished his malicious lie.

No wonder Porter and his cronies couldn't let those security camera tapes surface. The camera tapes were damning evidence. Visual evidence that, in my opinion, would have shown the appalling misbehavior of Danny Garth Hunt, Jerry Jay Gage, and Sherrie A. Lewis.

On April 16, 2019, my attorney filed PLAINTIFF'S FIRST AMENDED PETITION with the 443rd Ellis County District Court. *Exhibit A- the scoresheet, Exhibit B-ECSC Bylaws*, and *Exhibit C- Notice of Representation of Anita Dickason and Litigation Hold* were added to support the *Factual Allegations* within my lawsuit.

<u>CAUSE NO. 99913</u>
<u>PLAINTIFF'S FIRST AMENDED PETITION</u>
<u>IV. FACTUAL ALLEGATIONS,</u>

Paragraph #11 was amended; *As demonstrated by the attached <u>Exhibit A</u>, Ms. Dickason did not, nor did any member of her team, change the official scores on the five-member team score sheet.*

Paragraph #12 was amended; *Prior to the filing of this lawsuit, despite being a paying member of the ECSC, Ms. Dickason had never been provided a copy of the ECSC bylaws, constitution, or any other documents that address the rights of club membership. On or about March 20, 2019, a copy of the ECSC constitution and bylaws were finally obtained through discovery and are attached as <u>Exhibit B</u>. This document conclusively established that the ECSC failed to follow its own policies and procedures with respect to both the handling of the scoring* *dispute, the decision to bar Ms. Dickason from the shooting league for a two-year period, and the subsequent refusal by the ECSC to provide Ms. Dickason with a copy of the club's rules and policies when requested on or about July 20, 2018. A copy of that request is attached hereto as <u>Exhibit C</u>.*

Paragraph #14 was added; *On December 21, 2018, Ms. Dickason received a letter from the ECSC that club member Russell Porter sought to have her membership rights terminated (in addition to her 2-year ban from trap league participation). The ECSC approved the termination of Ms. Dickason's membership on January 14, 2019. She appealed the termination and her appeal was held on March 2, 2019, where her ECSC membership was officially and finally terminated.*

Paragraph #15 was added; *Defendant Hunt's defamatory statements have resulted in irreparable and incalculable harm and loss of standing and good will in the ECSC and among fellow club members, friends, and competitors. These statements, along with the actions of ECSC, have not only caused tremendous mental and emotional harm to Ms. Dickason, but the defamatory statements, along with Ms. Dickason's expulsion from the ECSC, have also jeopardized her ability to join similar sports clubs in the area, leaving her barred from meaningful participation in a sport that has been her life-long passion.*

Emergency! Paging Dr. Porter!

Chapter Ten

Shawn and I read and followed the ATA rules. We expected the same from other competitors. We expected the same from ECSC shoot management. We simply spoke up and asked that the rules be followed. This was about loaded guns, firearms safety, and what happens when competitors and shoot management fail to follow the rules and misbehave in a live-fire shooting competition. According to the meeting minutes of July 12, 2018, ATA rules governed the trap league.

On the last night of the 2018 Spring trap league, I filed a valid ATA protest regarding the opposing team's misbehavior and violations of ATA rules and procedures that resulted in the scoring errors to the individual charged with the oversite of the trap league, shoot management Dan Hunt. As a competitor, this was the proper procedure. I followed the rules, Dan Hunt didn't.

Instead, Dan Hunt's subsequent actions escalated my valid ATA protest into a contentious issue with six other people in the trap league. The six consisted of two men on the losing second-place team and four members of the misbehaving team. Though Dan Hunt would subsequently attempt to claim it was "over half the damn league" that wanted Shawn thrown out of the trap league.

Because of Dan Hunt's misbehavior with firearms, incompetence in running the trap leagues, and his action against Shawn, we took the issue to the Board of Directors. Once again, it was the proper procedure.

The result was that Dan Hunt, a vindictive Duncanville narcotics detective and incompetent, unqualified ECSC leagues manager, turned the July 2, 2018, meeting into an ongoing confrontation with his false accusations, physical aggression, and a threat. I was subjected to a lengthy, gesticulating, abusive tirade by Director Jerry Jay Gage.

In a subsequent meeting on July 12, 2018, of which I had no knowledge, nor even knew I had been accused of wrongdoing, I was kicked out of the trap league. According to Vice President Chris Rose, it was for "Uh, changing scoresheets without you know talking to anybody." A bogus accusation of cheating that destroyed my reputation and credibility.

The minutes of the meetings on July 2, 2018, and July 12, 2018, didn't become a problem until I filed a lawsuit against the ECSC and Dan Hunt. The 2018 Board of Directors had already ignored a lawful request from my attorney for a copy of the minutes. Porter and his cronies had no intention of allowing me to see their minutes.

Once I filed my lawsuit, it all changed. Minutes of a corporation's meetings are the legal record of the actions of the elected officers. As part of the judicial proceedings, ECSC would be forced to produce the legal minutes of their corporations' board meetings. Porter and his cronies couldn't make their minutes disappear like they did the security camera tapes. It appeared to me they had a problem. If they produced minutes that accurately depicted what transpired, it would be damning evidence against them in court.

After studying the minutes of the two meetings, I believe they were doctored to whitewash their malicious, unprincipled conduct, mitigate the club's liability, and cover up the misbehavior of their leagues manager. What it says about the lack of integrity and ethical conduct of the ECSC leadership is a damning indictment.

In the July 2, 2018, monthly board meeting minutes, there is a blatant attempt to support Dan Hunt by making Shawn the fall guy, the culprit. I saw the same pattern repeated in their minutes for the July 12, 2018, clandestine *Board Meeting-Emergency Meeting*, kangaroo court.

However, this time, the Board added me to their hit list.

Their legal minutes of the July 2, 2018, meeting do not reflect that I informed the Board that I had filed a valid ATA protest with shoot management, Dan Hunt. Their legal minutes do not reflect Hunt's instructions to me to note the errors in the margin of the scoresheet. Their legal minutes do not reflect that Dan Hunt changed my scores.

Their legal minutes do not reflect Shawn refused to proceed until everyone stipulated to a confidentiality agreement to ensure what was said stayed in-house, so no one's reputation, including the club's, would be damaged.

Their legal minutes do not reflect that Dan Hunt turned the meeting into a confrontation with his lies and threats. When Shawn simply asked Hunt to explain why he kicked him out of the trap league, Hunt angrily responded, "I don't have to tell you a damn thing." Their legal minutes do not detail Dan Hunt erupting from his chair, lunging toward the table as he threatened Shawn, "Nobody calls me a liar and gets away with it."

Their legal minutes do not reflect Director Jerry Jay Gage's gesticulating, verbally abusive tirade, wrongly ranting I didn't have a right to protest.

This is why I believe the security camera tape disappeared. The tape would have shown the disparity between what occurred in the July 2nd meeting and their written, legal record, the corporation's minutes.

Since the minutes were not signed, who doctored them is another interesting question. Was this another ECSC Duck & Cover to avoid accountability? If I had to speculate, the Grand Poobah was likely responsible. Porter didn't hesitate to change the terms of my suspension in his email on July 16, 2018, adding further restrictions the Secret 7 didn't vote on. It's my belief Porter wouldn't hesitate to doctor the minutes.

Porter was Defendant ECSC's respondent to the Interrogatories submitted the same day by Defendants' attorneys, as were the club documents. I wonder if Poobah Porter ever realized how their minutes demonstrated the duplicity and vindictiveness of Duncanville narcotics detective, ECSC leagues manager Dan Hunt, and the 2018 ECSC Board of Directors.

Oh, what a tangled web we weave, when first we practice to deceive! Sir Walter Scott, 1808.

July 2, 2018, Monthly Board Meeting Minutes

My first thought reading their minutes was, did Porter and his cronies attend the same meeting I did?

Excerpt: July 2, 2018, Monthly Board Meeting Minutes,

Members Present: Charlie Beard, Don Henslee, Sherrie Lewis, Tap Haley, Rusty Porter, and Jay Gage

Whoever prepared the minutes couldn't get Director Haley's name correct. It's Raymond "Tab" Haley, III, formerly of Dallas, now Daingerfield, Texas. I found it interesting these elected officers were not referred to by their positions on the ECSC Board. Another ECSC Duck & Cover? Then, there is instigator Sherrie Lewis, who wasn't listed as an elected director, according to the *ECSC Board of Directors Summary 2015-2019.*

Excerpt: July 2, 2018, Monthly Board Meeting Minutes,

Trap league scoring issue discussion began and Shawn George requested reading a 15 page analysis which was not allowed.

The truth is, Shawn did read a great deal of his presentation, and it wasn't 15 pages. Who came up with 15 pages that Shawn wasn't allowed to read? Was Poobah Porter counting? What actually happened was when Shawn reached the part about Hunt's misbehavior with firearms, President Beard stopped him, refusing to allow him to continue. We were told that if we wanted to talk about gun safety and other concerns, we would have to file a complaint at another meeting. I immediately told President Beard I would file a formal complaint at the next board meeting. This was conveniently left out of their legal minutes.

Excerpt: July 2, 2018, Monthly Board Meeting Minutes,

Shawn George made numerous accusations about the league manager and called him a liar.

This should have read: *Dan Hunt made numerous false accusations about Shawn, and Shawn called Duncanville narcotics detective Danny Garth Hunt a liar to his face.* Dan Hunt accused Shawn of browbeating the scorer, then used another competitor in the first week of the trap league as an example. The real problem was Shawn made a fool of Hunt before the Board. This was the incident with the falsely alleged "helpless" new competitor described in Chapter One. This wasn't in their legal minutes, nor was Hunt's refusal to call the competitor, letting the Board listen to Hunt's "helpless" new shooter's side of the story.

When Dan Hunt couldn't back up any of his false accusations, he finally became so irate that he told Shawn, "If you (Shawn) want to shoot the trap league, you can run it yourself." Shawn immediately and clearly accepted Hunt's offer, not once, but twice. That, of course, didn't make it into their legal minutes.

Excerpt: July 2, 2018, Monthly Board Meeting Minutes,

Dan Hunt explained the sequence of events that started on the field after the event was finished regarding Shawn aggressively going after the assigned scorer and that this discussion spilled over into the clubhouse afterwards where scorecards were changed. Shawn claimed that both the scorer and Dan told him to change whatever event scores he wanted to which he did.

First, Dan Hunt's above rendition didn't happen in the meeting I attended. Second, Dan Hunt's explanation of the *sequence of events* is a fabrication. It never happened. Third, my scores on the official scoresheet have not been changed. So, how could Shawn have changed them? Fourth, Dan Hunt himself later refuted the above description of the *sequence of events* in his own court filings.

As a reminder, I told Vice President DVM Chris Rose in the recorded July 15, 2018, phone call: "But ah, Chris, we didn't change any score, scoresheets. All we did was follow what Dan told us to do, and that was to note the scores onto the outer edge of the scoresheet. We didn't actually change any scores." Vice President DVM Chris Rose said, "Well, that's you know not how it was reported."

The following is what Dan Hunt stated in two Defendants' court filings to the 443rd Ellis County District Court and in *Appellees' Brief* to the Court of Appeals, Tenth District of Texas.

On the evening of June 28, 2018, after the competition, Plaintiff approached Hunt and said the scores recorded for two of her rounds were not accurate on the official score sheet. Hunt asked Plaintiff to mark the targets she was protesting on the border of the score card. After serving dinner to the club members, Hunt gathered the completed scorecards and began the process of reviewing scores, determining award winners and preparing awards.

Dan Hunt's latest version, some two years later, certainly wasn't what Hunt reported to the ECSC Board of Directors, as recorded in their official legal corporation minutes of the July 2, 2018, monthly board meeting. Hunt's admissions in his court filings raised a serious question regarding ECSC's liability for defamatory statements in a legal corporation document that had far-reaching consequences for a paid member of the ECSC. According to Vice President DVM Chris Rose's recorded statements on July 15, 2018, we were kicked out of the league based on what was reported to the Board. What was reported to the Board by Duncanville narcotics detective and ECSC leagues manager Danny Garth Hunt was clearly a lie, according to none other than Danny Garth Hunt himself. With his court filings, Hunt labeled himself a liar.

So, how damaging were Dan Hunt's accusations, as recorded in the July 2, 2018, monthly board meeting minutes?

Shawn never talked to Dan Hunt as described in their minutes. There was no spillover into the clubhouse. Shawn was outside loading the trap house. Shawn never spoke to Dan Hunt after the match and didn't even enter the clubhouse until after Hunt left to run other side matches once the league had finished. The only reason Shawn was involved was because he was my squad leader, and I told him what Hunt, as shoot management, said to do.

Dan Hunt's statement to the Board of Directors about Shawn *aggressively going after the assigned scorer* is what I would call a bald-faced lie. In Dan Hunt's email on July 1, 2018, Hunt wrote that Larry Degal had changed a score at the *request* of the shooter. During the July 2, 2018, monthly board meeting, *request* escalated into Dan Hunt loudly proclaiming that Shawn had **"browbeat"** his scorer and another competitor two months prior. When Shawn challenged Hunt to get his "helpless" competitor on the phone, even offering Hunt the man's phone number to allow Hunt's approximately six-foot-three, some 275 pounds, falsely alleged "browbeaten" individual to explain to the Board what really happened, Hunt refused to make the call.

According to their minutes, a vindictive Duncanville cop and incompetent ECSC leagues manager further embellished his fabrication of the event. Shawn was falsely accused of *aggressively going after the assigned scorer*. Hunt had gone from **request** to **browbeat** to **aggressively going after the assigned scorer.** Dan Hunt, a vindictive, incompetent, misbehaving leagues manager, was making good his threat. "Nobody calls me a liar and gets away with it."

Shawn didn't threaten anyone. Shawn didn't browbeat anyone. Shawn didn't aggressively go after the scorer. Shawn and I didn't lie about any of this. Neither I nor Shawn did anything wrong. We followed the rules. We followed Hunt's instructions.

Shawn never changed the scores. The scoresheet and Dan Hunt's July 1, 2018, email are the proof. In his email, Hunt reported that Larry Degal changed one score at the request of the shooter. Degal was the only person changing the score on the official scoresheet. The scores and totals recorded by the misbehaving official scorekeeper Larry Degal have not been changed. My two contested targets, as recorded by Degal, have not been changed. They are still recorded as misses.

Shoot management Dan Hunt ruled in my favor, giving me credit for my two contested targets. Hunt changed my scores when he entered the individual competitor scores into myskeet.com.

Of course, none of this was recorded in the minutes. Instead, the minutes were written to make Shawn the culprit and, what I believe, was a blatant attempt to cover up their leagues manager's misbehavior. It should also be noted that Dan Hunt does not mention ATA rules and procedures.

Excerpt: July 2, 2018, Monthly Board Meeting Minutes,

Shawn George brought an AR-15 rifle and laid it on the conference room table. Dan Hunt arrived later.

In previous chapters, I referenced instigator Sherrie Lewis' slanderous accusation that Shawn slammed an assault rifle onto the table to intimidate the Board. Before bringing the target rifle as evidence about Hunt's misconduct with firearms into the meeting room, Shawn obtained the permission of President Charlie Beard, along with Porter, with no objections from any directors. Here's the kicker. According to their minutes, it wasn't an assault rifle slammed on the table that alarmed Director Sherrie Lewis.

Excerpt: July 2, 2018, Monthly Board Meeting Minutes,

During the discussion Shawn slammed a trash can onto the table, alarming one of our board members.

Not satisfied with Hunt's false accusation of Shawn *aggressively going after the assigned scorer,* Shawn was then falsely accused of slamming a small plastic container on the table, alarming a board member. The board member was instigator Sherrie Lewis. Yes, a small plastic container was what alarmed instigator Sherrie Lewis. Lewis, a Life Member of the Dallas Safari Club and DIVA WOW shotgun instructor, was afraid of a clinking sound from a small plastic container. Not the falsely alleged assault rifle that, according to instigator Sherrie

Lewis, Shawn had slammed onto the table to intimidate the Board.

Shawn had brought the container as part of his presentation to refute Dan Hunt's false accusations about another incident during the league. This is the non-event described in Chapter One. Shawn was looking over his reading glasses and misjudged the distance to the tabletop. The container clinked when he set it on the Formica tabletop, a meaningless accident. And again, nary a scratch. Yet, instigator Sherrie Lewis made a production out of it, just as she falsely did with the assault rifle intimidation.

Just how absurd could a situation become? Shawn and I attempted to address serious issues of gun safety and alcohol problems within the leagues and during the use of the club's facilities. This isn't in their minutes. Then, add that Dan Hunt, a police officer, exploded from his chair, physically lunged toward the table and verbally threatened Shawn. I was subjected to a lengthy, abusive, wildly gesticulating tirade by Director Jerry Jay Gage because he wrongly claimed I didn't have a right to protest. Yet, their egregious misbehavior isn't in the minutes. Instead, what made it into their minutes was the clinking of a small plastic container that alarmed Dallas Safari Club Life Member, ECSC instigator Sherrie Lewis.

Ridiculous? Absolutely. You can't make this stuff up. It's in their official, legal, unsigned corporation minutes.

Excerpt: July 2, 2018, Monthly Board Meeting Minutes,

Anita Dickason read a prepared statement defending herself and the suspension.

This statement added to my belief their minutes were doctored. I wasn't at the meeting to defend myself. I had done nothing wrong. I had not been accused of any wrongdoing. I had not been kicked out of the trap league. During the June 30th phone call with Dan Hunt, I specifically asked if I had been kicked out. Hunt said no, just Shawn. I was there to support Shawn and refute Dan Hunt's false accusations. What I told the Board were legitimate concerns grounded in fact about Dan Hunt's administration of the leagues, his mishandling of my valid ATA protest, and the misbehavior of the opposing team that resulted in the scoring errors. My statements were based on ATA rules and procedures.

Excerpt: July 2, 2018, Monthly Board Meeting Minutes,

Club president advised both members that the board would investigate the suspension and the many accusations to determine at a later date if the board would overturn the trap league manager's decision. All visitors were excused.

This statement was on par with the rest of the whitewash of the misbehavior of their leagues manager, Dan Hunt, during the meeting. Like Dan Hunt's rendition of the *sequence of events* in their minutes was a lie, so is the above statement. It never happened. Because I was visibly upset from Gage's unwarranted, abusive, gesticulating, lengthy verbal attack, all President Beard said to reassure me before we walked out was, "Don't worry about it. We deal with this all the time."

No one, including the President, said anything about a later date to determine *if the board would overturn the trap league manager's decision.* As a reminder, I had not been kicked out of the league, only Shawn.

At the close of the meeting, we thought Shawn was now the trap leagues manager. Hunt had resigned in front of six board members. Shawn's suspension by Hunt should have been a moot point.

The meeting actually ended not long after Dan Hunt stormed from the room furious, following Shawn twice, clearly accepting Dan Hunt's offer to let Shawn run the trap league. Shortly thereafter, Hunt admitted to nearly one hundred people, some children, that he was suffering from mental whatever after *intense and severe exposures at work.* Somehow, the Danny Garth Hunt family, between Hunt storming out of the meeting and some three hours later sending his whining pity email at thirty-four minutes before midnight, were, according to Dan Hunt, placed in *a position of discomfort.* Had Danny Garth Hunt continued his misbehavior at home as he had in the meeting?

The ECSC was faced with a lawsuit. Dan Hunt was their codefendant. It's my opinion their minutes were intentionally written to make Shawn the fall guy, while supporting Dan Hunt, their deceitful, vindictive, incompetent, unqualified, hothead leagues manager, admittedly suffering from mental whatever.

It should be noted that the individual Porter and his cronies supported, Dan Hunt, would throw the ECSC leadership under the bus in his future court filings to the 443rd Ellis County District Court and the Court of Appeals, Tenth District of Texas. Dan Hunt's own statements in the *Background* of Defendants' filings to the Courts prove Dan Hunt's rendition of the sequence of events as recorded in the July 2, 2018, monthly board meeting minutes are a lie. Dan Hunt's accusation of cheating was bogus, just as I have repeatedly claimed since I got the July 15, 2018, phone call from Vice President DVM Chris Rose, that "straight-up" former mayor of Cedar Hill, Texas.

Porter and his cronies weren't finished. They had another problem to fix. Vice President DVM Chris Rose told me I had been kicked out of the leagues for "Uh, changing scoresheets without you know talking to anybody." They had no evidence to back up their bogus charge of cheating. This brings us to the next set of legal corporation minutes.

The unsigned, legal corporation minutes of their July 12, 2018, clandestine *Board Meeting-Emergency Meeting*, kangaroo court were another seriously flawed attempt by the Board of Directors to mitigate their liability and cover for Dan Hunt. It appeared to me, poor ol' "straight-up" Christopher Lyons Rose, the former mayor of Cedar Hill, Texas, was about to become Poobah Porter's sacrificial lamb.

Buses, Dogs & Fleas

Chapter Eleven

On July 12, 2018, the ECSC Secret 7 held their clandestine *Board Meeting-Emergency Meeting,* kangaroo court. A kangaroo court in which I was falsely accused, secretly judged, wrongly convicted, and sentenced. As of the July 2, 2018, monthly board meeting, I had not been accused of anything. Dan Hunt was after Shawn, not me. Yet, ten days later, I am thrown out of the leagues on a bogus charge of cheating.

Their meeting was presided over by the former mayor of Cedar Hill, Texas, Vice President DVM Christopher Lyons Rose. The same individual who called me on July 15, 2018, to tell me what the Board had done to me during a secret meeting of which I had no knowledge.

As the presiding officer, Vice President DVM Chris Rose was the official ECSC spokesman. Rose's official reason for why I had been kicked out of the leagues was: "Uh, changing scoresheets without you know talking to anybody." Furthermore, after protesting I didn't change any scores, only followed Dan Hunt's instructions to note the errors in the margin of the scoresheet, Rose stated, "Well, that's you know not how it was reported." As I have already identified, the person doing the reporting was their incompetent, unqualified, vindictive leagues manager, Dan Hunt.

Vice President DVM Chris Rose refused to discuss the details of their meeting, stating, "So like I said that's the action that's been taken and uh we can't argue about it right now."

In my July 24, 2018, *Notice of Representation of Anita Dickason and Litigation Hold,* my attorney lawfully requested a copy of their July 12, 2018, board meeting minutes. The Grand Poobah and his cronies refused to provide a copy. It took a lawsuit and thousands of dollars to obtain their clandestine meeting minutes, which I finally received in March 2019. Once more, I was astounded by what I read, especially what was clearly missing in their minutes.

ECSC Vice President DVM Chris Rose's recorded statements are quoted verbatim in the *Factual Allegations* of my lawsuit. On December 19, 2018, when the Board was served with the notice of my lawsuit, they received a copy of the document filed with the court. They certainly knew Rose's statements were one of the reasons for my lawsuit. Yet, the minutes of their clandestine July 12, 2018, *Board Meeting-Emergency Meeting,* kangaroo court do not support what their official spokesman, ECSC Vice President DVM Chris Rose told me on the phone.

In the minutes is a glaring omission. There is no reference to scoresheets, or changing scoresheets, as put forth by the official spokesman for the ECSC, Vice President DVM Chris Rose on July 15, 2018. In my opinion, their July 12th legal minutes depict Vice President DVM Chris Rose a liar. Had Rose become expendable? Just throw "straight-up" Rose under the bus and come up with another reason for kicking me out of the trap leagues.

According to their minutes, their latest reason came from the Amateur Trapshooting Association (ATA) rules they now stated governed their trap leagues. An incomprehensible twist since I never observed Dan Hunt enforce any ATA rules and procedures. What was conspicuously missing in Dan Hunt's match bulletins and his so-called investigation of my valid ATA protest was any mention of ATA rules and procedures. During the July 2, 2018, monthly board meeting, it's what I told the Board. There were no rules in Dan Hunt's trap leagues. It was why so many problems existed within shoot management Dan Hunt's oversite of the trap leagues.

Just as in their July 2nd minutes, they clearly made Shawn and me the culprits while supporting their incompetent, unqualified, vindictive leagues manager Dan Hunt. In doing so, whoever wrote their minutes hung ECSC Vice President DVM Chris Rose, that former mayor of Cedar Hill, Texas, a "straight-up" guy, out to dry.

What follows is the ECSC's official legal record; the minutes of their clandestine *Board Meeting-Emergency Meeting*, kangaroo court.

Excerpt: July 12, 2018, Board Meeting-Emergency Meeting Minutes,

Quorum-Chris Rose, David McDaniel, Rusty Porter, Jay Gage, Sherrie Lewis, Wayne Johnston, Don Henslee. This was the Secret 7.

The absent board members were President Charlie Beard, Secretary Shannon Edwards, and Director Tab Haley. When you add them up, it's ten, not nine elected Directors as stipulated by the ECSC Bylaws and the *ECSC Board of Directors Summary, 2015-2019.*

The absence of President Charlie Beard raised another valid question. Who called their clandestine kangaroo court? Per their Bylaws, only the president was authorized to call *special meetings.* If President Beard called their secret emergency meeting, why didn't he attend? Did Beard do the ECSC Duck & Cover, or was Poobah Porter running the show as usual?

Four of the seven board members, Henslee, Gage, McDaniel, and Johnston, were low to mid-level ATA registered trap competitors. Yet, in combination, these four ATA registered competitors either had no idea what the rules stated or intentionally chose to overlook them.

Excerpt: July 12, 2018, Board Meeting-Emergency Meeting Minutes,

Meeting was called to order by Chris Rose, Vice President, to resolve the trap scoring issue solely caused by member Anita Dickason and her guest, Shawn George.

Note the phrase; *solely caused*. According to their unsigned minutes, when Rose called the meeting to order, they had already judged the falsely accused, unnotified, uninvited and unrepresented—guilty. As the former mayor of Cedar Hill, Texas, was this how Rose had operated as mayor of Cedar Hill?

To me, this was a defining statement about Poobah Porter, "straight-up" Rose, and their cronies' leadership. The more they tried to cover up their unprincipled conduct, the deeper they dug their hole.

Since this was a *trap scoring issue*, the intentional violations of the ATA scoring rules by the opposing team, Larry Degal, Barbara Parks, and Susie Thompson, are certainly relevant.

ATA Trap Line Training Manual, page 8, *G. Scorer's Safety Rules Summary*, #8: *In singles and doubles, keep your chair 3 yards behind the firing line.*

The misbehaving scorekeeper, Larry Degal, positioned himself approximately fifty measured feet out of position, entirely outside the trap field, behind and to the left of firing position #1, surrounded by his intentionally and loudly laughing, misbehaving teammates.

Upon being asked by Shawn, my squad leader, to take a proper scoring position behind the sixteen-yard line, Larry Degal refused. Upon a second request to take a proper scoring position, official scorer Larry Degal again arrogantly refused, stating, "I'll score from wherever I want." As squad leader, Shawn then informed Degal that any mistakes in scoring were on the scorekeeper and not the shooters.

ATA Trap Line Training Manual, page 8, *G. Scorer's Safety Rules Summary*, #5: *Insist that the trap area is quiet -no-talking- when you are pulling or scoring.*

Official scorekeeper Larry Degal was surrounded by constant chatter from his misbehaving teammates. Susie Thompson wouldn't shut up, and a laughing Barbara Parks screamed, "Lost." Had Degal taken a proper scoring position some three yards behind the shooters and called the lost shots as stipulated by ATA scoring rules, there would have been no reason for anyone to scream.

ATA Trap Line Training Manual, page 6, D. Starting a Squad and Event #6: When scoring, do not talk to anyone. Do not allow anyone to talk to you. Do not allow anyone to stand near you and talk. You will be blamed for the poor scoring, not them. Ask them to please move away. Be respectful but firm. If they still interfere so that you cannot perform your duties without interruption, the best thing to do is to stop the squad and tell the offender they must clear the area so the squad may progress.

This section clearly defines the scorer's conduct and responsibility to ensure the accuracy of the scores. The disruptive and unsportsmanlike conduct of the opposing team was a clear violation. As the official scorekeeper, it was Larry Degal's responsibility. Larry Degal was *solely* responsible for the scoring violations, not Shawn and me.

Yet, according to their minutes, "straight-up" Rose and the rest of the Secret 7 willfully ignored the ATA rules for the proper scoring of a match, along with the egregious violations and unsportsmanlike conduct by Larry Degal and his misbehaving teammates. ATA rules, the Board clearly stipulated within their minutes, governed their matches.

During the ECSC sponsored trap leagues, it wasn't unusual for non-firing competitors to gather around a scorekeeper, laughing and joking. The competitors' misbehavior was an infraction of the ATA scoring rules Dan Hunt, as shoot management and leagues manager, never corrected.

As a reminder, this was Rusty Porter's response to an official interrogatory, *League managers are tasked with the responsibility of ensuring that the club's rules, policies and bylaws are followed.* Leagues manager Dan Hunt's failure to enforce ATA rules and procedures within the leagues was a blatant dereliction of his responsibilities, as evidenced by the Grand Poobah, Rusty Porter's statement.

During the July 2nd board meeting, Dan Hunt admitted he received complaints about the disruptive behavior of our opposing team from competitors on adjoining trap fields. Did Hunt do anything? No. Did Hunt investigate? No. Instead, cook Dan Hunt stayed in the clubhouse setting up dinner for the awards banquet. That was more important to ECSC shoot management Dan Hunt than correcting a dangerous situation on the trap field.

In Hunt's official capacity as shoot management, he ignored the complaints from competitors shooting on other trap fields, condoning the misbehavior of our opposing team. This is why shoot management must be both competent and qualified. I believe this is what you get when your cook oversees forty people with loaded guns from the kitchen.

ATA Trap Line Training Manual, page 7, D. Starting a Squad and Event, #7: Call all lost targets. Be sure the "lost" is said distinctly but not yelled out so loud that it startles the next shooter or causes the release of extra targets.

There is no co-scoring in the ATA rules. Once the shooter fires, the official scorer is responsible for watching the bird and accurately recording the score as a hit or miss. If the target is missed, then the scorer calls "lost." The official scorer, Larry Degal, wasn't calling the missed targets. That was a laughing, screaming Barbara Parks. All Degal did was write what Barbara Parks screamed.

ATA Trap Line Training Manual, page 6, C. Reporting for Work: Assure that the shooter can see the board so he can check his scores during each change.

When Larry Degal twice refused to assume a proper scoring position three yards behind the firing line, instead sitting in a chair some fifty measured feet away, completely off the trap field in a crowd of misbehaving, laughing teammates, my team couldn't check our scores at each change.

ATA Trap Line Training Manual, page 8, G. Scorer's Safety Rule Summary: Above all other responsibilities of your job, safety is the most important. #4: When the shooters move to the next post, call 'Rotate please.' It is your responsibility to see that the guns are unloaded and open before allowing the shooters to rotate to their next position.

This built-in ATA safety precaution was impossible because of the intentional, unsportsmanlike attitude and misbehavior of Larry Degal, who, when asked by my squad leader to take up a proper scoring position, arrogantly stated, "I'll score from wherever I want," which wasn't even on the trap field.

The ATA rules and procedures were created over the one-hundred-plus years of the Amateur Trapshooting Association's existence. These rules and procedures ensure the safe, efficient, sportsmanlike conduct within the sport of trapshooting. Rules Larry Degal, Barbara Parks, and Susie Thompson willfully ignored.

Degal's insolence reflected the unsafe conditions, arrogant, unsportsmanlike, I'll do what I damn well please, know-it-all attitudes that permeated the ECSC trap leagues run by an incompetent and unqualified shoot management, leagues manager, cook Dan Hunt.

It was the same arrogant, unsportsmanlike conduct that occurred during the first week of the trap league. I attempted to correct Laura McGee and some of her teammate's unsafe handling of their shotguns. Laura McGee told me to mind my own business. This was the unsafe, unsupervised environment within the ECSC trap leagues managed by their ECSC leagues manager, Danny Garth Hunt, their cook.

The misconduct by Degal's team that violated numerous ATA rules and procedures for scoring a match was inexcusable and unwarranted. Yet the ECSC Board intentionally ignored Degal and his team's misbehavior, which caused the entire mess. All I did was file a valid protest according to the ATA rules.

Excerpt: July 12, 2018, Board Meeting-Emergency Meeting Minutes,

Discussion of the various interviews and information, gathering we agreed to complete at the end of the July 2 meeting followed. All board members had the opportunity to speak about the issue. (Note, the comma after information is not a misprint.)

What an enlightening statement. No wonder this was all done in secret. If you hold a clandestine kangaroo court, all while trampling the reputation and rights of a paid member, you might as well have a secret Porter/Henslee kangaroo investigation.

According to their minutes, all the board members got to speak. Who didn't get to speak? The falsely accused. Who didn't hear the false accusations? The falsely accused.

In his phone call, even Vice President DVM Chris Rose refused to discuss what the Secret 7 had done. Rose stated, "So like I said that's the action that's been taken and uh we can't argue about it right now." When did the former mayor of Cedar Hill, Christopher Lyons Rose, think I should have an opportunity to defend myself?

Three of the Secret 7, Chris Rose, David McDaniel, and Wayne Johnston, were absent at the July 2, 2018, monthly board meeting. These three individuals, Rose, McDaniel, and Johnston, relied on what Dan Hunt and the rest of the Secret 7 told them. Rose stated in his phone call, "From what I understand and what was reported to the board."

As the Secret 7's presiding officer, Rose had no idea as to the truth of what happened. Yet, "straight-up" Rose allowed a vote on a motion that would have far-reaching, adverse consequences for an innocent member in good standing. But at least Christopher Lyons Rose, former council member and mayor of Cedar Hill, Texas, is a "straight-up" kind of guy. Just ask him.

Treasurer Rusty Porter's response to one of my interrogatories didn't support the statement *various interviews*. Porter stated only one person was interviewed, Larry Degal. Porter's secret kangaroo investigation hinged on the word of one person, Larry Degal, the intentionally misbehaving official scorekeeper who *solely caused* the *trap scoring issue*. Which statement is false? What's recorded in the legal minutes or Porter's response in an official court document? I believe it's a valid question.

Excerpt: July 12, 2018, Board Meeting-Emergency Meeting Minutes,

Since our club relies on the national organizations for rules, we asked Don Henslee to clarify the ATA scoring rules.

This is what I referred to as the incomprehensible twist, especially after what I told the Board during the July 2, 2018, monthly board meeting. The problem with Hunt's leagues was that there were no rules.

Not once did I observe any reference to ATA rules in shoot management, leagues manager Dan Hunt's poorly managed, bordering on unsafe, trap leagues or read such in Hunt's match bulletins.

If the Board *relies on the national organizations for rules,* and Dan Hunt was *tasked with the responsibility of ensuring the club's rules, policies and bylaws are followed,* where were the ATA rules in shoot management Dan Hunt's so-called investigation of my legitimate ATA protest? As shoot management, Dan Hunt was responsible for ruling on a scoring dispute involving infractions of ATA rules and procedures. Instead, Hunt ignored the misbehavior of a group of competitors that caused the scoring errors and jeopardized the safety of the participants. Yet, according to Poobah Porter, Dan Hunt was *tasked* with knowing and applying the rules.

Not once before I filed my lawsuit did Dan Hunt admit I walked into the clubhouse and told him about the errors in my scores. Not once before I filed my lawsuit did Dan Hunt admit he told me to note the errors in the margin of the scoresheet. Not once before I filed my lawsuit did Dan Hunt admit he, himself, ruled in my favor, then changed my scores.

Instead, Dan Hunt blamed Shawn, making him the culprit. A vindictive rendition Hunt would continue to perpetuate with false accusations and lies in his future court filings.

Excerpt: July 12, 2018, Board Meeting-Emergency Meeting Minutes,

Don Henslee reported the official ATA scoring rules that scores are accepted by the shooter before leaving each post: not at the end of the round. All board members concluded that this issue was a clear scoring violation.

By asserting I didn't have a right to protest at the end of the round, this was how whoever wrote the minutes ignored Vice President DVM Chris Rose's bogus claim I cheated. Were they actually implying I didn't have a right to walk into the clubhouse and file an official ATA protest with shoot management, Dan Hunt? Unfortunately for Porter and his cronies, it's not what the ATA rules state. Their rules clarifier was as incompetent as their leagues manager.

I wonder if it ever occurred to the Secret 7 that their *clear scoring violation* was just as damning of their shameful, malicious conduct as was their bogus charge of cheating. I believe their latest official reason for my suspension was an act of desperation meant to bury their defamatory bogus charge of cheating. Still, not a single reference about what Rose told me, "Uh, changing scoresheets without you know talking to anybody." If Poobah Porter was responsible for the minutes, it would seem Porter just conveniently parked his bus on top of "straight-up" Rose.

Did the Secret 7 believe anyone with even a rudimentary knowledge of competitive shooting would buy into their asinine excuse for their shameful, unprincipled conduct? Did it ever occur to them that someone might have read the ATA rules and know what they state?

What are the ATA rules and procedures governing a scoring dispute that ATA registered shooter, their so-called rules clarifier, Director Don R. Henslee, and ATA registered shooters, Directors David C. McDaniel, Jerry Jay Gage, and Wayne Johnston, conveniently ignored or were too ignorant of the rules to know?

ATA Official Rules, *Section VII, Official Scoring: A. Procedure, #1: The referee/scorer's decision on whether a target is dead or lost is final, subject to review only by the shoot committee or other governing body.*

The operative words; ***subject to review.*** Director Don R. Henslee conveniently failed to mention this when he was requested *to clarify the ATA scoring rules*. There was no *clear scoring violation,* as claimed in their minutes. Furthermore, this next ATA rule was a doozy. Could it get any clearer?

ATA Official Rules, Section VII, Official Scoring: A. Procedure, #15: Any protest concerning a score or scores must be made before or immediately after the close of the competition to which such scores relate. A valid protest may only be made by a contestant who competed in the event.

I had a right to protest. I followed the rules. Determining my scores were wrong, *immediately* following *the close of the competition,* I walked to the kitchen in the clubhouse and filed my valid ATA protest with ECSC's shoot management, the cook, Dan Hunt.

Once I filed my protest, it was shoot management Dan Hunt's responsibility to competently rule on the validity of my protest based on ATA rules and procedures. Of course, none of that happened.

Dan Hunt decided to give me credit for the two points, as he would later state in a court filing *because there was no consequences to the final results.* Just as Dan Hunt was ignorant of the ATA rules for the proper scoring of a match, Dan Hunt was ignorant of the ATA rules for a scoring dispute. Dan Hunt's vindictiveness, ignorance, and incompetence perpetuated the *trap scoring issue.* In my observations, Dan Hunt was as clueless about the ATA rules as was Director Jerry Jay Gage. I can now add Director Don R. Henslee.

Furthermore, I believe I had the right to protest the entire match because of the opposing team's intentional, disruptive, unsafe conduct. The earlier ATA Trap Line Training Manual excerpt stated: *When scoring do not talk to anyone. Do not allow anyone to talk to you. Do not allow anyone to stand near you and talk. You will be blamed for the poor scoring, not them.* This clearly put the scoring errors on the shoulders of the misbehaving official scorekeeper, Larry Degal.

ATA Official Rules, Section VII, Official Scoring: A. Procedure, #3: The referee/scorer shall distinctly announce, 'Lost' when the target is missed.

Larry Degal, as the official scorer, was not calling the lost targets.

ATA Official Rules, *Section VII, Official Scoring: A. Procedure, #11: The official score sheet must be available for shooter inspection at all times.*

Available is behind the firing line, within three yards, not seated fifty-plus feet away, completely off the trap field.

I would suggest to ATA registered shooter and ECSC Director Don R. Henslee that he read the ATA rule book before spouting his so-called, seriously flawed expert opinion. To quote Abraham Lincoln, "Better to remain silent and thought a fool, than to speak and remove all doubt."

I followed the ATA rules and procedures. Degal, Parks, Thompson, Hunt, and the Secret 7 didn't. Since the Secret 7 couldn't support Dan Hunt's bogus accusation of cheating, I believe Henslee's misleading snippet of an ATA rule was nothing more than an attempt to justify the Board's unprincipled conduct. In my opinion, the Secret 7 appeared desperate to cover their seriously exposed backsides.

The following section was the most revealing. Registered competitor David McDaniel, the complaining second-place competitor, and ATA registered competitor Don Henslee, who clearly demonstrated his ignorance of ATA rules and procedures, led the way with their motion.

Excerpt: July 12, 2018, Board Meeting-Emergency Meeting Minutes,

A motion was made by David McDaniel and seconded by Don Henslee to uphold the decision made by the trap league manager which suspended member Anita Dickason and her guest, Shawn George, for a total of two years from only league competition, this does not include other shooting venues or club activities. Motion passed with a unanimous vote.

When did I get suspended? As of the July 2, 2018, meeting, I had not been suspended. I had not been accused of any wrongdoing. Then ten days later, I'm added to Dan Hunt's hit list. I believe what the Board did was meant to stop me from filing a formal complaint at the next meeting, strip me of my rights as a member in good standing. My belief was certainly reinforced by Porter's threat to extend my suspension in his July 16, 2018, email if I caused any further controversies, and that I couldn't watch a match.

As for Dan Hunt's decision, it was all about Shawn, not me. I believe Dan Hunt felt he had to get rid of Shawn, and Hunt was willing to lie to do it. Shawn simply tried to make Hunt behave himself with firearms. When Hunt falsely accused Shawn of "browbeating," Shawn made a fool of Hunt in the July 2nd monthly board meeting. Shawn rightfully called Hunt a liar to his face. It totally surprised Hunt when Shawn accepted Hunt's offer to let him run the trap leagues. Dan Hunt's *decision* was nothing more than getting rid of Shawn. Dan Hunt's malicious vindictiveness would become even more clear in his future court filings. I was the one who sued him, not Shawn. Yet, in Dan Hunt's latest rendition of the scoring issue in Defendants' court filings, it was Shawn, not me, that Hunt went after with his defamatory accusations and outright lies.

Quite frankly, I believe the Secret 7's statement, *to uphold the decision made by the trap league manager,* should have read: *to uphold the decision made by our vindictive, threatening, trap-shooting-from-the-hip like a buffoon with a loaded gun, our cook, a Duncanville cop admittedly suffering from mental whatever "after intense and severe exposures at work," the hothead who most likely himself placed his family "in a position of discomfort," our incompetent, unqualified, deceitful ECSC trap leagues manager, who has already resigned not once, but twice.*

This was who Vice President DVM Chris Rose, that "straight-up" kind of guy and his backstabbing cronies supported. Their vindictive leagues manager would eventually throw "straight-up" Rose along with ECSC leadership under the bus. It's all in Dan Hunt's future court filings before the 443rd Ellis County District Court and the Court of Appeals, Tenth District of Texas. More on this in subsequent chapters.

There was another glaring contradiction between the motion the

Secret 7 approved and Porter's July 16, 2018, email to me. The motion stipulated: *for a total of two years from only league competition, this does not include other shooting venues or club activities.*

During the July 15, 2018, phone call, Vice President DVM Chris Rose specifically emphasized that my two-year suspension only applied to the trap leagues. Rose said, "No. Just the trap league. You just, you can go out and do all the other things you just can't play in the trap league."

Yet, the Grand Poobah, in his July 16, 2018, email, changed my suspension to include *any league competition.* I was now *suspended* from not only the trap league but all the club-sponsored leagues. A sanction not voted on by the Board. The motion didn't include Porter's other stipulations I couldn't watch or score and that my suspension would be extended if there were further controversies. Porter intentionally exceeded his authority with what I believe was malicious intent. Did Poobah Porter think he didn't have to abide by a vote of the Board, any more than he had to follow Texas law or their Bylaws?

Excerpt: July 12, 2018, Board Meeting-Emergency Meeting Minutes,

A short discussion followed and it was decided Chris Rose would make a courtesy call to the member, Anita Dickason, and Rusty Porter would confirm our ruling with a written e-mail.

Seriously? We'll make ourselves feel good after intentionally and maliciously destroying her reputation and credibility without giving her a chance to defend herself. Let's be polite and pat ourselves on the back by giving her a courtesy call.

Merriam-Webster defines a courtesy call as; *a visit made because it is the polite thing to do.* There was no way Vice President DVM Chris Rose would make a courtesy call. This former mayor of Cedar Hill, Texas, presided over a clandestine kangaroo court where an innocent woman was falsely accused, secretly judged, wrongly convicted, and then sentenced, in absentia. Rose wouldn't face me in a meeting, and he wasn't about to face me in a courtesy call. Dallas/Ft. Worth area clay shooter, Cedar Hill DVM Christopher Lyons Rose is a lot of things, but he isn't what I would consider a "straight-up" kind of guy.

Instead, Vice President DVM Chris Rose made a cowardly phone call. And how long did it take that self-proclaimed, "straight-up" kind of guy, the former council member and past mayor of Cedar Hill, Texas, ECSC Vice President DVM Chris Rose to work up the nerve to make his cowardly call? Three days. Even then, "straight-up" Rose just wanted to give me the bad news, explain he was being "straight-up" with me, and end the call as quickly as possible. Rose refused to discuss what he had done to an innocent woman, all behind her back, or the details of his clandestine board's actions.

Never was Porter's version of *fostering good fellowship* at the Ellis County Sportsmans Club more alive and well than in the destructive, malicious actions of Vice President DVM Chris Rose and his band of cronies in his clandestine kangaroo court on July 12, 2018.

So, which is true? The bogus charge of cheating as put forth by Vice President DVM Chris Rose in a recorded phone call, or the ATA rule put forth by their incompetent ATA rules clarifier Don Henslee, that didn't even apply.

If I were forced at gunpoint to choose, I'd probably pick former Cedar Hill mayor and Vice President DVM Christopher Lyons Rose. Remember, Christopher Lyons Rose is a "straight-up" kind of guy. I expect a reasonable, prudent individual would believe Rose's statements since he presided over the ECSC kangaroo court, and his cowardly phone call occurred only three days after the meeting. Chris Rose had no reason to lie. Rose only wanted to give me the bad news and get off the phone.

Not once within the July 12th board meeting minutes was there a reference to changing scoresheets or even a mention of the scoresheet. If the Board had indeed enacted a seriously skewed ATA rule as their reason for kicking me out of the trap league, why wouldn't Rose have told me? Instead, Christopher Lyons Rose directly accused me of cheating, "Uh, changing scoresheets without you know talking to anybody." It was a bogus cheating scandal that certainly wasn't supported by any evidence. In fact, both Dan Hunt and Rusty Porter refused to accuse me of cheating in response to my court-ordered interrogatories.

After I filed my lawsuit, Porter, Rose, and their cronies were about to face the consequences of their malicious, unprincipled conduct. The minutes didn't appear until nearly nine months later. Whoever doctored the minutes wasn't concerned about supporting what their Vice President DVM Chris Rose told me during our recorded phone call. With Henslee's skewed ATA rules violation they threw their own Vice President under the bus. In my opinion, "straight-up" Rose became Porter's sacrificial lamb. Porter, the Grand Poobah, was good at driving the bus.

I would politely ask Cedar Hill DVM Christopher Lyons Rose, the self-proclaimed "straight-up" kind of guy, to look in a mirror. I wonder how Rose thinks he looks with Porter's tire tracks on his back.

Danny Garth Hunt, a Duncanville cop, admittedly suffering from mental whatever *after intense and severe exposures at work,* their incompetent leagues manager, the guy Rose supported, was about to take over driving the bus. Rose would get hit again, this time by Danny Garth Hunt in Defendants' future filings before the 443rd Ellis County District Court and the Court of Appeals, Tenth District of Texas.

According to the minutes of the February 4, 2019, board meeting, newly appointed ECSC President Chris Rose resigned and walked out. I wonder if "straight-up" Rose resigned because Porter was such a good bus driver, or perhaps Christopher Lyons Rose simply began to itch.

Being a highly educated, self-styled "straight-up" kind of guy, surely Cedar Hill Doctor of Veterinary Medicine Christopher Lyons Rose, noted Dallas/Fort Worth area clay shooter, the former council member and former mayor of Cedar Hill, Texas, had heard an old saying.

If you don't want fleas, don't lie with dogs.

Heigh-Ho, Heigh-Ho, A Marshaling They Go!

Chapter Twelve

In March 2019, I received Defendants Dan Hunt and ECSC's responses to Plaintiff's Interrogatories. The phrase *marshal all evidence* is repeatedly used to avoid a direct answer to a simple question.

Defendant Dan Hunt's Objections and Answers to Plaintiff's First Set of Interrogatories,

INTERROGATORY NO. 3: *With the exception of your attorney(s), please identify the names and telephone numbers of all individuals you have spoken with regarding the scoring dispute described in Plaintiff's Original Petition, the suspension of Plaintiff's membership rights, and/or the termination of Plaintiff's membership.*

ANSWER: *Wyatt and Tina Hunt, Nathan Roach, Clay Hinds, Russell "Rusty" Porter, Sherry Lewis.*

Wyatt is Dan Hunt's son. Tina Hunt is Dan Hunt's wife. Nathan Roach works for the Duncanville Police Department. Clay Hinds is a local Waxahachie attorney.

A noticeable omission in Hunt's response is the intentionally misbehaving scorekeeper Larry Degal, who was responsible for the *scoring dispute* as described in *Plaintiff's Original Petition*. The results of Dan Hunt's so-called investigation of the *scoring dispute*, as recorded in Dan Hunt's July 1, 2018, email, hinged on the word of one person, Larry Degal. Degal wasn't the only significant omission.

Dan Hunt failed to mention the other four of the six club members who complained at the awards banquet after Dan Hunt ruled in my favor, Director David McDaniel, Tommy Nations, Jeff Gregory, and Susie Thompson. Dan Hunt failed to mention the other board members as recorded in the July 2, 2018, monthly board meeting, President Charlie Beard, and Directors Jerry Jay Gage, Don Henslee, and Tab Haley.

The recipients of Dan Hunt's June 29, 2018, and July 1, 2018, emails regarding the scoring dispute are missing. The first one he wrongly sent to the skeet league competitors instead of the trap league competitors.

Acting in his official capacity as leagues manager, on July 2, 2018, Dan Hunt sent out a vicious, libelous, whining pity email, *Immediate resignation,* to nearly one hundred club members, guests, and children at thirty-four minutes before midnight. Dan Hunt had spread his malicious, false accusations about Shawn and me far and wide to club members, guests, and even children through his multiple emails.

In his *Immediate resignation* email, Hunt proclaimed; *I hereby resign any responsibilities or commitments related to the ECSC leagues that I have previously committed to. This includes any past, present, or future events.* Hunt further proclaimed; *I cannot justify participation in these events to the detriment of my well being or the well being of my family.* Yet, less than twenty hours later, Dan Hunt returned to the club to participate in the skeet league.

Despite his resignation, according to the July 12, 2018, meeting minutes, the July 15, 2018, phone call from Vice President DVM Chris Rose, the July 16, 2018, email from the Grand Poobah, Rusty Porter, and Dan Hunt's August 16, 2018, email to trap league competitors about the start of a new trap league, Dan Hunt was obviously still in charge.

What fool would believe Dan Hunt wasn't inundated with questions about the scoring dispute from club members and guests who received his multiple emails or from other members using the facility?

Dan Hunt was literally front and center at the Ambush, otherwise known as the membership appeal meeting. Dan Hunt was positioned right in front of the doors leading into the clubhouse, cooking breakfast for club members clustered around his grill. These club members were about to vote on whether to kick me out of the club. The Board had sent a copy of my lawsuit and the formal complaint Porter filed against me to all club members. They knew I had sued Dan Hunt along with the ECSC. What fool would believe the club members weren't questioning Dan Hunt about the *scoring dispute described in Plaintiff's Original Petition, the suspension of Plaintiff's membership rights, and/or the termination of Plaintiff's membership* described in my interrogatory?

Yet, Dan Hunt claimed he only spoke to six people. In nearly nine months from when the scoring dispute arose and Dan Hunt's answer to my interrogatory, what fool would believe Dan Hunt only spoke to six people? Hunt had ongoing contact with ECSC club members for nearly nine months to continue spreading his malicious, false accusations. I believe Duncanville narcotics detective and ECSC leagues manager Dan Hunt's answer was nothing but a blatant attempt to mitigate Hunt's liability and culpability for the irrevocable damage he caused to my and Shawn's reputations and credibility.

INTERROGATORY NO. 4: *Do you contend that Plaintiff and/or a member of Plaintiff's team altered the official score on the Stockholder Team's official scoresheet for week eight (8), June 28, 2018, of the 2018 Spring Trap League? If so, please state the factual basis for this contention.*

ANSWER: *Defendant objects to the extent that the Interrogatory requests that Defendant marshal all evidence. Defendant further objects that the Interrogatory is premature, as discovery is still ongoing. Subject to the foregoing objections and without waiving same: will supplement.*

Defendant Dan Hunt wouldn't answer the question. Leagues manager Dan Hunt was responsible for the bogus charge of cheating. Vice President DVM Chris Rose told me I was kicked out of the league because "Uh, changing scoresheets without you know talking to anybody." I protested, saying, "But ah, Chris, we didn't change any score, scoresheets. All we did was follow what Dan told us to do and that was to note the scores on the outer edge of the scoresheet. We didn't actually change any score." Rose responded, "Well, that's you know not how it was reported." Dan Hunt did the reporting.

This time, Hunt couldn't get away with his false accusation. Not when the interrogatory required *the factual basis for this contention.* Danny Garth Hunt, a vindictive, incompetent, unqualified ECSC leagues manager, was between the proverbial rock and a hard place with nowhere to go. If Hunt answered yes, he had to produce the evidence. Hunt couldn't because there was none. If Hunt answered no, it would be a confession he lied to the ECSC Board of Directors. Hunt's refusal to answer didn't make Vice President DVM Chris Rose look good. "Straight-up" Rose went under the bus—again.

INTERROGATORY NO. 5: *To the extent you are aware, please identify: (1) the name(s) and telephone numbers of all individuals who claim Plaintiff and/or a member of Plaintiff's team altered the official score on the Stockholder Team's official scoresheet for week eight (8), June 28, 2018, of the 2018 Spring Trap League: and (2) any and all non-privileged documents that evidence said claims.*

ANSWER: *Defendant objects to the extent that the Interrogatory requests that Defendant marshal all evidence. Defendant further objects that the Interrogatory is premature, as discovery is still ongoing. Subject to the foregoing objections and without waiving same: will supplement, if any.*

Considering the scoresheet had not been altered, it's not surprising Dan Hunt didn't answer.

INTERROGATORY NO. 6: *To the extent you are aware, please identify: (1) the name(s) and telephone numbers of all individuals who observed Plaintiff and/or a member of Plaintiff's team alter the official score on the Stockholder Team's official scoresheet for week eight (8), June 28, 2018, of the 2018 Spring Trap League: (2) any and all non-privileged documents that evidence any alleged "observations."*

ANSWER: *None.*

Dan Hunt would contradict this answer in a later rendition of the events in Defendants' filings before the 443rd Ellis County District Court and the Court of Appeals, Tenth District of Texas.

Dan Hunt couldn't get his stories straight. It was an appalling pattern throughout Dan Hunt's own words describing the scoring dispute. To quote Sir Walter Scott, "Oh, what a tangled web we weave, when first we practice to deceive." This Duncanville vindictive cop and incompetent ECSC leagues manager Danny Garth Hunt would entangle himself in his web of deceit within future court filings.

INTERROGATORY NO. 7: *Please: (1) identify the name and telephone number of all individuals who lodged a complaint to you against the Plaintiff and/or a member of Plaintiff's team regarding the scoring dispute, and (2) identify any and all-non privileged documents which evidence such complaint(s).*

ANSWER: *Defendant objects that the Interrogatory is vague and ambiguous. Subject to the foregoing objections and without waiving same: David McDaniel, Tommy Nations, Larry Degal, Susie Thompson, Sherry Lewis, and Jeff Gregory.*

What was vague and ambiguous? Was this another legal tap dance? It seems to me it's a straightforward question. Who complained? Hunt's initial statements that it was over "half the damn league" boiled down to six individuals. Two ATA mid-level registered competitors on the second-place team and four on the misbehaving, scoring team whose numerous infractions of ATA rules and procedures led to the scoring errors and unsafe conditions. I would point out that instigator Director Sherrie Lewis was in the thick of it.

INTERROGATORY NO. 8: *For any and all statements you have made about the Plaintiff from 2017 to present, please: (1) describe with reasonable particularity the content of the statement; (2) identify the name and telephone number for each person to whom the statement was made; and (3) identify any documents that evidence such statements. Please note that statements made to your attorney are expressly excluded from this request.*

ANSWER: Defendant objects that the Interrogatory requests information that is not relevant nor reasonably calculated to lead to the discovery of admissible evidence. Defendant further objects that the Interrogatory is vague, ambiguous and constitutes an impermissible fishing expedition. Lastly, Defendant objects that the Interrogatory is overbroad as to time and scope. Subject to the foregoing objections and without waiving same: see documents produced by Defendants for information responsive to this Interrogatory.

The *documents produced by Defendants for information responsive to this Interrogatory,* included emails Dan Hunt sent to league competitors on June 29th and July 1, 2018. The emails identified the recipients.

Curiously, the *documents produced by Defendants* did not include Defendant Dan Hunt's vicious, libelous, vindictive, whining pity email, *Immediate resignation.* Why was it missing along with the names of the nearly one hundred unsuspecting club members and guests receiving Dan Hunt's malicious, libelous email at thirty-four minutes before midnight? Hunt's July 2nd whining pity email was just as relevant, if not more so, than the two emails Dan Hunt sent on June 29th and July 1, 2018. Like the security camera tapes that Porter and his cronies never produced, it appeared Dan Hunt didn't want his libelous, whining pity email to see the light of day. Had Dan Hunt's email, *Immediate resignation,* become a liability?

****

Defendant Desoto Gun Club D/B/A Ellis County Sportsman's Club's Objections and Answers to Plaintiff's First Set of Interrogatories, Treasurer Russell "Rusty" Porter was the respondent.

INTERROGATORY NO. 5: *Please identify the names and telephone numbers of all individuals interviewed regarding the scoring dispute described in Plaintiff's Original Petition, the suspension of Plaintiff's membership rights, and/or the termination of Plaintiff's membership.*

ANSWER: *Defendant objects that the Interrogatory is vague and ambiguous. Defendant further objects to the extent responsive information is protected pursuant to the attorney-client privilege or work product doctrine. Subject to the foregoing objections and without waiving same: Larry Degal, address and telephone number – will supplement.*

The Porter/Henslee kangaroo investigation consisted of one individual. The intentionally misbehaving scorekeeper Larry Degal. There was not a lot of credibility there, but then, the truth evidently wasn't important to Porter and his cronies. The July 12, 2018, board meeting minutes contradict Porter's response to the interrogatory.

Excerpt from minutes: *Discussion of the **various interviews** and information gathering we agreed to complete at the end of the July 2 meeting followed.* Who were the other individuals interviewed? Why was Larry Degal the only one listed?

INTERROGATORY NO 6: *Do you contend that Plaintiff and/or a member of Plaintiff's team altered the official score on the Stockholder Team's official scoresheet for week eight (8), June 28, 2018, of the 2018 Spring Trap League? If so, please: (1) state the factual basis for this contention, and (2) identify any and all non-privileged documents that support this contention.*

ANSWER: *Defendant objects to the extent that the Interrogatory requests that Defendant marshal all evidence. Defendant further objects that the Interrogatory is premature, as discovery is still ongoing. Subject to the foregoing objections and without waiving same, will supplement.*

ECSC Treasurer Rusty Porter knew what his Vice President Chris Rose told me on July 15, 2018. "Uh, changing scoresheets without you know talking to anybody." I told Porter and his cronies in two documents, *Anita Dickason's Notice of Representation and Litigation Hold* and the *Factual Allegations* in my lawsuit.

This time, the Grand Poobah couldn't get away with hiding behind his Vice President, Chris Rose's phone call or an email. If

Porter answered yes, supporting what his Vice President told me, Porter had to produce the evidence. He had none. The scoresheet and Dan Hunt's July 1, 2018, email proved otherwise. If Porter answered no, it would be an admission the Secret 7 wrongly convicted me of cheating, as reported to me by their official spokesman, ECSC Vice President Chris Rose. A false accusation that resulted in irrevocable damage to my reputation and credibility. It's no wonder the Grand Poobah refused to answer the question. Of course, none of this made his crony, Vice President DVM Chris Rose, look good.

INTERROGATORY NO 7: *To the extent you are aware, please identify: (1) the name(s) and telephone numbers of all individuals who claim Plaintiff and/or a member of Plaintiff's team altered the official score on the Stockholder Team's official scoresheet for week eight (8), June 28, 2018, of the 2018 Spring Trap League, and (2) any and all non-privileged documents that evidence said claims.*

ANSWER: *Defendant objects to the extent that the Interrogatory requests that Defendant marshal all evidence. Defendant further objects that the Interrogatory is premature, as discovery is still ongoing. Subject to the foregoing objections and without waiving same, will supplement, if any.*

Whoever wrote the July 2, 2018, board meeting minutes recorded Dan Hunt's bogus charge of cheating. It's in an official ECSC legal document. Yet, Porter refused to identify Dan Hunt in his answer to this interrogatory. It appeared that Porter kept covering for Hunt while he hung Rose out to dry. Poor ol' "straight-up" Rose. He never got to drive the bus. Rose was simply too busy being under it.

INTERROGATORY NO. 8: *To the extent you are aware, please identify: (1) the name(s) and telephone numbers of all individuals who observed Plaintiff's and/or a member of Plaintiff's team alter the official score on the Stockholder Team's official scoresheet for week eight (8), June 28, 2018, of the 2018 Spring Trap League; (2) any and all non – privileged documents that evidence any alleged "observations."*

ANSWER: *None.*

How could I be accused, then convicted, of "Uh, changing scoresheets without you know talking to anybody," if someone didn't observe *Plaintiff's and/or a member of Plaintiff's team alter the official score on the Stockholder Team's official scoresheet?* Of course, the scoresheet was the evidence the official scores were not altered.

INTERROGATORY NO. 9: *Please: (1) identify the name and telephone number of all individuals who lodged a complaint with Defendant Hunt and/or a member of ECSC Board of Directors against the Plaintiff and/or a member of Plaintiff's team regarding the scoring dispute, and (2) identify any and all nonprivileged documents which evidence such complaint(s).*

ANSWER: *Defendant objects that the Interrogatory is vague and ambiguous. Subject to the foregoing objections and without waiving same: David McDaniel, Tommy Nations, Larry Degal, Susie Thompson, Sherry Lewis, and Jeff Gregory.*

Porter provided the same response as did Dan Hunt. Two second-place competitors, neither of which had any first-hand information, and four competitors from the misbehaving scoring team.

INTERROGATORY NO. 11: *For an ECSC League Manager, please: (1) identify the ECSC's qualifications for the position; (2) describe the duties and responsibilities of an ECSC League Manager; and (3) identify any documents which evidence the qualifications, duties, and/or responsibilities of an ECSC League Manager.*

ANSWER: *Defendant objects that the Interrogatory requests information that is not relevant nor reasonably calculated to lead to the discovery of admissible evidence. Defendant further objects that the Interrogatory is vague and ambiguous. Subject to the foregoing objections and without waiving same: all of the club's shooting league managers are volunteers. There are no official qualifications for the position. League managers are tasked with the responsibility of ensuring that the club's rules, policies and bylaws are followed.*

How could anyone consider a question regarding the qualifications to run a live-fire shooting competition consisting of forty-armed men, women, and children, some with little to no experience, as not relevant or that the question was vague or ambiguous? There again was the word, *volunteers,* as if that fact negated the necessity for competent, qualified oversite of forty armed individuals. Dan Hunt, an incompetent, vindictive leagues manager the ECSC Board allowed to oversee their trap leagues, was at the center of the controversy. Dan Hunt's vindictiveness, false accusations, and misconduct exposed the club to a lawsuit. ECSC's qualifications for league managers were undoubtedly relevant.

Porter's response; *There are no official qualifications for the position,* was enlightening, though not surprising. Based on my extensive competitive experience and observations, the lack of qualifications was evident from how Dan Hunt ran the trap leagues and later his so-called investigation.

Then Porter had the audacity to claim, *League managers are tasked with the responsibility of ensuring that the club's rules, policies and bylaws are followed.* Since I had to file a lawsuit, spending thousands of dollars to obtain the *club's rules, policies, and bylaws,* I had to question if Porter's response was an attempt to mitigate the club's liability.

Either way, I've got news for Treasurer Rusty Porter. The buck stops with the ECSC Board of Directors. Using Porter's answer, it follows the Board of Directors was responsible for ensuring their leagues manager complied with ECSC *club's rules, policies, and bylaws* for managing a trap league governed by the ATA rules. It also follows it was the Board's responsibility to ensure Dan Hunt behaved himself with a loaded shotgun, especially in front of parents and children. The ECSC Board of Directors was ultimately responsible for their misbehaving, admittedly suffering from mental whatever, incompetent, unqualified, vindictive leagues manager, Dan Hunt.

What was astounding was the failure of ECSC leadership to

recognize they had liability hanging out their wazoo. I tried to tell them. Shawn tried to tell them. Look at what they did to us. A false accusation of cheating, we were thrown out of the trap leagues, my paid membership rights to participate in club-sponsored events wrongfully suspended, and our reputations and credibility destroyed. Why? To silence us. Porter, Rose, and their cronies were not concerned with liability or the welfare and safety of club members, guests, and the many children using the ECSC facility. They obviously weren't concerned with their leagues manager misbehaving like a buffoon with a loaded weapon in front of parents and children. I believe all they cared about was their social atmosphere and how much money they made. Don't upset club members and guests by correcting their misbehavior or dangerous mishandling of weapons. Let's just ignore the danger of mixing guns, alcohol, and children.

They could have easily corrected these serious gun and alcohol-related issues, along with the incompetent management of their leagues, in a closed meeting with us. Instead, they tried to bury their problems by destroying our reputations and credibility with their unprincipled, clandestine conduct.

So what did Porter and his cronies' unprincipled conduct get them? What it didn't get them was another meeting under a confidentiality agreement. Instead, it got them sued. It got them a book, where the unsafe handling of firearms and alcohol consumption on their property now becomes a matter of public awareness and concern. The unwarranted mixing of guns, alcohol, and children, along with the contemptible behavior of Dan Hunt, Rusty Porter, Chris Rose, and the rest of their cronies, are now in the Library of Congress.

If anyone, especially a child, is seriously injured or killed at the ECSC due to the negligence of the Board of Directors or unqualified leagues managers, plaintiffs and their attorneys will perhaps have a road map of why it happened.

48 Bucks - A Banker's Integrity

Chapter Thirteen

The next phase of the judicial proceedings was mediation, scheduled for April 17, 2019. It was voluntary, not mandated by the Court. My attorney had instructed me to prepare my list of demands. My list did not include money. I wanted a public apology from Defendants and reinstatement of my ECSC membership. Even though I had no plans to ever set foot again on ECSC property, I believed reinstating my membership would help minimize the damage the ECSC Board of Directors and their vindictive leagues manager Dan Hunt did to my reputation and credibility.

Instead, the mediator tossed my list across the desk toward me, saying, "This is a non-starter." The entire process went downhill from there. Eventually, we hammered out a settlement. I settled because I had accomplished what I set out to do with the lawsuit. The settlement amount would recoup my attorney fees I was forced to pay to obtain the evidence I didn't cheat, as reported to me by the former mayor of Cedar Hill, Texas, ECSC Vice President DVM Christopher Lyons Rose. The documents clearly demonstrated Dan Hunt's malicious, vindictive misbehavior and the unprincipled leadership of the ECSC. While I could never fully eradicate their damage to my reputation and credibility, at least I had my proof.

I signed, along with Defendants Dan Hunt and Waxahachie banker, ECSC President Mike Lee, a contract, a *Rule 11 and Settlement Agreement*. Hindsight being twenty-twenty, I wish I had never signed.

Instead, I would have been better off with a jury trial. But I did, believing a horrific chapter in my life was over. I had my evidence. The lawsuit was supposedly settled. Was I ever wrong! Instead, a new, expensive chapter was about to begin. One that would extend the lawsuit for another four-plus years, costing me tens of thousands more dollars and a great deal more stress.

What happened was another episode in the unbelievable saga of reprehensible conduct and false accusations by Duncanville narcotics detective, ECSC leagues manager Dan Hunt and the unprincipled leadership of the ECSC. Dan Hunt and ECSC leadership reneged on the contract, *Rule 11 and Settlement Agreement* they mediated and willingly signed on April 17, 2019.

The contract, *Rule 11 and Settlement Agreement* contained a confidentiality clause regarding just the settlement terms. I couldn't talk about it, nor could Defendants. The confidentiality clause subsequently became a moot point when the contract, *Rule 11 and Settlement Agreement* became part of the open records in multiple court filings after I was forced to file a second Breach of Contract against Defendants. The settlement terms were now public record and openly discussed by the attorneys in Court.

According to the contract, *Rule 11 and Settlement Agreement*, I was to receive the settlement check on or before May 2, 2019. On May 8, 2019, after the deadline for receipt of the settlement check came and went without any word from my attorney, I sent an email asking about the status. My attorney responded with an email. No check, but she'd received a document she was revising. I expected a typed version of the contract, *Rule 11 and Settlement Agreement*. I even indicated such in my response to my attorney. It wasn't what I got.

On May 15, 2018, I received Defendants' *Settlement and Release Agreement* from my attorney. It was version #2 since I didn't get the original document, version #1, until after I received version #2. I read the document in disbelief. It wasn't a typed version of the contract, *Rule*

11 and Settlement Agreement Defendants and I signed. It was a new contract containing provisions not agreed upon or even discussed during mediation. Provisions that were not included in the contract, *Rule 11 and Settlement Agreement* Defendants mediated and willingly signed.

Defendants' attorneys also refused to send my settlement check until I signed Defendants' new contract, *Settlement and Release Agreement*.

In the next chapter, I will detail the specifics of the *Order of The Supreme Court of Texas and The Court of Criminal Appeals: The Texas Lawyer's Creed–A Mandate for Professionalism*. Within this document governing the conduct of a lawyer, I discovered what I believe were multiple violations of *The Texas Lawyer's Creed* by Defendants lawyers. Though here, I will cite one stipulation from *The Texas Lawyer's Creed* pertinent to the actions by Defendants' attorneys. Note the stipulation is the *agreement of the parties,* not the attorneys.

III. Lawyer to Lawyer: *4. I will attempt to prepare documents which correctly reflect the agreement of the parties. I will not include provisions which have not been agreed upon or omit provisions which are necessary to reflect the agreement of the parties.*

Defendants' new contract, *Settlement and Release Agreement*, did not *correctly reflect the agreement of the parties.* Instead, it contained provisions *which have not been agreed upon.*

I received my attorney's email at 3:48 p.m. At 4:12 p.m., less than thirty minutes after receiving Defendants' new contract, I responded, telling my attorney I wouldn't sign Defendants' new contract. I also explained why.

When I queried my attorney about the reason for Defendants' actions, I was told Dan Hunt and the ECSC were dissatisfied with the contract, *Rule 11 and Settlement Agreement* they mediated and willingly signed.

I'd spent over $3200 in attorney and mediation fees. Why bother with mediation if Defendants could willy-nilly change the contract because they didn't like the one they had already signed? No one with any sense would sign a contract under such conditions. You can't just decide to change the terms like Defendants Dan Hunt and ECSC tried to do.

The first issue dealt with the settlement amount. It now included the balance on my ECSC debit card. My $48. Where the devil did that one come from? It was never addressed in mediation. The contract, *Rule 11 and Settlement Agreement* did not stipulate the settlement amount included the balance on my ECSC debit card.

The $48 on my ECSC debit card was my money. It didn't belong to the club. The club had acquired the money from a charge to my credit card. On January 14, 2019, the ECSC Board of Directors voted to *refund* the balance on my ECSC debit card, then notified me of the Board of Directors' intended *refund* in ECSC Secretary Shannon Edwards' letter dated January 15, 2019. To quote; *Please return your gate key card, your clay card and your keys to the club house and the trap and skeet houses as soon as possible. Upon our receipt of your clay card, we will send you a refund check of the amount remaining on your card.*

I complied with Secretary Shannon Edwards' instructions at the Ambush, otherwise known as the membership appeal meeting. I handed my *clay card* to then ECSC President Mike Lee. Waxahachie banker, ECSC President Mike Lee, told me in person, to my face, that he would refund the balance on my debit card, my $48, and send me a check.

The Board of Directors had no right to arbitrarily add my $48 to the settlement amount. My $48 didn't belong to them. Payment of the settlement amount, by the way, wasn't coming from the ECSC. Their 830-plus billion-dollar French insurance conglomerate was writing the check for the settlement amount. I doubt the insurance adjustor cared if the Board used the settlement payment as an excuse to avoid refunding my $48 as promised. I viewed it as a win-win for the club.

They'd found a way to keep my money. They intentionally stole it. As of the date of this book, I have never received the *refund* as voted and approved by the ECSC Board of Directors and promised two times. I believe that I discovered what Waxahachie banker and ECSC President Mike Lee's integrity was worth, 48 bucks.

When I obtained the minutes of several ECSC Board meetings, I discovered Mike Lee was present at the January 14, 2019, ECSC board meeting when the Board voted to *refund* the balance on my debit card. Yet, like Treasurer Rusty Porter, who disregarded a vote of the Board by adding his stipulations to my suspension, the new President, Mike Lee, also ignored a vote of the board.

Was this how Mike Lee transacted business as an executive vice president of my local Waxahachie bank? To me, it didn't say much about Waxahachie banker Mike Lee's ethics.

What did I say earlier about a line from an old Bret Maverick episode, "If you can't trust your banker, who can you trust?" How chintzy can a Waxahachie banker get? The ECSC Board of Directors wrongly ruined my reputation, humiliated me, lied to my face, then intentionally stole my $48.

The next issue with Defendants' new contract was adding Shawn as a party to the lawsuit. He wasn't. There was a place in the contract, *Rule 11 and Settlement Agreement,* to add another party to the proceedings if they had so chosen during mediation. A stipulation I could and would have disagreed with at the time. This section of the contract, *Rule 11 and Settlement Agreement* was clearly left blank.

Their next new provision, a non-disparagement provision, was a doozy. This time, Hunt and ECSC leadership wanted to deny me my First Amendment Rights. Defendants' non-disparagement provision was nothing but another gag order. One meant to penalize me, just as Grand Poobah Porter did with his gag order of July 16, 2018. Porter informed me my suspension would be extended if I caused further controversies. In other words, shut up about the gun safety issues and the inherent danger of mixing guns, alcohol, and children. Porter and his cronies wanted me silenced.

Defendants attempted it again in their new contract, *Settlement and Release Agreement*. They wanted to deny me my right to speak out. Their new non-disparagement provision would prevent me from discussing gun safety issues and the dangers of mixing guns, alcohol, and children at the ECSC. Legitimate concerns every participant and parent of any child participating in events at a gun club allowing the consumption of alcoholic beverages has not only, in my opinion, a right to express, but a moral obligation.

Their new non-disparagement provision would stop me from exposing the malicious, vindictive misbehavior of Duncanville narcotics detective and ECSC leagues manager Danny Garth Hunt, and the ECSC Board of Directors' unprincipled conduct that destroyed my reputation. Considering the Board had already tried to silence me, it shouldn't have come as a surprise they would attempt the same tactic again.

I never asked for compensation from their 830-plus billion-dollar French insurance conglomerate for Defendants damage to my reputation, the humiliation I was subjected to before fellow club members and competitors, the mental and physical anguish I endured because of their malicious false accusations and unprincipled conduct. No, I was willing to settle for what it cost me in attorney fees to obtain the evidence of their deceitful and unprincipled conduct. Yet, these unprincipled individuals, Dan Hunt and ECSC leadership, weren't satisfied. They tried to kick me again. This time, they wanted to take away my First Amendment Rights. Silence me once and for all. Stop me from speaking out.

Here is another interesting point. In Defendants' original version of their new contract, *Settlement and Release Agreement*, their new non-disparagement provision only applied to Shawn and me. It wasn't reciprocal. They could keep badmouthing us, yet we couldn't tell the truth about them. It was just like "straight-up" Rose and his cronies' clandestine kangaroo court. They got to talk. Shawn and I didn't. In version #2, the provision was changed to be reciprocal, applying to Defendants as well.

The problem was Dan Hunt's and Sherrie Lewis' propensity to ignore confidentiality agreements. I'd already been down this road with these two before. Why would I trust Duncanville narcotics detective, ECSC leagues manager Dan Hunt, or ECSC instigator Sherrie Lewis after their statements that were not only false, but violated the confidentiality agreement everyone in the July 2nd board meeting agreed to? Dan Hunt and the ECSC Board of Directors had already reneged on one contract, *Rule 11 and Settlement Agreement* they mediated and willingly signed. Defendants' attorneys now wanted me to believe Dan Hunt and the ECSC Board of Directors would suddenly see the light and honor their new contract, including a condition they couldn't say anything about me.

ECSC leadership, Vice President DVM Christopher Lyons Rose, Grand Poobah, Russell Alvin (Rusty) Porter, Jr., and their cronies had already tarred and feathered me. It was not quid pro quo. It was not tit for tat. Dan Hunt and the ECSC Board of Directors weren't giving up anything. The club's insurance carrier, the 830-plus billion-dollar French insurance conglomerate, was covering their misconduct.

Not only did Defendants attempt to deny me my First Amendment Rights, they also augmented the confidentiality agreement in the signed contract, *Rule 11 and Settlement Agreement,* stipulating the settlement terms had to be kept confidential.

Their new confidentiality agreement denied me the right to use documents not in the public record, in addition to the existing stipulations within the signed contract, *Rule 11 and Settlement Agreement.* The new stipulation would deny me the use of documents the ECSC initially refused to provide in response to a lawful request from my attorney, *Litigation Hold,* in July 2018. I had to sue them and spend thousands of dollars to obtain these documents. Porter and his cronies now wanted to stop me from using the documents I lawfully obtained to refute their false accusations and malicious behavior.

On May 29, 2019, J. Richard Harmon, Defendants' attorney, responded to my refusal to sign their new contract, *Settlement and Release Agreement,* firing off an email to my attorney. The high-powered attorney hired by the 830-plus billion-dollar French insurance conglomerate, the "Big Dog," as had been described to me, had entered the picture. Up to this point, my attorney had been dealing with another lawyer, Regan G. Pearson, in the Dallas multi-state law firm.

As a reminder, *The Texas Lawyer's Creed*, an *Order* by the *Supreme Court of Texas*, stipulated: **III. Lawyer to Lawyer:** *4. I will attempt to prepare documents which correctly reflect the agreement of the parties. I will not include provisions which have not been agreed upon or omit provisions which are necessary to reflect the agreement of the parties.*

The stipulation clearly stated; *to reflect the agreement of the parties,* not the agreement of the attorneys. It should also be noted the referenced emails were attached as exhibits in two court filings by Defendants before the 443rd Ellis County District Court.

In his email, Harmon, the "Big Dog," wrote; *Regan informed me that Ms. Dickason is refusing to sign the settlement agreement even though you agreed to the language. She apparently has three issues with the settlement agreement. First, she is refusing to sign the agreement because the settlement does not include the $48 that was left on her shooting card. The Rule 11 agreement Ms. Dickason and you signed at mediation was for a total settlement amount of $15,000, not $15,048 or any other amount. We have a binding agreement at the number.*

The "Big Dog," J. Richard Harmon, considered the existing contract, *Rule 11 and Settlement Agreement,* a *binding agreement* regarding the money, but not the other provisions in the contract his clients mediated and willingly signed.

Harmon's arguments about the $48 didn't make sense. Harmon wrote: *First, she is refusing to sign the agreement because the settlement does not include the $48 that was left on her shooting card.* According to Defendants' new contract, *Settlement and Release Agreement*, the settlement amount included my $48. All I did was point out this was a false fact. My $48 was never brought up in mediation and was not stipulated in the contract, *Rule 11 and Settlement Agreement* his clients mediated and willingly signed. Then Harmon raised the issue that the settlement amount wasn't $15,048. The "Big Dog," J. Richard Harmon, is the one who changed the settlement amount to $15,048 in his email. I never changed the settlement amount, nor did my attorney.

Which raised the question, why all the insistence about my $48? It seemed ridiculous at the time, considering the ECSC Board of Directors voted to refund it and promised to do so two other times. I even wondered what the "Big Dog" charged the 830-plus billion-dollar French insurance conglomerate to write his email, arguing over what I considered my intentionally stolen $48. So, why would a downtown Dallas attorney argue about it?

Harmon's actions had a much broader significance. In subsequent documents filed by Defendants before the 443rd Ellis County District Court and argued in two court hearings, opposing counsel falsely claimed I requested my intentionally stolen $48 be added to the settlement amount, making the total $15,048. This false statement to the Court echoed the "Big Dog," J. Richard Harmon's May 29, 2019, email. *The Rule 11 agreement Ms. Dickason and you signed at mediation was for a total settlement amount of $15,000, not $15,048 or any other amount. We have a binding agreement at the number.*

Using Harmon's altered settlement amount, Defendants and their attorneys would later attempt to convince the 443rd Ellis County District Court to throw out the contract, *Rule 11 and Settlement Agreement*. They would mislead the Court by claiming I changed the settlement amount. When, in fact, it was the "Big Dog," J. Richard

Harmon, who changed the settlement amount.

Next, the "Big Dog" addressed Shawn's signature.

Second, Ms. Dickason is refusing to sign the agreement because Mr. George is a signatory to the document. Mr. George is a party to the Rule 11 agreement, has obligations under that agreement, and signed it. It should come as no surprise that he is a signatory on the actual settlement agreement, and he needs to sign the document.

Shawn was not listed as a party within the contract, *Rule 11 and Settlement Agreement*, nor was he a party to the lawsuit. Shawn signed the *Rule 11 and Settlement Agreement* because he was in the room and a witness to the proceeding. His only obligation was to abide by the confidentiality provision, not to talk about the settlement terms. Shawn never had any obligations or liabilities regarding the lawsuit or any claims. This was how Defendants attempted to manipulate a new contract in their favor.

The "Big Dog," J. Richard Harmon, finished with;

Third, and most disturbing, I understand from Regan that Ms. Dickason is refusing to sign the agreement because of the reciprocal anti-disparagement provision. Really? Does your client understand that disparagement is illegal and actionable? The fact that Ms. Dickason and Mr. George are taking this position is causing my clients great concern that they have every intent to make publicly disparaging and defamatory remarks about them once the settlement is funded. We are absolutely not removing that provision from the settlement agreement. If Ms. Dickason and Mr. George do not sign the settlement agreement as written, my clients will add a breach of contract claim to the counterclaim and will pursue all available relief including my firm's and Mr. Bunch's attorney fees and costs. Let us know as soon as possible whether we have a deal as agreed or we need to move forward with the litigation. Thanks. Rick.

The "Big Dog," J. Richard Harmon, was obviously incensed. The "Big Dog, not only threatened me but also Shawn, a nonparty to the lawsuit. Defendants weren't satisfied with going after my First

Amendment Rights. Now, they attempted to strip Shawn of his First Amendment Rights. The overriding question was why the insistence on an *anti-disparagement provision* was so critical after the *Rule 11 and Settlement Agreement* had been signed. There had been no discussion during mediation concerning an *anti-disparagement provision*. Did someone on Defendants' legal team screw up? Was there a come-to-Jesus meeting afterward? Or was it deliberately left out, expecting they could get away with sliding it into their new contract, *Settlement and Release Agreement*? Was this why the "Big Dog, J. Richard Harmon entered the fray when I refused to sign—to fix their problem? Harmon was adamant about not removing any of Defendants' new provisions.

I would have refused to sign the contract, *Rule 11 and Settlement Agreement* if it had contained an *anti-disparagement* provision or any of their other new provisions. I wasn't about to sign a new contract containing provisions to which I had not agreed. I was not going to be silenced no matter what the "Big Dog" demanded. I was not giving up my First Amendment Rights.

After reading the "Big Dog's" threats, another question arose. Had Harmon even read my original petition? I knew defamation was illegal and actionable. It's why I filed a defamation lawsuit against Harmon's unprincipled clients. Disparagement was a different issue, far broader and more encompassing than defamation. I wouldn't be able to speak out about gun safety infractions or the inherent dangers of mixing guns, alcohol, and children at the ECSC. I wouldn't be able to say anything about the conduct of a vindictive Duncanville cop and ECSC leagues manager, Dan Hunt, and the unprincipled leadership of the ECSC. I wouldn't be able to defend myself against their malicious, false accusations.

Here was another point to consider. According to the contract, *Rule 11 and Settlement Agreement*: Paragraph 6. *It is contemplated that counsel for defendant shall deliver drafts of any further settlement* *documentation to the other parties by <u>April 24, 2019</u>. The parties agree to cooperate with each other in the drafting and execution of such additional documents.*

The underlined entries were written on the form by the mediator. What was significant in this quote was the word *contemplated*. There is a difference between *contemplated* and required. The contract, *Rule 11 and Settlement Agreement*, which Defendants mediated and willingly signed, did not stipulate I was required to sign further documents. Still, I attempted to cooperate. I explained why their new contract, *Settlement and Release Agreement* was unacceptable. They just didn't like my answer. Then, instead of cooperation from Defendants and their attorneys, I was threatened and bullied. If I didn't sign, Defendants would come after me with a breach of contract lawsuit, asking for their attorney fees. They refused to send my settlement check until I signed their new contract. Defendants and their attorneys were holding my settlement check hostage.

On June 5, 2019, my attorney responded to the "Big Dog," J. Richard Harmon.

My client is not in breach of anything at this point. She is agreeing to be bound by the terms of the mediated Rule 11 agreement. With respect to the three issues raised in your email: First, with respect to the $48 on the card. I would first note that the Rule 11 makes no mention of the money left on her card so I'm not sure why it is part of the agreement. This being said, the settlement agreement drafted by your office requires her to release the $48 on her card. That is $48 of her money that she paid to the club as part of a credit account to purchase items at the club, and so any remaining funds belong to her. You are correct that the amount of the settlement was $15,000, not $15,048, but by requiring her to give up funds to the club rightfully belonging to her, she is in actuality getting paid $14,952. Second, you are incorrect that my client is refusing to sign the agreement because Mr. George is a signatory. Both my client and Mr. George signed the Rule 11 agreement, wherein they agreed not to enter *the gun club premises and to be bound by a confidentiality agreement. Mr. George and my client are willing to be bound by whatever they agreed to in the Rule 11. Third, I really don't want to get into the weeds on this, but you are a respected and experienced attorney and know very well that: (1) not every disparaging comment is defamatory and therefore "illegal," particularly in the context of my client's ability to exercise her First Amendment rights and the growing anti-SLAPP case law on this subject, and (2) a non-disparagement provision is not boilerplate add-on language; rather, it is a material term that would likely require additional/carved out consideration to be enforceable. If it is so central to the deal that you are threatening to sue my client for breach of contract, then it should have been included (in) the Rule 11 agreement, as were the terms regarding the settlement amount, confidentiality, and the agreement not to enter onto the property. Finally, as you are also aware from reviewing the Rule 11 agreement, any issues that arise concerning the Rule 11 agreement are to be taken up first with Judge Fifer by phone, then in a second mediation if necessary. While I understand your frustration, threats of litigation and attorney fees are counterproductive. I am happy to reach out to Burdin to set up a phone conference with Judge Fifer so we can try and talk through and hopefully resolve these issues.* (Fifer was the individual who referred to Defendants' attorney, J. Richard Harmon, as the "Big Dog.")

My attorney never claimed I changed the settlement amount to $15,048. Instead, my attorney agreed with the "Big Dog" that the settlement amount was not $15,048. Yet, opposing counsel would claim in Defendants' two filings before the 443rd Ellis County District Court, during two hearings, and in *Appellees' Brief* filed before the Court of Appeals, Tenth District of Texas, that I requested the balance on my shooting card be added to the settlement amount, changing it to $15,048. I found opposing counsels' assertions were nothing but a deliberate false representation of the facts to mislead the Court.

The contract, *Rule 11 and Settlement Agreement* stipulated a second round of mediation if any issues arose. If a party refused to participate in the mediation, court and attorney fees could not be recovered in subsequent litigation to enforce the agreement.

Excerpt: ***Rule 11 and Settlement Agreement,***

If one or more disputes arise with regard to the interpretation and/or performance of this agreement or any of its provisions, the parties agree to attempt to resolve same by phone conference with the Mediator who facilitated the settlement. If the parties cannot resolve their differences by phone conference, then each agrees to schedule a one-half day of mediation with the Mediator within thirty (30) days to resolve the disputes and to share the cost of same equally. If a party refuses to mediate, then that party may not recover the attorneys fees or costs in litigation brought to construe or enforce this agreement. Otherwise, if mediation is unsuccessful then the prevailing party or parties shall be entitled to recover reasonable attorneys fees and expenses, including the cost of the unsuccessful mediation.

Per the dispute stipulation, my attorney attempted to schedule a conference call with the mediator. In an email dated June 5, 2019, Defendants' attorney, the "Big Dog," J. Richard Harmon, ordered my attorney: *Do not contact Judge Fifer, and I can guarantee you that there will not be another mediation.* The "Big Dog's" arrogant refusal was yet another intentional breach of the contract, *Rule 11 and Settlement Agreement,* Defendants mediated and willingly signed.

On June 24, 2019, my attorney received an email from Defendants' attorney Regan G. Pearson.

We have discussed your client's issues with the language in the proposed settlement agreement with Mr. Hunt and the gun club. First, we can agree that Mr. George does not need to sign any settlement agreement but maintain that he is bound by the Rule 11 Agreement he previously signed at the mediation. Second, our clients will not agree to any settlement that does not contain the anti-disparagement language previously-included in the settlement agreement and lastly, our clients insist that Ms. Dickason's $48 shooting card balance is included in the $15,000 settlement. If your client cannot agree, then our position will be that there was no, "meeting of the minds" at the mediation, no valid agreement was reached and we will continue to litigate this case.

I spent hours in mediation. I paid over $3200 in attorney and mediation fees to finalize a contract, *Rule 11 and Settlement Agreement*, Defendants mediated and willingly signed. They'd already agreed to the terms of the settlement, and it didn't include my intentionally stolen $48 or the *anti-disparagement language*. Now, they threatened to throw out a signed contract because I wouldn't agree to their new provisions. Still no settlement check. I believed Regan G. Pearson's threat to extend the litigation was another egregious violation of *The Texas Lawyer's Creed*, an *Order* by the *Supreme Court of Texas*. Defendants weren't paying the tab for their extended litigation. It was their 830-plus billion-dollar French insurance conglomerate.

II. Lawyer to Client: *7. I will advise my client that we will not pursue conduct which is intended primarily to harass or drain the financial resources of the opposing party.*

Despite what Regan G. Pearson asserted in his June 24, 2019, email, Defendants would renege again. Defendants did not remove Shawn as they agreed. Their final version, #3, of their new contract, *Settlement and Release Agreement*, was attached as an exhibit in their filings to the 443rd Ellis County District Court. Shawn was still listed as a party and required to sign the agreement.

After Defendants and their attorneys refused to send the settlement check, on July 29, 2019, my attorney filed *Plaintiff's Second Amended Petition* with the 443rd Ellis County District Court to add a second breach of contract to my lawsuit against Dan Hunt and the ECSC.

There was no response from Defendants to the second breach of contract filing. On August 14, 2019, my attorney filed *Plaintiff's Motion for Summary Judgment*, resulting in a hearing before the 443rd Ellis County District Court. The purpose of the hearing was to force Defendants to comply with the contract, *Rule 11 and Settlement Agreement* they mediated and willingly signed.

Shortly after my filing, and on the same day, Defendants' attorney, Regan G. Pearson reacted, informing my attorney his clients had abandoned their positions regarding the new provisions. So much for the "Big Dog," J. Richard Harmon's statement regarding the anti-disparagement provision: *We are absolutely not removing that provision from the settlement agreement,* or their threats to file a breach of contract if I refused to sign their new contract.

Defendants had now seemingly agreed to abide by the original terms of the contract, *Rule 11 and Settlement Agreement* their clients mediated and willingly signed. The only problem was they planned to send a third version of their new contract, *Settlement and Release Agreement.* As I later discovered, their third version still contained provisions to which I had not agreed. Still no check.

To force Defendants to comply with the contract, *Rule 11 and Settlement Agreement* they signed, I had to sue them again. The problem was my attorney fees. While Defendants wanted to claim timeout, saying we'll go along with the original contract, *Rule 11 and Settlement Agreement*, they refused to pay my attorney fees and court costs I had to expend to force their compliance. According to the *Rule 11 and Settlement Agreement*, I was entitled to recover my attorney fees and court costs. Defendants couldn't. Their threatening attorney, the "Big Dog," J. Richard Harmon, had clearly, in writing, refused to go back into mediation.

In an August 15, 2019, email from Regan G. Pearson to my first attorney, Pearson refused to pay my attorney fees. My settlement check was still held hostage. I wouldn't get it until I signed their third version of Defendants' new contract, *Settlement and Release Agreement.*

After the issues with Defendants' new contract, *Settlement and*

Release Agreement, I believed hiring another firm specializing in contracts and breach of contract lawsuits was in my best interest.

On October 31, 2019, my new attorney filed *Plaintiff's Amended Motion for Summary Judgment to Enforce Rule 11 Settlement Agreement* with the 443rd Ellis County District Court. A hearing was subsequently scheduled for January 16, 2020.

At the time, my new attorney expected the enforcement of the *Rule 11 and Settlement Agreement* would be a mere formality. The Court could enforce the terms and conditions once a *Rule 11 and Settlement Agreement* was filed with the Court.

As events played out, it didn't happen. Instead, I believe Defendants' attorneys violated another section of *The Texas Lawyer's Creed*, an *Order* by the *Supreme Court of Texas*, within Defendants' filing and during a hearing before the 443rd Ellis County District Court.

IV. Lawyer and Judge: *6. I will not knowingly misrepresent, mischaracterize, misquote or miscite facts or authorities to gain an advantage.*

Within two court filings by Defendants and two court hearings before the 443rd Ellis County District Court, I would be subjected to further defamation and false accusations. Dan Hunt's false statements and accusations would again rear their ugly head, not only in Defendants filings but also by opposing counsels' statements to the Court. The ECSC would do the same with their false claims. All for one reason—*to gain an advantage.*

Dan Hunt's false statements and accusations, along with those of the ECSC, would ultimately reach the Court of Appeals, Tenth District of Texas.

Dan Hunt and the ECSC would reach new lows in their unprincipled conduct. Once again, I would be forced to stand my ground while continuing to pay a heavy price.

Affidavits! What Affidavits?

Chapter Fourteen

Dare I say, the January 16, 2020, hearing before the 443rd Ellis County District Court was nothing but another kangaroo court under the guise of the Texas Judicial System? Dare I say, Defendants, Defendants' attorneys, and the 443rd Ellis County District Court made a mockery of the very foundation of the tenants of the Texas Judicial System?

Two attorneys, Regan G. Pearson and the "Big Dog," J. Richard Harmon, hired by the 830-plus billion-dollar French insurance conglomerate, represented Dan Hunt and ECSC. The ECSC had also hired a local Waxahachie, Texas, attorney Ronald E. Bunch. During the hearing, Regan G. Pearson and Ronald E. Bunch represented Defendants. This was a hearing on my motion to enforce the contract, *Rule 11 and Settlement Agreement,* Defendants mediated and willingly signed. The *Rule 11 and Settlement Agreement* finalized the lawsuit.

The number of attorneys for Defendants had always appeared to be overkill. Why would the ECSC need a third attorney, Ronald E. Bunch, when their 830-plus billion-dollar French insurance conglomerate picked up the tab for a massive, multi-state law firm in downtown Dallas? It was a valid question, especially after Treasurer Rusty Porter filed his charges with the ECSC Board of Directors to have me thrown out of the club. In his formal complaint to the Board, Porter wrote; *this lawsuit will cost the club money.* If Porter was so concerned about the expense to the club, why hire an additional small-town local attorney? They had free legal services from a massive, multi-state law firm. Why would the ECSC Board of Directors spend club money on a small-town Waxahachie attorney when it wasn't necessary? Or was it?

Did Ronald E. Bunch provide the local connection Porter referred to when he implied he wasn't concerned with lawsuits because of the club's connection to the Ellis County legal community? Bunch's office was only a few blocks from the Waxahachie Courts Building. Ronald E. Bunch, a long-time Waxahachie attorney, would certainly have been known to the 443rd Ellis County District Court, as opposed to the attorneys from the downtown Dallas, big city, multi-state law firm hired by the 830-plus billion-dollar French insurance conglomerate. Was Bunch's involvement an attempt to influence the Court? It was another question that begged to be answered.

Based on what I read in two documents filed by Defendants before the 443rd Ellis County District Court and the transcript of two court hearings, it's my belief Regan G. Pearson, J. Richard Harmon, and Ronald E. Bunch compromised their professional integrity and ethics to win at any cost.

To quote an old saying; *If you have the facts on your side, pound the facts; if you have the law on your side, pound the law; if you have neither the facts nor the law, pound the table.* Regan G. Pearson and Ronald E. Bunch pounded the table before the 443rd Ellis County District Court. Was I dealing with Rambo-style lawyers willing to do whatever was necessary to win? Consider the excerpts from court documents and transcripts within this and the following chapters, then decide.

Texas Judicial System: Judicial Conduct and Discipline:
All persons who serve as judges in this State must be knowledgeable in the law and dispense justice in a fair and impartial manner.
ORDER OF
The Supreme Court of Texas and The Court of Criminal Appeals
The Texas Lawyer's Creed–A Mandate for Professionalism

The conduct of a lawyer should be characterized at all times by honesty, candor, and fairness. In fulfilling his or her primary duty to a client, a lawyer must be ever mindful of the profession's broader duty to the legal system.

The Supreme Court of Texas and the Court of Criminal Appeals are committed to eliminating a practice in our State by a minority of lawyers of abusive tactics which have surfaced in many parts of our country. We believe such tactics are a disservice to our citizens, harmful to clients, and demeaning to our profession.

The abusive tactics range from lack of civility to outright hostility and obstructionism. Such behavior does not serve justice but tends to delay and often deny justice. The lawyers who use abusive tactics, instead of being part of the solution, have become part of the problem.

I am a lawyer. I am entrusted by the People of Texas to preserve and improve our legal system. I am licensed by the Supreme Court of Texas. I must therefore abide by the Texas Disciplinary Rules of Professional Conduct, but I know that professionalism requires more than merely avoiding the violation of laws and rules. I am committed to this creed for no other reason than it is right.

II. Lawyer to Client: *6. I will treat adverse parties and witnesses with fairness and due consideration.*

II. Lawyer to Client: *7. I will advise my client that we will not pursue conduct which is intended primarily to harass or drain the financial resources of the opposing party.*

II. Lawyer to Client: *8. I will advise my clients that we will not pursue tactics which are intended primarily for delay.*

III. Lawyer to Lawyer: *4. I will attempt to prepare documents which correctly reflect the agreement of the parties. I will not include provisions which have not been agreed upon or omit provisions which are necessary to reflect the agreement of the parties.*

III. Lawyer to Lawyer: *7. I will not serve motions or pleadings in any manner that unfairly limits another party's opportunity to respond.*

IV. Lawyer and Judge: *6. I will not knowingly misrepresent, mischaracterize, misquote or miscite facts or authorities to gain an advantage.*

The hearing for *Plaintiff's Amended Motion for Summary Judgment to Enforce Rule 11 Settlement Agreement* was scheduled for Thursday, January 16, 2020. My motion was filed on October 31, 2019, giving Defendants and their attorneys more than two months to prepare for the hearing.

On Thursday, January 9, 2020, at 2:41 p.m., opposing counsel pulled another underhanded tactic when Defendants filed *Defendants' Response to Plaintiff's Amended Motion for Summary Judgment to Enforce Rule 11 Settlement Agreement* with the 443rd Ellis County District Court.

My attorney was given seven (7) calendar days' notice with their late filing of Defendants' Response. Since opposing counsel didn't file Defendants' Response until Thursday afternoon, that left four (4) business days, Friday, Monday, Tuesday, and Wednesday. With other cases on his schedule, my attorney had only four days to evaluate a sixty-one-page document and prepare his response for the hearing at 9:00 a.m. on Thursday.

On January 13, 2020, my attorney filed *Plaintiff's Motion to Strike Facts not in Evidence and Exhibits contained in Defendants' Response to Plaintiff's Amended Motion for Summary Judgment to Enforce Rule 11 Settlement Agreement.* In my Motion, my attorney rebuked opposing counsel.

Excerpt: Plaintiff's Motion to Strike,

I: Introduction and Facts

On October 31, 2019, Plaintiff filed Plaintiff's Amended Motion for Summary Judgment to Enforce Rule 11 Settlement Agreement. Plaintiff set this Motion for hearing on January 16, 2020.

On January 9, 2020, (7 days prior to the above-referenced hearing date), the Defendants filed a written response to Plaintiff's Amended

Motion for Summary Judgment to Enforce Rule 11 Settlement Agreement that contained multiple exhibits, and alleged statements from Defendants that were not produced timely to Plaintiff. This constitutes unfair surprise and is absent good cause from not producing, thus the following exhibits and facts that support Defendant's Response should be stricken and excluded pursuant to the exclusionary rule per Tex. R. Civ. Pro 193.6. Fort Brown Villas III Condo, Ass'n v. Gillenwater, 284 S.W.3d 879, 882 (Tex.2009).

In addition to the cited violation of *Texas Rules of Civil Procedure* governing discovery, opposing counsels' actions also violated *The Texas Lawyer's Creed, A Mandate for Professionalism,* an *Order* by the *Supreme Court of Texas.*

III. Lawyer to Lawyer: *7. I will not serve motions or pleadings in any manner that unfairly limits another party's opportunity to respond.*

Considering what I had already experienced when Defendants reneged on a contract they mediated and willingly signed, *Rule 11 and Settlement Agreement,* along with Defendants attorneys' threats and bullying, Defendants' improper filing was just more of the same, par for the course. I believe my question regarding Rambo-style lawyers was valid. Especially when opposing counsels' obstructive conduct wasn't the only legal issue with Defendants' Response.

Dan Hunt and the ECSC weren't satisfied with the damage they'd already done to my and Shawn's reputations and credibility with their false accusations and unprincipled conduct. Defendants and their attorneys used the judicial system to continue their malicious, defamatory accusations.

In addition to the rebuke of opposing counsel, my attorney requested the following.

Excerpt: Plaintiff's Motion to Strike,

Additionally, the following Exhibits contain rank hearsay and are not properly authenticated by both Mr. Hunt or Desoto Gun Club, thus the Exhibits B through F should be precluded from consideration in regard to Plaintiff's Motion for Summary Judgment.

The entire "Background Facts" Section (page 1 to 5) of Defendant's Response should be stricken as facts not in evidence. The statements and evidence are not directly supported or cited by Exhibits, Affidavits, or testimony by the Defendants and is simply testimony with authenticating source.

The *"Background Facts" Section (page 1 to 5)* within Defendants' Response included Dan Hunt's latest version of the scoring dispute that occurred months before I filed my lawsuit in December 2018. None of which had anything to do with the purpose of the hearing, to enforce the *Rule 11 and Settlement Agreement,* a contract Defendants and I signed at mediation on April 17, 2019. The contract finalized the lawsuit.

Defendants used their Response to establish a false version of the issues leading up to the lawsuit without providing evidence, signed, notarized affidavits from Defendants' or witnesses. This was a hearing involving only the attorneys, not a trial. In a trial, I could have taken the witness stand to defend myself against their defamatory and false accusations. Once again, I wasn't allowed to defend myself, as had happened in the ECSC clandestine, *Board Meeting-Emergency Meeting,* kangaroo court.

Since this wasn't a trial, Dan Hunt didn't have to worry about taking the witness stand where his false accusations and misconduct would be exposed. Instead, Hunt could put forth his vindictive, malicious, false facts and accusations within Defendants' Response without fear of consequences or reprisal.

The Court allowed Defendants to enter their irrelevant *Background,* putting a false version of events leading up to my lawsuit into the court records. A lawsuit that had already been settled.

During the January 16, 2020, hearing, Defendants' attorneys reiterated, even embellished their false facts and malicious accusations, before the 443rd Ellis County District Court. Despite my attorney's multiple objections, the 443rd Ellis County District Court allowed it.

The Court gave free rein to Defendants' attorneys to put forth their *misrepresentations, mischaracterizations, misquotes and miscites of facts.* The 443rd Ellis County District Court required no *Exhibits, Affidavits, or testimony by the Defendants.* The 443rd Ellis County District Court ultimately denied my motion to strike. In my opinion, the Court wasn't concerned about the unethical timing of Defendants' filing or opposing counsels' unprofessional, damaging conduct that could adversely affect my case. Nor was the Court concerned with allowing unsupported, malicious, defamatory, false facts to remain in the record.

A statement in an email from the "Big Dog," J. Richard Harmon, to my first attorney was prophetic. *Does your client understand that disparagement is illegal and actionable?* Harmon's words should have been directed at his clients, as well as the statements of his co-counsel, Regan G. Pearson and Ronald E. Bunch. It was what his clients did in Defendants' Response and Regan G. Pearson and Ronald E. Bunch did during the court hearing. It was okay when Dan Hunt, ECSC, and their lawyers did the disparaging and defaming. Was the "Big Dog" saying, do as I say, not as I do?

As I said earlier in this book, my lawsuit was never about two properly contested points in a poorly managed, bordering on unsafe, haphazardly overseen ECSC live-fire shooting competition.

My reputation is far more important than those two points could ever be. I was willing to fight to defend it, spending tens of thousands of dollars in legal fees. It should convey I wouldn't roll over and play dead. It is why I would never have signed a contract in any form or fashion that denied my First Amendment Rights to defend myself with the truth. It was a battle I waged for nearly five years. Talk about David and Goliath. How about an elderly woman fighting a big, multi-state law firm hired by a massive French insurance conglomerate with reported assets of 830-plus billion dollars?

The reasons for my lawsuit were clearly outlined in the body of the *Factual Allegations* in *Plaintiff's Original Petition*, filed on December 10, 2018, with the 443rd Ellis County District Court. Defendants were served with a copy of the filing. Defendants' Dan Hunt and ECSC and their attorneys knew why I filed a lawsuit, and it didn't have anything to do with two points. In fact, two points were never referenced in my petition.

IV. Lawyer and Judge: 6. *I will not knowingly misrepresent, mischaracterize, misquote or miscite facts or authorities to gain an advantage.*

What did Defendants' attorneys do? They misrepresented the facts of my lawsuit to the 443rd Ellis County District Court by trivializing it, claiming it was about two points. Why? To *gain an advantage,* to unduly influence the Court. What was truly disturbing was this wasn't the reason we were in Court. It was a hearing on a breach of contract. Yet, over my attorney's valid objections, this was what the Court heard from the attorney of record for the ECSC, Ronald E. Bunch.

Excerpt: Court Transcript,

MR. BUNCH: I mean we are talking about two targets. They say - - she says she hit them, the official scorekeeper says they missed them - - And not only that, but the official scorekeeper says she missed them. And what's crazy about this is their team won first place, and then she turns around and files a lawsuit on this. The club says, all right, that's not good sportsmanship.

This wasn't the only time Ronald E. Bunch misled the Court with mischaracterizations and false, defamatory statements during the hearing. Was this why Porter and his cronies used club funds to hire Ronald E. Bunch at an added expense?

Ronald E. Bunch wouldn't be the only one to deliberately misrepresent facts to the Court. Attorney Regan G. Pearson, the ECSC and Dan Hunt would go even further.

Dan Hunt's latest version, a reversal from his previously

documented statements, was not supported by any evidence, signed, notarized witness affidavits, or a signed, notarized affidavit from Dan Hunt affirming the truthfulness of his statements.

Likewise, there were no signed, notarized affidavits from the ECSC Board of Directors affirming the accuracy of so-called facts within Defendants' Response.

The only affidavit attached as an exhibit in Defendants' Response was the *Controverting Affidavit of Ron Bunch Regarding Attorney Fees.* By contrast, my Motion, *Plaintiff's Amended Motion for Summary Judgment to Enforce Rule 11 and Settlement Agreement,* contained five affidavits, including mine.

When it came to protesting my attorney fees, what I had paid to force Defendants' to comply with a contract they mediated and willingly signed, Defendants had an affidavit from opposing counsel. When it came to Defendants' false facts and false accusations, there were no signed, notarized affidavits from Defendants attesting to their truthfulness. I believe Defendants' failure to affirm their document with any signed, notarized affidavits was a telling, significant omission.

Dan Hunt hid behind his whining pity email, his family, and his job to air his cowardly, malicious, and false accusations. There were no consequences or accountability for the damage he did. In fact, ECSC leadership condoned Hunt's despicable behavior. This time, within Defendants' Response, Dan Hunt hid again, using my hearing to enforce a contract, *Rule 11 and Settlement Agreement* Dan Hunt signed. Dan Hunt launched another cowardly, defamatory, libelous attack against Shawn. As before, there were no consequences or accountability for the damage Dan Hunt did. This time, the Court condoned Hunt's deceitful misconduct.

In addition to the glaring omission of signed, notarized affidavits or evidence, another notable document was missing in Defendants' Response, Dan Hunt's libelous, whining pity email, *Immediate resignation.* Why was this vindictive leagues manager's *Immediate resignation* not attached as an exhibit with a signed, notarized affidavit affirming its truthfulness? After all, Dan Hunt had sent it to nearly one hundred unsuspecting men, women, and children. Why would the accusations in Hunt's email not be part of Defendants' *Background?* Hunt even ended his malicious email with this statement; *Having said that, any and all false allegations or slanderous events will be met with legal action.*

Dan Hunt never backed up his threat with *legal action* for the alleged grievances within his whining pity email. Dan Hunt never took *legal action* after he was served with a *"Cease and Desist"* notification in which I accused Dan Hunt of malicious defamation in his whining pity email and his bogus charge of cheating he made to the ECSC Board of Directors.

Here was Dan Hunt's chance to include all his alleged grievances from his whining pity email. Dan Hunt didn't even have to spend a dime on *legal action* to bring forth his alleged grievances. The club's 830-plus billion-dollar French insurance conglomerate paid the attorney fees for Hunt's defense.

Within the *Background* of Defendants' Response, Dan Hunt certainly availed himself of the opportunity to attempt to whitewash his actions. Dan Hunt certainly availed himself of the opportunity for another vicious, vindictive attack against Shawn and the competition target rifle Hunt pointed in the direction of competitors on the last night of the Spring trap league. The attack could only be viewed as a new low in Dan Hunt's vindictive behavior. Yet, there was no mention of Hunt's *Immediate resignation* email or any of his so-called grievances.

Why? Was it because Hunt's libelous, whining pity email would define and discredit Dan Hunt as the self-serving, threatening, vindictive individual he is? Had Hunt's vicious false accusations within his whining pity email become a liability?

Or was Dan Hunt attempting to hide his vindictive misconduct and avoid his false accusations coming back to roost? Through his libelous, false accusations and his written words, I found Danny Garth Hunt's email of July 2, 2018, at thirty-four minutes preceding midnight, clearly defined his true character.

A vindictive Duncanville narcotics detective and ECSC leagues manager who cowardly used his family and his employer to justify his attack. The same person who most likely placed his own family *in a position of discomfort* and admitted suffering from mental whatever *after intense and severe exposures at work*. I believe this was why Hunt's whining pity email, *Immediate resignation* was not in his court filings. Like the security camera tapes, Hunt's *Immediate resignation,* his libelous, whining pity email had conveniently disappeared.

Hunt wasn't the only one who didn't have to worry about consequences or accountability for his libelous, false accusations. During the hearing before the 443rd Ellis County District Court, attorney Regan G. Pearson would regurgitate Hunt's false facts and accusations without fear of reprisal. After all, Pearson didn't have to worry about his client being exposed on the witness stand, or my testimony refuting Dan Hunt's false accusations and deceitful misbehavior. Remember, the 443rd Ellis County District Court let attorney Regan G. Pearson get away with it.

Before the 443rd Ellis County District Court, unfair surprise, no problem. Affidavits, no problem. And to paraphrase another famous line from a movie, Defendants didn't "need no stinking" affidavits.

Hunt's Tangled Web

Chapter Fifteen

Even though the Court's ruling would take over two months, it only took reading a few pages of the January 16, 2020, court transcript of the hearing to realize I lost. It seemed to me the Court had little to no knowledge of the filings nor demonstrated any expertise regarding my case's legal issues during the hearing. The judge's résumé didn't reference any legal expertise in civil law, only criminal. Based on what I read in the transcript, the Court relied on opposing counsel to explain what was going on and direct the Court's actions.

The transcript wasn't what I would refer to as a shining example of the stipulation by the Texas Judicial System: *All persons who serve as judges in this State must be knowledgeable in the law and dispense justice in a fair and impartial manner.*

Excerpt: Court Transcript,

THE COURT: So we are here on two things. Motion to Strike Facts not in Evidence and Exhibits Contained in Defendant's Response to Plaintiff's Amended Motion for Summary Judgment to Enforce Rule 11 Settlement Agreement, and also Plaintiff's Amended Motion for Summary Judgment to Enforce Rule 11 Settlement Agreement.

Obviously, the Court knew the purpose of the hearing. It was about the contract, *Rule 11 and Settlement Agreement*, not my lawsuit that had been settled nearly nine months earlier. Yet, the Court would allow Defendants' irrelevant, false facts and accusations regarding the events leading up to my lawsuit into the official court records.

At the start of the hearing, my attorney asked several times for a ruling on *Plaintiff's Motion to Strike Facts Not in Evidence*. The Court wouldn't rule. Instead, the Court allowed Defendants' irrelevant, false facts and accusations of events that occurred before I filed my lawsuit into the record. All without evidence or signed, notarized affidavits from witnesses or Defendants. Did I not say I was concerned about a fair and impartial hearing in Ellis County? Perhaps Porter was correct in what he bragged.

The damaging consequences to Shawn and my reputations from *Defendants' Response to Plaintiff's Amended Motion for Summary Judgment to Enforce Rule 11 Settlement Agreement,* and statements by Defendants' attorneys, started with what the 443rd Ellis County District Court refused to strike. Defendant Dan Hunt's latest version of the scoring dispute was in the *Background Facts Section (page 1 to 5).*

I didn't believe statements from this vindictive Duncanville cop and ECSC leagues manager Dan Hunt could become more contemptible. I was mistaken. What Dan Hunt did within Defendants' Response only emphasized my belief Hunt is a coward and a bully. Dan Hunt used my motion to enforce a contract, *Rule 11 and Settlement Agreement,* to further his revenge on Shawn. I was the one who sued Dan Hunt in the original lawsuit. When Dan Hunt reneged on the contract, *Rule 11 and Settlement Agreement* he mediated and willingly signed, I sued Dan Hunt again for breach of contract. Shawn was never a party to the original lawsuit. Shawn had nothing to do with why Defendants and I were in court. Yet, that didn't stop Dan Hunt's cowardly attack or his false facts and accusations to make Shawn the culprit.

IV. Lawyer and Judge: *6. I will not knowingly misrepresent, mischaracterize, misquote or miscite facts or authorities to gain an advantage.*

Dan Hunt's attorneys allowed damaging, false accusations and defamation into Defendants' filing that were refuted by documents in opposing counsels' possession. Opposing counsels' conduct was what I viewed as egregious violations of *The Texas Lawyer's Creed*. Even worse, attorney Regan G. Pearson would not only continue the unwarranted defamation during the hearing but embellish it, all *to gain an advantage* to unduly influence the Court.

Excerpt: *Defendants' Response to Plaintiff's Amended Motion for Summary Judgment to Enforce Rule 11 and Settlement Agreement,*

On the evening of June 28, 2018, after the competition, Plaintiff approached Hunt and said the scores recorded for two of her rounds were not accurate on the official score sheet. Hunt asked Plaintiff to mark the targets she was protesting on the border of the score card. After serving dinner to the club members, Hunt gathered the completed scorecards and began the process of reviewing scores, determining award winners and preparing awards.

These statements are not what Dan Hunt told the 2018 ECSC Board of Directors, as recorded in the board meeting minutes for July 2, 2018. These statements are not what Vice President DVM Chris Rose told me on the phone. In fact, Rose implied I was lying when I protested I had followed Dan Hunt's instructions. Rose said, "Well, that's you know not how it was reported."

Once again, poor ol' former Cedar Hill mayor, ECSC Vice President DVM Chris Rose went under the bus. This time, "straight-up" Chris Rose had company, the ECSC Board of Directors. But then, this was Dan Hunt, the "guy" Rose, Porter and their cronies supported.

After approximately eighteen months, Dan Hunt finally admitted that he had told me to note the errors on the margin of the scoresheet. While attempting to whitewash his actions, I wonder if Hunt even knew how damning his statement was. I had been thrown out of the trap leagues, and my reputation was destroyed by what Dan Hunt falsely told the Board. Vice President DVM Chris Rose clearly stated in our recorded phone call that I was kicked out of the trap league for; "Uh, changing scoresheets without you know talking to anybody."

Keep in mind Dan Hunt's statements in Defendants' Response.

Plaintiff approached Hunt and said the scores recorded for two of her rounds were not accurate on the official score sheet. Hunt asked Plaintiff to mark the targets she was protesting on the border of the score card. Unbelievably, within this document, Hunt contradicts his own words.

Excerpt: ***Defendants' Response to Plaintiff's Amended Motion for Summary Judgment to Enforce Rule 11 and Settlement Agreement,***

He determined that there was no impact to the outcome of the league, team standings or any individual awards as a result of the two contested targets and elected to give credit to Plaintiff for the targets since there were no consequences other than to Plaintiff's own personal score.

Dan Hunt's admission he changed my scores was another significant statement. Hunt's problem was that he should have read his own emails. Hunt sent out two, one on June 29, 2018, about suspending the league results and having to re-enter all the league scores. Hunt's second email was on July 1, 2018. Hunt wrote, *I recreated the league and reviewed the impact of the two disputed targets by comparing the scores and the standings did not change.*

According to ECSC shoot management, leagues manager Dan Hunt's own words, he didn't determine the impact to the league results until between June 29th and July 1, 2018. It didn't happen on the night of June 28, 2018, as Hunt proclaimed in his latest rendition.

Dan Hunt's statement there were *no consequences* further emphasized his lack of knowledge concerning ATA rules. There is no mention in the ATA rules and procedures about giving credit for errors in scoring a target since there were *no consequences.* I would point out that nothing in Dan Hunt's latest version of events within Defendants' Response was based on any ATA rule for the proper scoring of a match, a competitor's right to file a protest, or the infractions and dangerous misbehavior of the opposing team. As a reminder, ATA rules governed the trap leagues according to the ECSC clandestine July 12, 2018, *Board Meeting-Emergency Meeting* minutes.

Therein was the problem. Dan Hunt, an incompetent, unqualified leagues manager and shoot management for the league competition, didn't know how to properly handle a valid ATA protest, according to the very rules the Board claimed governed their leagues. This is why shoot management must be competent and qualified. There is no good ol' boy system in the ATA rules and procedures. I didn't ask for any favors. As with every shooting discipline I've competed in, I followed the rules. I filed a legitimate protest based on ATA rules and procedures. I expected shoot management Dan Hunt to competently render a knowledgeable decision based on ATA rules. It didn't happen.

Excerpt: *Defendants' Response to Plaintiff's Amended Motion for Summary Judgment to Enforce Rule 11 and Settlement Agreement,*

After the league meeting to issue awards, Hunt was confronted by several ECSC members who reported that Plaintiff's boyfriend, Shawn George (George), appeared to be altering scores on the scorecard. Hunt explained that George was likely merely making notations at his own directions, but the members persisted, claiming that George "browbeat" the scorekeeper into changing scores.

Dan Hunt, a vindictive Duncanville narcotics detective and ECSC leagues manager, was now tangled in his own words. In an official court document, Dan Hunt was asked who *observed* Plaintiff or a member of Plaintiff's team alter the official scores. Hunt answered: *NONE*. In his latest rendition, Dan Hunt's *None* turned into *several ECSC members*. (Previously identified by Dan Hunt and Rusty Porter as Director David McDaniel, Tommy Nations, Director Sherrie Lewis, Larry Degal, Susie Thompson, and Jeff Gregory.)

Within Defendants' Response, Dan Hunt admitted my two contested scores were not changed as recorded by Larry Degal on the scoresheet. Dan Hunt admitted he told me to note my two contested targets in the margin of the scoresheet. Dan Hunt had the scoresheet, where my two targets were noted in the margin as Hunt had instructed. Dan Hunt admitted he changed my scores when he entered them into the computer.

When *confronted by several ECSC members* who falsely accused Shawn of *altering scores on the scorecard*, why didn't Dan Hunt produce the scoresheet? Why didn't Dan Hunt man up and tell them he changed my scores? According to Hunt's latest rendition, all Hunt told them was that *George was likely merely making notations at his own directions.*

So, let's get this straight. First, these *ECSC members* falsely accused Shawn of *altering scores on the scorecard.* Not liking Hunt's answer, these *ECSC members* shifted gears and falsely accused Shawn of browbeating the scorekeeper to change the scores. These scores were my two contested targets that were not altered on the scoresheet.

What's wrong with this picture? I'll tell you. It was all about Dan Hunt making Shawn the culprit. It was all about Dan Hunt's revenge for Shawn attempting to make Hunt behave himself with firearms, then twice making a fool of Hunt in front of the Board. Dan Hunt used my breach of contract lawsuit to get back at Shawn.

Dan Hunt's convoluted explanation of what happened after he handed out the awards on June 28, 2018, was the crux of the scoring dispute. It didn't happen on the trap field. It didn't happen when I walked into the clubhouse to file a legitimate ATA protest over the disruptive, unsportsmanlike violations of ATA rules by the opposing team's co-scorekeepers, resulting in errors to my score and my two contested targets. It didn't happen when Dan Hunt ruled in my favor and elected to give me credit for my two contested targets, changing my scores when he entered them into the software program that generated the league reports. It didn't happen until Dan Hunt handed out the league results at the award ceremony.

It's my belief the consumption of alcoholic beverages played a role in the behavior of the remaining competitors. As I previously identified, alcohol affects judgment and exacerbates disputes. Based on the subsequent events, the dispute was further aggravated by the incompetence of shoot management Dan Hunt, who failed to run the trap leagues according to ATA rules and procedures. The same rules the Board of Directors declared in their legal minutes of the July 12, 2018, clandestine kangaroo court, *Board Meeting-Emergency Meeting,* governed the matches. Rules that, according to Rusty Porter, the league manager was tasked to follow but didn't.

Then there was the false accusation, *but the members persisted, claiming that George "browbeat" the scorekeeper into changing scores.*

Was this another Dan Hunt fabrication as he had done in the July 2, 2018, board meeting? That was when the false accusation of "browbeat" initially surfaced. Hunt falsely tried to prove Shawn "browbeat" the misbehaving scorekeeper by falsely accusing Shawn of browbeating another competitor. Shawn made a fool of Hunt before the Board. Even Hunt's email dated July 1, 2018, in which he reported Larry Degal changed **one score** at the *request* of the shooter, demonstrated Dan Hunt had embellished. *Request* became "browbeat." Hunt's next false embellishment was in the July 2, 2018, board meeting minutes when Dan Hunt accused Shawn of *aggressively going after the scorekeeper.* The more this vindictive Duncanville narcotics detective and ECSC leagues manager Dan Hunt commented about the misbehaving scorekeeper, the more egregious Shawn's false transgression became. *Request* became *browbeat,* and then *aggressively going after the scorekeeper.*

Excerpt: ***Defendants' Response to Plaintiff's Amended Motion for Summary Judgment to Enforce Rule 11 and Settlement Agreement,***

The scorekeeper later confirmed that he changed the score for the two contested targets from lost targets to hit targets because he did not want to get into an argument with George and that he had previously properly called the targets as lost.

What a doozy of a lie. The two contested targets are my scores. Degal never changed my two contested targets. The proof is the scoresheet and Dan Hunt's July 1, 2018, email. Dan Hunt should have read his own email. If that's not enough, how about Dan Hunt's words in the first paragraph of Defendants' Response, proving it's a lie? *On* *the evening of June 28, 2018, after the competition, Plaintiff approached Hunt and said **the scores recorded for two of her rounds were not accurate on the official score sheet.** Hunt asked Plaintiff to **mark the targets she was protesting on the border of the score card.*** Within the same court filing, Dan Hunt falsely claimed just the opposite. Larry Degal changed the scores for my two targets.

To this date, the zeros entered on the scoresheet by Larry Degal for my two contested targets have not been changed. They are still marked zeros. Scores are written in pencil. An erased score is clearly visible.

Excerpt: *Defendants' Response to Plaintiff's Amended Motion for Summary Judgment to Enforce Rule 11 and Settlement Agreement,*

League participants from multiple teams demanded that ECSC investigate. On June 29, 2018, Hunt sent an email to all league participants advising that the Week 8 results were being suspended pending an investigation due to a scoring dispute. Shortly after sending the email, Hunt received a telephone call from Shawn George. George asked about the email, and Hunt explained the allegations and investigation. The conversation shortly thereafter devolved into an argument. A few days later, on July 1, 2018, Hunt sent an email to the league members providing finalized league scores and stating that two contested targets were officially being changed to lost targets because the scorekeeper confirmed that he changed the scores at the request of the shooter to avoid confrontation.

What a compilation of false facts and accusations. Shawn wasn't the one to call Dan Hunt. Trying to be helpful, I called Hunt. Of course, that minor detail didn't fit with Hunt's agenda to lay all the blame on Shawn. There was another doozy of a fabrication. For a second time, Dan Hunt falsely claimed Degal changed my two contested targets on the scoresheet. This time, Hunt attempted to justify his false accusation with a reference to his email. Once again, Dan Hunt, or maybe his attorney, should have read Hunt's July 1, 2018, email. The scoresheet and Hunt's email show Dan Hunt's statements in Defendants' Response are false. It's no surprise Hunt's email and the contested scoresheet were not included as exhibits in Defendants' Response. They would refute Hunt's false statements and accusations.

Let's try to keep up with Dan Hunt's Abbott and Costello routine, *Who's on First*, or, in this case, who changed my scores.

- ✓ Hunt changed my scores. On June 28, 2018, shoot management, leagues manager Dan Hunt ruled in favor of my valid ATA protest. Instead of entering the scores as written on the scoresheet by Larry Degal, Hunt changed my scores, giving me credit for my two contested targets when he entered the league results into the software program, myskeet.com.

- ✓ Hunt changed my scores a second time. Hunt's July 1, 2018, email sent to trap league competitors stated, *The scorekeeper reported that the two targets in question were* **correctly recorded as lost targets**. *The targets remain lost.* In the computer software program, Hunt changed my scores again, removing the credit for my two contested points after he had ruled in my favor. Hunt re-entered the scores as written on the scoresheet by Larry Degal.

- ✓ I changed my scores. Vice President DVM Chris Rose informed me during the July 15th phone call that I was kicked out of the league for "Uh, changing scoresheets without you know talking to anybody." Now, I am the one changing the scoresheet.

- ✓ Shawn changed the scores. Hunt falsely accused Shawn of changing the scores as recorded in the July 2nd board meeting legal minutes; *Shawn claimed that both the scorer and Dan told him to change whatever event scores he wanted to which he did.* Another false accusation as the scores are not changed on the scoresheet.

- ✓ Dan Hunt changed my scores. In Defendants' Response, Hunt admitted he *elected to give credit to Plaintiff for the targets.*

- ✓ Shawn changed my scores. In Defendants' Response, Dan Hunt stated, *ECSC members who reported that Plaintiff's boyfriend,*

Shawn George (George), appeared to be altering scores on the scorecard. A false accusation easily refuted by the scoresheet.

✓ Larry Degal changed my two contested targets. In Defendants' Response, Dan Hunt claimed Larry Degal said he changed my two contested targets. It was another false statement refuted by the scoresheet.

✓ Larry Degal changed my scores. For a second time within Defendants' Response, it's Larry Degal who changed my scores. This time in reference to Dan Hunt's email on July 1, 2018. A false statement easily refuted by the email itself.

The bottom line is that Dan Hunt was the only person who changed my scores. Within Defendants' Response, a legal court document, Hunt repeatedly made false statements and accusations. As a veteran police officer, I had to question whether Danny Garth Hunt, a Duncanville narcotics detective, pulled the same stunts while testifying in criminal cases. What competent prosecutor would want to use this type of individual to make a case? Have people been imprisoned because of Hunt's embellishments and outright false statements?

Why would a so-called competent attorney have allowed these false and contradictory statements from his client into an official court filing? Attorney Regan G. Pearson had the documents that evidenced Hunt's false statements. Pearson had the scoresheet along with Hunt's emails. Yet, opposing counsel ignored the facts while allowing his client to introduce false details and defamatory accusations to unduly influence the Court. Based on what I read in Defendants' Response and the court transcript, Regan G. Pearson and Ronald E. Bunch struck me as the type of lawyers willing to do anything to get a ruling in their favor. The following is what transpired in the court hearing.

My attorney went first. His comments were articulate, an accurate recital of the facts, defining why the parties were in Court, the contract, *Rule 11 and Settlement Agreement* Defendants mediated and willingly signed, then reneged on.

When Regan G. Pearson began to talk, it wasn't about the legal issues my attorney addressed, the mediated contract, the *Rule 11 and Settlement Agreement*, or even the purpose of the hearing. What did Pearson do? I believe attorney Regan G. Pearson defied *The Texas Lawyer's Creed*, an *Order* by the *Supreme Court of Texas*.

IV. Lawyer and Judge: 6. *I will not knowingly misrepresent, mischaracterize, misquote or miscite facts or authorities to gain an advantage.*

Attorney Regan G. Pearson started down the path of *misrepresentations, mischaracterizations, misquotes, and miscites of facts,* all to unduly influence the Court throughout the hearing.

A vindictive Duncanville cop, ECSC leagues manager, the individual admittedly suffering from mental whatever *after intense and severe exposures at work,* along with his counsel, misled the Court into believing I had filed a lawsuit over two points and the so-called culprit was Shawn for his falsely alleged treatment of the intentionally misbehaving scorekeeper. In studying the court transcript, it appeared their goal was to get their false version into the court record and ensure it was what the Court heard. All under the guise of a hearing for a breach of contract.

Attorney Regan G. Pearson launched into the irrelevant *Background* within Defendants' Response that my attorney had petitioned the Court to strike. Irrelevant, unsubstantiated false details that had nothing to do with why we were in court. This was what the Court heard. This was what the 443rd Ellis County District Court allowed.

Excerpt: Court Transcript

MR PEARSON: Your Honor, I would like to start with some background because I think it's particularly important in this case that the parties understand now—or that the Court understand how the parties got to this point.

An argument Regan G. Pearson would use more than once to justify his irrelevant, unsubstantiated false facts and false accusations.

My attorney began to object. Throughout the approximately fifty-seven (57) minute hearing, my attorney objected approximately eighteen (18) times to the irrelevancy, hearsay, and lack of proper substantiation for opposing counsel's statements. My attorney kept trying to bring the hearing back to why we were in court, the contract, the *Rule 11 and Settlement Agreement*. The Court overruled all of my attorney's objections. The Court even ruled before opposing counsel could argue against my attorney's objection. The Court allowed opposing counsel to freely put forth unsubstantiated false facts and accusations. My attorney finally asked for a running objection. That's right, a running objection. How bad is a hearing when an attorney is forced to request a running objection?

What did I quote about the rules of the *Texas Judicial System: Judicial Conduct and Discipline? All persons who serve as judges in this State must be knowledgeable in the law and dispense justice in a fair and impartial manner.*

Next came Regan G. Pearson's regurgitation of the details in Dan Hunt's latest rendition of events in Defendants' Response.

Excerpt: Court transcript,

MR. PEARSON: There was a dispute as to whether or not Plaintiff hit two targets in a shooting competition. Plaintiff says she did; others said she didn't. It was eventually determined by the lead manager that my client, Dan Hunt, that Plaintiff's team would have won first place regardless of the dispute, so she was given credit for these two targets. (In line 3, *lead* was a misprint. It should be *league*.)

I would point out there was no mention of the ATA rules and procedures governing the trap league. ATA rules governed the league according to the ECSC board meeting minutes of July 12, 2018. Rules that according to Rusty Porter, *League managers are tasked with ensuring the club's rules, policies, and bylaws are followed.*

What did opposing counsel's false representation of the scoring dispute have to do with a breach of contract hearing regarding a mediated contract, *Rule 11 and Settlement Agreement?* Absolutely nothing other than opposing counsel wrongly influencing the Court.

IV. Lawyer and Judge: 6. *I will not knowingly misrepresent, mischaracterize, misquote or miscite facts or authorities to gain an advantage.*

Excerpt: Court Transcript,

MR. PEARSON: Hunt was later confronted, however, by several members of the club who said that Plaintiff's boyfriend had coerced the scorekeeper during the competition to change some scores.

COERCED! Dan Hunt wasn't the only individual with an inexcusable propensity for embellishment. Opposing counsel Regan G. Pearson changed *browbeat* to **coerced**—an indefensible and unwarranted act of defamation by an officer of the Court. The definition of coercion is using threats or force. That's what the Court heard. Attorney Regan G. Pearson misled the Court with his damaging, defamatory accusation, this *mischaracterization,* to which he had no evidence, no signed, notarized affidavit from a witness or Defendant Dan Hunt.

It didn't stop Regan G. Pearson or his unjustified attack on the character of an individual who wasn't even a party to the lawsuit or who, to this day, has never been allowed to refute Pearson's malicious accusation. In my opinion, this was an egregious, unethical violation of *The Texas Lawyer's Creed,* an *Order* by the *Supreme Court of Texas.* Yet, the 443rd Ellis County District Court allowed it.

Shawn had done nothing wrong. Shawn simply pointed out an error, one target, in his scores to the intentionally misbehaving, out-of-position scorekeeper, which the scorekeeper voluntarily corrected. Hunt's July 1, 2018, email stated, **at the request.** There was no confrontation. *Request* isn't *browbeat, aggressively go after,* or *coerce.*

Before the 443rd Ellis County District Court, Regan G. Pearson had no qualms about blackening a man's good name and reputation. An innocent man who was never allowed to defend himself. Worse still,

Regan G. Pearson and Defendant Dan Hunt never backed up their defamation or mischaracterization with any evidence or signed, notarized affidavits.

Excerpt: Court transcript,

MR. PEARSON: So Defendant Hunt later met with the scorekeeper, and the scorekeeper confirmed that he had changed scores during the competition to avoid confrontation. So Hunt then sends an e-mail to the entire league members advising that the competition results were going to be investigated due to a scoring dispute. A few days later, Hunt sends another e-mail to the league saying that the two contested targets were being changed to lost targets because the scorekeeper had confirmed that he changed the scores at the request of Plaintiff's boyfriend to avoid confrontation.

This was what the Court heard. Another false statement from Regan G. Pearson that was controverted by the second email Pearson referenced and the scoresheet. Neither of which were attached as exhibits to Defendants' Response. Was Pearson so incompetent that he allowed his client to make not only false, but contradictory statements within Defendants' Response? Was Pearson so incompetent that he disregarded the scoresheet or failed to read Dan Hunt's email? Or was it an intentional attempt to mislead the Court?

Here's another point to consider. Dan Hunt's statements within Defendants' Response and Regan G. Pearson's arguments before the Court clearly indicated that Larry Degal stated, **at the request** of Plaintiff's boyfriend. How did **at the request** become **browbeat,** then **COERCED?** Because Dan Hunt and Regan G. Pearson's false accusations were nothing more than an attempt to whitewash Dan Hunt's actions. They made Shawn the culprit, without proof or allowing the falsely accused an opportunity to defend himself.

Statements such as this by Regan G. Pearson became a pattern throughout the hearing; *misrepresentations, mischaracterizations, misquotes, and miscites of facts, all to gain an advantage.* This was a hearing on a breach of contract. Yet, the 443rd Ellis County District

Court allowed falsely alleged, irrelevant, defamatory allegations into the court record over my attorney's proper objections. None of which was supported by any evidence or signed, notarized affidavits.

It seemed there was no end to the lack of integrity, truthfulness, and professionalism I encountered from not only Defendants but their attorneys. This was how Dan Hunt and the ECSC leadership operated, attacking without allowing the injured party to defend themselves. Defendants' attorneys carried the vicious attack forward into court. It's one thing to challenge the legal issues. The mischaracterization and defamatory remarks opposing counsel made to the 443rd Ellis County District Court were inexcusable and unwarranted.

In my opinion, this was nothing more than another kangaroo court in which the falsely accused was denied an opportunity to defend himself. It was another kangaroo court on a grander stage, a District courtroom in Ellis County, not a small meeting room in the ECSC clubhouse.

Our court system works best when people tell the truth. That's why there are severe penalties for perjury. Attorneys are officers of the Court. They are expected to be truthful. Judges cannot competently conduct court proceedings when misled or have no idea what's happening. In Dallas County, there is a list of police officers, known as the Brady list, who are not allowed to testify. What was so egregious in this hearing was what the Court heard didn't come from a vindictive Duncanville cop, Dan Hunt, but instead from his attorney, an officer of the Court. Perhaps the Texas judicial system needs a similar list for attorneys.

Dan Hunt's latest rendition of events in the *Background* of Defendants' Response was a win-win situation for Dan Hunt. Using the *Background* of an official court document filed before the 443rd Ellis County District Court, Dan Hunt could vilify and defame Shawn without worrying about consequences or reprisals. Dan Hunt was good at hiding behind his whining pity email, his family, his job, and now the elderly woman who filed a second breach of contract against him because he reneged on a contract he mediated and willingly signed. Dan Hunt could claim whatever he wanted since this was a breach of contract hearing, not a trial. And he did.

This vindictive Duncanville cop and ECSC leagues manager wasn't finished making good his threat. "Nobody calls me a liar and gets away with it." While I didn't believe Dan Hunt's behavior could become any more despicable, once again, Hunt proved me wrong. Within Defendants' Response was another false and inexcusable accusation by Duncanville narcotics detective and ECSC leagues manager Dan Hunt, which in my professional opinion, went far beyond the actions of a mentally stable individual who carries a badge and gun.

Excerpt: *Defendants' Response to Plaintiff's Amended Motion for Summary Judgment to Enforce Rule 11 and Settlement Agreement,*

The next day, Hunt responded to a request to appear before the ECSC board to discuss the dispute. Upon entering the meeting, Plaintiff and Shawn George were present with the members of the club's board. At some point during this meeting, Shawn George retrieved an assault rifle he brought to the club previously and set it on the table as some sort of perceived intimidation tactic.

Dan Hunt described an event that never happened. The target rifle, as clearly described in Chapter One (pages 1-2 and pages 11-13) was not an assault rifle. Dan Hunt damn well knew it wasn't an assault rifle, but he had to embellish the event to make it look ominous to unduly influence the Court. Just as Sherrie Lewis lied, so did Dan Hunt. Can you imagine a Duncanville PD narcotics detective, Dan Hunt using this type of tactic to convict people within the Dallas County court system?

The falsely alleged assault rifle Hunt described had already been on the table for approximately an hour when Hunt entered the room. Dan Hunt's malicious accusation was a vicious, inexcusable lie. What I viewed as another damning indictment of Dan Hunt's character. Dan Hunt's defamatory, malicious accusation was a cowardly act that Hunt evidently believed he could get away with. After all, this was a hearing, not a trial, where Hunt would be under oath and cross-examined on a witness stand.

It would get worse. Dan Hunt would further embellish his false accusation in Defendants' irrelevant *Background Facts* in *Appellees' Brief* to the *Court of Appeals, Tenth District of Texas,* when Dan Hunt had his attorney change *perceived* to *apparent.* Dan Hunt's level of despicability had no bounds.

I have already referenced the damage from Director Sherrie Lewis' malicious false accusations regarding assault rifle intimidation, and the truth of what occurred during the July 2, 2018, ECSC board meeting. It bears repeating.

This was the same target rifle that, on June 28, 2018, Dan Hunt shouldered, pointed it in the direction of the staging area behind the trap fields where competitors were gathering, and placed his finger on the trigger. A Class A misdemeanor per the *Texas Penal Code.*

Before the meeting began, Shawn asked the Board for permission to bring the target rifle into the conference room as evidence against Dan Hunt. Upon permission from President Beard and Poobah Porter, with no objections from any board member, Shawn left, then returned with the inert evidence he carefully laid on the Formica table. Again, this all occurred before the start of the meeting. Dan Hunt didn't enter the room for approximately an hour or so after the meeting started. The July 2, 2018, ECSC Board meeting minutes confirm the sequence of events. The security camera tape the ECSC was ordered to preserve would have been visual evidence of what occurred.

Danny Garth Hunt, a Duncanville narcotics detective and ECSC leagues manager made false accusations concerning the target rifle in Defendants' two filings to the 443rd Ellis County District Court and Defendants' filing to the Court of Appeals, Tenth District of Texas. Dan Hunt's false statements concerning the target rifle he mishandled were an intentional attempt to sway the Courts.

After Shawn made a fool of Hunt in the meeting, Dan Hunt didn't have the backbone to confront Shawn face to face. Instead, a vindictive Duncanville cop, Danny Garth Hunt, hid behind his near midnight whining, libelous email, his innocent family, his mental whatever at work, then maliciously lied in a court document. Regan G. Pearson produced no signed, notarized affidavit from his client, Defendant Dan Hunt, attesting to the truthfulness of Hunt's malicious, false accusation.

Even more egregious, ECSC leadership, especially Porter, knew Dan Hunt's accusation within Defendants' filings was false. Once again, Porter and his cronies condoned the malicious lies of their deceitful leagues manager.

As I stated earlier, Dan Hunt's defamatory accusations were nothing but a kangaroo court all over again, only this time in an official filing before the 443rd Ellis County District Court. Dan Hunt's false accusation of assault rifle intimidation was nothing more than a malicious tactic to prejudice the Court in a manner that denied Shawn due process to refute Hunt's false accusation. Of course, Hunt didn't have the backbone to put his name on a signed, notarized affidavit to back up his egregious lie. This was another reason my attorney filed my Motion to Strike, which the Court denied.

Consider these facts about Dan Hunt's words and actions.

✓ According to Dan Hunt's fabrication, he didn't know the difference between an assault rifle and a target rifle. For a police officer with arrest powers for criminal offenses, including those involving weapons this would be inexcusable, a deplorable ignorance. Yet, this was the same narcotics detective who picked up said target rifle, pointing it in the direction where fellow competitors were beginning to gather, a criminal violation. The same narcotics detective suffering from mental whatever *after intense and severe exposures at work.* The same narcotics detective who admitted he needed the gun club's activities to help him cope. The same narcotics detective, a children's shooting coach, and ECSC leagues manager who continuously misbehaved with a loaded shotgun, firing from his hip, acting like a laughing buffoon in front of parents and children. The same Duncanville narcotics detective most likely responsible for placing his family *in a position of discomfort,* Danny Garth Hunt.

✓ There was no mention of intimidation with an assault rifle in Dan Hunt's July 2, 2018, whining pity email, *Immediate resignation.* An email Dan Hunt sent less than three hours following the meeting. Considering the number of false and malicious accusations Hunt used in his whining pity email, if intimidation with an assault rifle had actually happened as Hunt described, surely Danny Garth Hunt would have used it in his near-midnight, libelous, self-serving email.

✓ Even in the doctored minutes of the July 2nd board meeting, minutes clearly written to support Dan Hunt and defame Shawn, there is no mention of intimidation with an assault rifle. What is mentioned? A small plastic container that alarmed Director Sherrie Lewis. Sherrie Lewis, Life Member of the Dallas Safari Club, a DIVA WOW shooting instructor and ECSC instigator, later made up the false accusation about assault rifle intimidation.

✓ Even in the doctored minutes of the clandestine July 12th *Board Meeting-Emergency Meeting,* kangaroo court, minutes clearly written to support Dan Hunt and make Shawn and me the culprit, there is no mention of intimidation with an assault rifle. Why didn't the Secret 7 use the Lewis and Hunt assault rifle intimidation story instead of a poorly skewed ATA rule by their incompetent rules expert, Don Henslee? Hunt would ultimately record his vicious assault rifle intimidation lie within two court filings before the 443rd Ellis County District Court. A vicious lie

Dan Hunt would further embellish in his filing to the Court of Appeals, Tenth District of Texas. If the Lewis/Hunt lie was good enough for the 443rd Ellis County District Court and the Court of Appeals, Tenth District of Texas, why wasn't it good enough for former Cedar Hill mayor, DVM Christopher Lyons Rose and his clandestine kangaroo court?

✓ Vice President DVM Chris Rose never mentioned intimidation with an assault rifle in his July 15, 2018, recorded phone call. Surely, had the Board been intimidated by an assault rifle as falsely alleged by Dan Hunt to the 443rd Ellis County District Court and the Court of Appeals, Tenth District of Texas, such an inexcusable act, perhaps an illegal act, would have been the reason we were suspended. Instead, the 2018 ECSC Board of Directors used Dan Hunt's bogus two-point cheating scandal, then two-stepped to Don R. Henslee's incompetent ATA rules clarification, to hopefully cover their exposed backsides.

✓ If indeed this assault rifle intimidation happened, why were we not then and there kicked out of the club during the July 2, 2018, board meeting? And why did those in the meeting room not immediately exit the room? The inert target rifle certainly didn't intimidate Jay Gage or stop his wildly gesticulating, lengthy verbal attack on me. The inert target rifle didn't stop Dan Hunt from exploding from his chair and lunging toward the table's edge as he threatened Shawn. Most importantly, why did Porter and his cronies not immediately save the security camera tapes to use against us? Why? Because it never happened. It's all a vicious, fabricated story by ECSC instigator Sherrie Lewis. One Dan Hunt would later use in his filings for a malicious attack to intentionally and wrongly influence a District Court and the Court of Appeals.

If this had been a trial, we could have taken the witness stand and, under oath, brought out the truth. It wasn't. It was a hearing about a summary judgment to enforce the *Rule 11 and Settlement Agreement,* Defendants voluntarily signed, then reneged on. In my opinion, a hearing the 443rd Ellis County District Court allowed to become a trial of my lawsuit—a trial with no witnesses, no evidence, and no signed, notarized affidavits from witnesses or Defendants.

Texas Judicial System: Judicial Conduct and Discipline:
All persons who serve as judges in this State must be knowledgeable in the law and dispense justice in a fair and impartial manner.

Even my attorney told the Court; *They are using the Rules of Civil Procedure as this is a final jury trial for evidence. That is not the same— that is not the same rules in regards to a summary judgment. For the summary judgment, only the evidence that have been properly verified through affidavits and everything else submitted to you can be examined by the Court for a determination.* The Court ignored my attorney.

I believe the irrelevant, false facts and false accusations by Dan Hunt and opposing counsel served one purpose; to further defame Shawn and me and wrongly influence the Court. The 443rd Ellis County District Court denied my motion to strike, allowing the irrelevant, false facts, and false accusations to remain in the court records.

What transpired in the hearing was beyond belief. What was truly appalling was the damage to Shawn's good name and reputation by a vindictive Duncanville narcotics detective, ECSC leagues manager Dan Hunt. Shawn was attacked and vilified within Defendants' Response and Pearson's statements. Attorney Regan G. Pearson didn't hesitate to embellish when he proclaimed Shawn *coerced* the scorekeeper.

My attorney objected to the hearsay and lack of proper documentation, but it made no difference. The 443rd Ellis County District Court overruled his every objection. *Misrepresentations, mischaracterizations, misquotes, and miscites of facts* were allowed to continue. This was how the Court conducted the hearing.

Ultimately, Dan Hunt's lies about intimidation with an assault rifle, the vicious defamation of an individual who wasn't even a party to the judicial proceedings, would be allowed to stand in three official court records, two filings before the 443rd Ellis County District Court and one before the Court of Appeals, Tenth District of Texas. Anyone can obtain a copy and read it. If it's in a court document, it must be true. That will be the perception, the reality. Whoever reads the documents won't know Danny Garth Hunt's statements are a lie.

I hold attorneys J. Richard Harmon, Regan G. Pearson, and Ronald E. Bunch accountable for Dan Hunt's malicious, vindictive defamation. These three attorneys are just as guilty as Dan Hunt in perpetuating the vicious defamation of an individual who was not a party to the lawsuit and had done nothing wrong to merit such a false, libelous accusation. All for one purpose, to further destroy Shawn's reputation and credibility, and wrongfully influence the Court. A malicious act the 443rd Ellis County District Court condoned.

Dan Hunt's June 29, 2018, email, June 30, 2018, phone call, July 1, 2018, email, threatening behavior and false accusations during the July 2, 2018, board meeting, distribution of his libelous, false accusations in his July 2, 2018, vicious, whining pity email *Immediate resignation,* false statements as recorded in the July 2, 2018, board meeting minutes, and now Hunt's malicious, false statements in Defendants' Response confirmed my opinion regarding Dan Hunt's character.

On July 2, 2018, Danny Garth Hunt, a Duncanville, Texas, narcotics detective, admitted to nearly one hundred people he suffered from mental whatever *after intense and severe exposures at work.* I observed Hunt suffered from something much worse, especially for an armed police officer. I found Duncanville, Texas, narcotics detective Dan Hunt suffered from a lack of honor, integrity, and a moral center grounded in truthfulness. As a veteran police officer, I believe Dan Hunt, formerly of Waxahachie, Texas, now of Tuscola, Texas, should never be allowed to testify against anyone in a court of law. Instead, Danny Garth Hunt's name, in my opinion, should be on all Brady-type lists.

Seriously? A Mulligan?

Chapter Sixteen

The issues with Dan Hunt's statements in Defendants' Response were not the only problems. Another quote from *The Texas Lawyer's Creed* is one I believe is applicable. *The lawyers who use abusive tactics, instead of being part of the solution, have become part of the problem.*

III. Lawyer to Lawyer: 4. *I will attempt to prepare documents which correctly reflect the agreement of the parties. I will not include provisions which have not been agreed upon or omit provisions which are necessary to reflect the agreement of the parties.*

Defendants' new contract, *Settlement and Release Agreement*, containing new provisions to which I had not agreed, I believe violated this stipulation in *The Texas Lawyer's Creed*. Please note the key phrase; *correctly reflect the agreement of the parties*. The *Creed* clearly states *parties*, not attorneys. This wasn't what Defendants' attorneys told the 443rd Ellis County District Court. Regan G. Pearson and Ronald E. Bunch repeatedly used the rationale that attorneys would routinely alter a *Rule 11 and Settlement Agreement* after it had been signed, adding new terms to the settlement agreement. Such arguments were used to justify their actions regarding Defendants' new contract, *Settlement and Release Agreement*. Opposing counsel even included an exhibit in Defendants' Response with twenty-five (25) attorney-to-attorney emails to support their arguments. In my opinion, Pearson and Bunch's arguments only highlighted their contravention of an *Order* by the *Supreme Court of Texas, The Texas Lawyer's Creed*.

Why would anyone be stupid enough to sign a contract if the attorneys could just willy-nilly change the terms after signing? Especially after several intolerable hours in mediation and spending over $3200 to hammer out a mediated settlement and signed contract. Yet, it was precisely what Defendants' attorneys would argue. According to Regan G. Pearson and Ronald E. Bunch, it's what lawyers routinely do—after the fact.

During the hearing before the 443rd Ellis County District Court, opposing counsel repeatedly used *reasonable, more than reasonable, cooperative,* and *finalize* to describe their and Defendants' actions after they mediated and willingly signed the contract, *Rule 11 and Settlement Agreement.* The problem, as I viewed it, was Defendants were not *finalizing a settlement.* They were reneging on a signed contract and replacing it with a new contract with new provisions that were never discussed during mediation. I certainly would not have signed the *Rule 11 and Settlement Agreement* had it contained such provisions.

By contrast, within Defendants' Response and opposing counsels' statements before the 443rd Ellis County District Court, I was falsely accused of causing delays, changing the settlement amount, and being unreasonable and uncooperative. They tried to label me as a difficult client. It was how Defendants' attorneys disparaged and defamed me in Defendants' Response and within their statements before the 443rd Ellis County District Court. It is beyond my comprehension how anyone could be viewed as unreasonable, uncooperative, or difficult for agreeing to abide by a signed contract.

They even used my delay in responding to their new contract, *Settlement and Release Agreement,* against me. How could I object to something I hadn't seen? Once I received and read what Defendants were attempting to do, it took me twenty-four minutes to notify my attorney of my objections. Their arguments about when I made my objections were a moot point. Whether I objected on April 23, 2019, or May 15, 2019, didn't make any difference.

For approximately four months, Defendants refused to remove their new provisions that I did not agree to during mediation. They held my settlement check hostage, trying to force me to sign their new contract. I believe what Defendants wanted was a mulligan. A sporting term meaning a do-over, a second try after your first has gone awry. In other words, we screwed up, and we demand you be dumb enough to let us fix it in our favor. Dan Hunt and the ECSC leadership had stuck it to me in their clandestine kangaroo court, then their ambush, and now they wanted to stick it to me again.

Within Defendants' Response and in the court hearing, opposing counsel argued the evidence showed they had complied with the settlement terms and had been more than reasonable in attempting to finalize the settlement.

The evidence opposing counsel used to hang their hat on were those twenty-five attorney-to-attorney emails they included as an exhibit. Yep, that was the total of their evidence. Regan G. Pearson and Ronald E. Bunch should have read their attached emails. More than one of the emails refuted statements within Defendants' Response and by opposing counsel before the Court during the hearing.

Since Defendants reneged on the contract, refused to remove their new provisions, and refused to send the settlement check, I had no choice but to go back into mediation. The contract, *Rule 11 and Settlement Agreement* contained a dispute clause. If any issues arose over the signed contract, *Rule 11 and Settlement Agreement*, all parties were required to participate in a second round of mediation.

The first mediation cost me over $3200. Defendants' refusal to abide by the contract they signed would now cost me several thousand more dollars for a second round of mediation. I had to pay for a conference phone call, then a second mediation session if the conference call didn't work. How much more cooperative could I get? How much more reasonable could I have been? Unlike Defendants, an 830-plus billion-dollar French insurance conglomerate did not pay my attorney and mediation fees. It was my money, out of my pocket.

Another point. I'm not the one who refused to abide by the dispute provision. It was the self-claimed *reasonable and cooperative* Defendants and their attorneys. My attorney tried to set up a telephone conference with the mediator. In a June 5, 2019, email, one of the twenty-five emails in Defendants' exhibit attached to Defendants' Response, the "Big Dog," J. Richard Harmon, flat out ordered my attorney, *Do not contact Judge Fifer, and I can guarantee you that there will not be another mediation.* The "Big Dog's" threat clearly violated the dispute clause within the contract, *Rule 11 and Settlement Agreement* his clients willingly signed. Yet, to the Court, they accused me of being uncooperative and unreasonable.

Regan G. Pearson, in an August 15, 2019, email to my first attorney, also included in Defendants' exhibit, had the unmitigated gall to label his actions as *nice*. Pearson wrote; *I've tried to be nice throughout this litigation.* Nice wasn't what I would term the threats and bullying from his co-counsel, the "Big Dog," J. Richard Harmon, to force me to sign their new contract, *Settlement and Release Agreement.* Nice wasn't what I would term attempting to force me to sign by holding my settlement check hostage. *Nice* wasn't what I would term Pearson's threats to file a lawsuit to have the *Rule 11 and Settlement Agreement* nullified if I didn't agree to sign their new contract. *Nice* wasn't what I would term opposing counsel extending the litigation, causing me unwarranted and unnecessary financial hardship. Yet, this was what Regan G. Pearson claimed was *nice*. I still have to wonder if this was nothing but Rambo-style tactics. Was this the behavior the *Supreme Court of Texas* intended to eliminate?

Neither I nor my attorney threatened anyone. I didn't change the settlement amount to $15,048, as opposing counsel, the "Big Dog," J. Richard Harmon and Regan G. Pearson, falsely claimed. My attorney's June 5, 2019, email to the "Big Dog" was the proof. This email was included in the twenty-five emails in Defendants' Response.

If Defendants' new provisions were so crucial, why weren't they brought up during mediation? Were their omissions deliberate? In mediation, Defendants didn't have a threat they could use. If I disagreed, I could have walked out. Instead, they waited. Once the contract was signed, I believe they had what they thought was leverage, the settlement check. Just refuse to send the check until I signed their new contract. If that didn't work, throw in a threat of a lawsuit or a threat to get the Court to throw out the existing contract, *Rule 11 and Settlement Agreement*. And, by the way, add Defendants' attorney fees to their threat. But then, according to Pearson, he was just being *nice*.

II. Lawyer to Client: *7. I will advise my client that we will not pursue conduct which is intended primarily to harass or drain the financial resources of the opposing party.*

What Defendants' intentional, unwarranted manipulation accomplished was to extend the litigation through two court hearings before the 443rd Ellis County District Court and the Court of Appeals, Tenth District of Texas. Defendants and their *nice* attorneys created a financial hardship for me, to the tune of tens of thousands of dollars. The financial hardship wasn't an issue for Defendants. The cost of the extended litigation wasn't coming from their pockets but from the deep pockets of their 830-plus billion-dollar French insurance conglomerate. Attorneys must love those oh-so-deep French pockets.

Excerpt: *Defendants' Response to Plaintiff's Amended Motion for Summary Judgment to Enforce Rule 11 Settlement Agreement,*

Following the exchange of initial written discovery, the parties mediated this case with the Honorable King Fifer on April 17, 2019. Even though Defendants believe the claims asserted against them were frivolous, Defendants agreed to settle all claims in exchange for the payment of $15,000.00 to Plaintiff and her boyfriend, Shawn George, in the spirit of compromise and to reach an early resolution of this case.

Shawn wasn't a party to the lawsuit. He had no claims to settle. He couldn't agree to such a condition. I'm the one that sued Dan Hunt and the ECSC, not Shawn.

Defendants' pats on their backs seemed never-ending, *frivolous, spirit of compromise, early resolution.* What a farce. Where was Defendants' *spirit of compromise* and *early resolution* when Defendants ignored my repeated attempts to amicably resolve the issues before they forced me to file a lawsuit? Where was Defendants' *spirit of compromise* and *early resolution* when Porter and his cronies refused to cancel their ambush, otherwise known as the membership appeal meeting in order to further humiliate me? Their *spirit of compromise* and *early resolution* was nothing but another; let's stick it to her while we make ourselves feel good about doing it. Much like Rose's so-called courtesy call.

When I have a backstabbing, vindictive Duncanville cop, ECSC leagues manager Dan Hunt, falsely accuse me of abusing him and his family in his late-night whining pity email, *Immediate resignation* to nearly one hundred fellow club members, guests, and children, then some ten days later, falsely claim I cheated, I take it seriously, very seriously. There was nothing *frivolous* about Dan Hunt's false accusations and vindictiveness. There was nothing *frivolous* about Dan Hunt's defamatory, whining pity email, *Immediate resignation.* There was nothing *frivolous* about leagues manager Dan Hunt's false accusations to the ECSC Board of Directors.

There was nothing *frivolous* about Director Sherrie Lewis falsely accusing Shawn of assault rifle intimidation.

There was nothing *frivolous* about the Board of Directors holding a clandestine kangaroo court, denying a paid member the right to defend herself. There was nothing *frivolous* about the wrongful suspension of my paid membership rights. There was nothing *frivolous* about my getting kicked out of the trap leagues, the humiliation, or the damage to my reputation because of a bogus charge of cheating. There was nothing *frivolous* about destroying the reputations of two innocent individuals who did nothing wrong nor caused harm to any individual at the ECSC. There was nothing *frivolous* about the Secret 7.

There was nothing *frivolous* about the tens of thousands of dollars it cost me to obtain proof of the destructive behavior of leagues manager Dan Hunt and the unprincipled conduct of the ECSC Board of Directors.

There was nothing *frivolous* about Dan Hunt's false statements and accusations in Defendants' Response. There was nothing *frivolous* about Dan Hunt falsely accusing Shawn of assault rifle intimidation in Defendants filings before the 443rd Ellis County District Court and ultimately to the Court of Appeals, Tenth District of Texas.

There was nothing *frivolous* about nearly five years of unwarranted stress, all caused by a vindictive Duncanville narcotics detective and ECSC leagues manager, Dan Hunt, and ECSC leadership's malicious, false accusations and unprincipled conduct.

Defendants now claimed my lawsuit was *frivolous.* Are you kidding me? Seriously? I wonder if attorneys Regan G. Pearson and Ronald E. Bunch, officers of the Court, consider their false statements and accusations to the 443rd Ellis County District Court *frivolous.*

Don't forget, this unnecessary, extended litigation was more billable hours for Pearson's law firm. I wonder if the 830-plus billion-dollar French insurance conglomerate considered it *frivolous.* Attorneys have to love those oh-so-deep French *frivolous* pockets.

Excerpt: Court Transcript,

MR. PEARSON: The parties agreed to mediate this case relatively early on in the litigation which resulted in what was thought to be a $15,000 settlement. The parties signed a Rule 11 settlement agreement while at the mediator's office. A few days after mediation, my office provided Plaintiff's prior counsel with a proposed settlement and release agreement. And that's attached to our response as Exhibit B.

THE COURT: Hang on just a second.

MR. PEARSON: Yes, Your Honor.

THE COURT: *When did you file the response? That's what I am looking for.*

MR. PEARSON: *Your Honor, it was filed on January 9th. And, I have a copy as well.*

THE COURT: *Yeah, I'm going to have to look at your copy. I do not have one.*

MR. PEARSON: *Yes, Your Honor.*

THE COURT: *Sorry. I was looking and looking and looking, I was like - -*

MR. PEARSON: *May I approach?*

THE COURT: *Yes, sir.*

MY ATTORNEY: *I have - - I have a response if the Judge wants one instead of your whole thing, so you can have your folder back.*

MR. PEARSON: *It's fine.*

MY ATTORNEY: *Okay.*

THE COURT: *Okay. So Defendant's response. Thank you. All right. I'm sorry, go ahead.*

This was unbelievable. The Court did not have a sixty-one-page document, *Defendants' Response to Plaintiff's Amended Motion for Summary Judgment to Enforce Rule 11 Settlement Agreement.* What's worse is the Court didn't even know it was missing for approximately fifteen minutes into the hearing, twelve pages of transcript. How could the Court not know, especially after the Court's statement at the start of the hearing?

Excerpt: Court Transcript,

THE COURT: *So we are here on two things. Motion to Strike Facts not in Evidence and Exhibits Contained in Defendant's Response to Plaintiff's Amended Motion for Summary Judgment to Enforce Rule 11 Settlement Agreement, and also Plaintiff's Amended Motion for Summary Judgment to Enforce Rule 11 Settlement Agreement.*

How could the Court not know when the Court and my attorney discussed Defendants' Response? This was the same document my attorney rebuked opposing counsel for its late filing and asked the Court to strike. The first four pages of the court transcript are about my motion to strike and Defendants' Response. Please note that my attorney and the Court specifically referenced Defendants' answer, *Defendant's Response to Plaintiff's Amended Motion for Summary Judgment to Enforce Rule 11 Settlement Agreement.*

Excerpt: Court Transcript,

MY ATTORNEY: Your Honor, in regards to the motion to strike, Exhibits B, C, D, E, and F, and all references to anything from Pages 1 through 5 that are purely speculative, hearsay, they are not relevant, but most importantly, they are not properly authenticated. There is no affidavit authenticating any of these exhibits. One affidavit is attached to which I did not apply to this which was their contention on reasonableness of attorney's fees and segregation.

So I asked at this juncture in regards to analyzing evidence in front of you to make a judgment for the summary judgment, that you strike all improperly authenticated evidence attached to Defendant's answer to Plaintiff's amended summary judgment petition.

THE COURT: And you say that was Exhibit A, B, through F?

MY ATTORNEY: Exhibit B, C, D, E, and F, I believe, Your Honor.

THE COURT: E and F, okay. Of Defendant's answer, right?

MY ATTORNEY: Yes, Your Honor.

THE COURT: All righty.

MY ATTORNEY: No affidavit has been submitted to verify any of these exhibits.

THE COURT: All righty.

MY ATTORNEY: And I believe for the bylaws of the DeSoto Gun Club. It is my understanding that those have not been produced in the prior discovery, thus exclusionary rule may apply to that.

THE COURT: And you said the bylaws?

MY ATTORNEY: Yes, of the DeSoto Gun club.

THE COURT: Okay. Okay. Anything - - is that it?

How could the Court analyze *evidence in front of you* when she didn't even have it? The Court even reaffirmed the document in which they were to be found. *THE COURT: E and F, okay. Of Defendant's answer, right?*

In four pages of the transcript, not once did the Court say, *hang on a second,* and advise my attorney that she didn't have Defendants' Response.

It wasn't until page fifteen of the transcript, when opposing counsel referenced an exhibit in Defendants' Response, that the Court said; *hang on just a second.* It's no wonder the Court wouldn't rule, despite my attorney's multiple requests for a ruling on my Motion to Strike sections within Defendants' Response. It's hard to rule on something you don't have. Even worse, the Court obviously didn't believe a missing sixty-one-page document was important until opposing counsel referred to it.

After studying the transcript, I believe this exchange only emphasized the Court's lack of knowledge or familiarity with the case and documents when she took the bench. The Court's unfamiliarity with the applicable documents or a civil hearing to enforce a *Rule 11 and Settlement Agreement* was a pattern throughout the hearing. What more can you say about the lack of fairness and impartiality by the Court?

Texas Judicial System: Judicial Conduct and Discipline: *All persons who serve as judges in this State must be knowledgeable in the law and dispense justice in a fair and impartial manner.*

Excerpt: Court Transcript,

MR. PEARSON: So about a month later, after making her revision to the agreement, Plaintiff's prior counsel e-mails us and says that her client is not going to agree to signing the agreement because, one, the agreement contained a nondisparagement provision; two, Plaintiff's boyfriend was included in the release; and three, the settlement amount included the $48 balance of her shooting card. And, importantly, Your Honor, the Plaintiff's motion fails to inform the Court that Plaintiff requested that the $48 balance of her shooting card be added to the settlement agreement, effectively making the settlement agreement, 15,048 bucks.

What the Court heard multiple times from opposing counsel were false facts regarding the $48 the club intentionally stole from me. As stipulated by the contract, *Rule 11 and Settlement Agreement*, the settlement amount did not include my stolen $48. I never attempted to add my stolen $48 to the settlement amount.

In reading the transcript, it appeared that Pearson was unfamiliar with the contents of Defendants' Response. The proof was my attorney's June 5, 2019, email, included in the twenty-five (25) emails in Defendants' Response.

Excerpt from my attorney's email dated June 5, 2019,

My client is not in breach of anything at this point. She is agreeing to be bound by the terms of the mediated Rule 11 agreement. With respect to the three issues raised in your email: First, with respect to the $48 on the card. I would first note that the Rule 11 makes no mention of the money left on her card so I'm not sure why it is part of the agreement. This being said, the settlement agreement drafted by your office requires her to release the $48 on her card. That is $48 of her money that she paid to the club as part of a credit account to purchase items at the club, and so any remaining funds belong to her. You are correct that the amount of the settlement was $15,000, not $15,048, but by requiring her to give up funds to the club rightfully belonging to her, she is in actuality getting paid $14,952.

My attorney clearly wrote; *She is agreeing to be bound by the terms of the mediated Rule 11 agreement.* I don't know how my intentions could be any clearer. The terms of the *mediated Rule 11 agreement* did not include my stolen $48 within the $15,000 settlement amount. This should have been Pearson's first clue as to why my motion didn't mention my intentionally stolen $48.

I never changed the settlement amount. My attorney didn't attempt to change the settlement amount. Instead, my attorney agreed that the "Big Dog" was correct. *You are correct that the amount of the settlement was $15,000, not $15,048.* Pearson misrepresented the facts, wanting the

Court to believe I changed the settlement amount. His statement was controverted by emails included in Defendants' Response.

IV. Lawyer and Judge: *6. I will not knowingly misrepresent, mischaracterize, misquote or miscite facts or authorities to gain an advantage.*

Excerpt: Court Transcript,

MR. PEARSON: Your Honor, my office responded and agreed to remove Plaintiff's boyfriend from the release but insisted on the antidisparagement language and that the $15,000 settlement amount including -- included the card balance. Plaintiff's prior counsel responded that she would meet with Plaintiff and discuss. She later responded and confirmed that Plaintiff would not agree to sign the settlement agreement if it contained antidisparagement language. And after conferring with our clients, my office responded to Plaintiff's prior counsel and advised that we would agree to remove the antidisparagement language from the agreement and a revised settlement agreement was send – to that effect was send, and that is attached as Exhibit E. (The word, *send*, was typed in the court transcript.)

Even though Pearson claimed Shawn was removed, he wasn't. Just like the contract, the *Rule 11 and Settlement Agreement*, they again reneged. *Exhibit E*, referenced by Regan G. Pearson, version #3 of Defendants' new contract, *Settlement and Release Agreement*, still included Shawn as a party to the lawsuit and required him to sign. Once again, Pearson misled the Court.

What Regan G. Pearson didn't tell the Court was Defendants didn't remove their non-disparagement language until after I filed *Plaintiff's Motion for Summary Judgment*. It took filing a second breach of contract lawsuit, then filing *Plaintiff's Motion for Summary Judgment* to force Defendants compliance.

On the same day my motion was filed, opposing counsel informed my attorney that Defendants had abandoned their position on the non-disparagement provision and would abide by the terms of the original mediated settlement. A new agreement, version #3, would be forthcoming. It should be noted, Regan G. Pearson continued to hold my settlement check hostage until I signed their new document.

Excerpt: Court Transcript,

MR. PEARSON: And then - - so Plaintiff filed a motion to substitute, and we spoke with (Plaintiff's attorney) regarding Plaintiff's now new raised issue of all these attorney's fees and whether we'd agree to pay for any attorney fees. And after speaking with our clients, we informed new counsel that - - that Defendants had no intention of paying any additional money for attorney's fees incurred during negotiations because the Defendants felt that they had been more than reasonable in trying to finalize the settlement.

Once the contract, *Rule 11 and Settlement Agreement* was signed, that was the end of negotiations. In fact, the *Rule 11 and Settlement Agreement* did not stipulate that I was required to sign another agreement. Still, Pearson attempted to justify his conduct in adding new provisions by stating all they tried to do was finalize the settlement. Not true. It was about a new contract. Defendants wanted their mulligan.

My *Motion for Summary Judgment,* filed in August 2019, included the attorney fees I incurred trying to force Defendants to comply with the *Rule 11 and Settlement Agreement,* they mediated and willingly signed. Just because Defendants capitulated in the removal of their unwarranted demands, it didn't negate the issue of my attorney fees.

After filing my motion, my first attorney contacted opposing counsel, requesting payment of my additional attorney fees. Opposing counsel refused. By the time my new attorney was on board, opposing counsel had already received two notifications regarding my attorney fees. It wasn't a new issue, as Pearson claimed.

It wasn't Pearson's clients, Dan Hunt and ECSC, who refused to pay my attorney fees, as Pearson told the Court. It was Regan G.

Pearson's other client, the insurance adjustor for the 830-plus billion-dollar French insurance conglomerate. Regan G. Pearson misled the Court. The proof was an email from Regan G. Pearson within the twenty-five emails attached to Defendants' Response. Please note, Regan G. Pearson refers to the adjustor, as *my adjustor.*

Excerpt, Regan G. Pearson's September 19, 2019, email,

As we discussed, I spoke with my adjuster regarding your client's claims for attorney's fees and whether she would be willing to offer anything on the fees. She advised that she is not inclined to pay on the attorney's fees.

Excerpt: Court Transcript,

MR. PEARSON: This case essentially involves a settlement which took longer than anticipated to be finalized due to objections by Plaintiff to traditional non disparagement language located in nearly all defamation settlements.

The settlement was finalized when Defendants signed the contract *Rule 11 and Settlement Agreement* on April 17, 2019. However, according to Regan G. Pearson, adding a new provision, *traditional non disparagement language,* was acceptable behavior after it was signed.

It should be noted there was one keyword; *nearly.* Regan G. Pearson admits that not all defamation settlements include *traditional non disparagement language.* If *traditional non disparagement language* was so essential, I still have to ask the same question my first attorney raised. Why wasn't it brought up during mediation?

Opposing counsel assumed I would know their non-disparagement provision would be added after the fact. I signed a contract. I didn't assume anything. If it wasn't in the signed contract, it wasn't applicable. Pearson also assumed I would agree to it. Just like he assumed, I would agree with ECSC's insistence on including my $48, money that didn't belong to the club, in the $15,000 settlement amount. It was an underhanded tactic to avoid honoring a vote of the Board to refund my money, my stolen $48.

There is an old saying about assume; ass-u-me. I'd like to know where attorneys are taught that once a contract is signed, it can be changed because of assumptions.

Excerpt: Court Transcript,

MR. PEARSON: *Defendants would show that any delay was due to Plaintiff or Plaintiff's prior counsel's own actions. For example, Plaintiff's objections to the agreement's language was not made known until one month after Plaintiff's prior counsel made what was thought to be all of her revisions to the agreement.*

It didn't matter whether I objected on April 23, 2019, when my attorney received the original version or a month later. For approximately four months, Defendants refused to remove their new provisions.

IV. Lawyer and Judge: 6. *I will not knowingly misrepresent, mischaracterize, misquote or miscite facts or authorities to gain an advantage.*

When it came to ECSC's legal liability for attorney fees, I believe Regan G. Pearson's violation of *The Texas Lawyer's Creed* was even more egregious.

Excerpt: *Defendants' Response to Plaintiff's Amended Motion for Summary Judgment to Enforce Rule 11 Settlement Agreement,*

In short, the reason that this case has not been resolved is Plaintiff's claim for attorney's fees. Plaintiff now claims over $13,000.00 in attorney fees incurred since May 3, 2019 under Chapter 38 of the Texas Civil Practice and Remedies Code. Chapter 38 allows attorney's fees to be recovered only from an "individual" or "corporation." Plaintiff cannot recover attorney's fees from ECSC under Chapter 38 because the club is organized as a non-profit organization and is not a corporation. See Club Bylaws attached as Exhibit F. I would point out the key phrase in the excerpt is; ***not a corporation.***

Excerpt: Court Transcript,

MR. PEARSON: *We – attorney fees are not recoverable against the Gun Club, Your Honor, because the Gun Club is organized a nonprofit organization and Chapter 38 only allows attorney's fees to be recovered from individuals or corporations on a breach of contract.*

The false and misleading information Regan G. Pearson fed to the Court seemed unending. There were several problems with what Regan G. Pearson, as an officer of the Court, told the Court. As an individual, Defendant Dan Hunt was equally liable for attorney fees. Regan G. Pearson conveniently ignored this fact in his statements to the Court. In my opinion, Regan G. Pearson's omission was a deliberate attempt to mislead the Court.

Defendants' assertion in Defendants' Response that the ECSC was **not a corporation,** and Regan G. Pearson's statements to the Court were what I would refer to as a bald-faced lie. I believe it was an intentional act by an officer of the Court. Regan G. Pearson tried to negate the club's liability for attorney fees.

Regan G. Pearson was trying to stop my recovery of tens of thousands of dollars in legal fees to which I was entitled, according to *Chapter 38 of the Texas Civil Practice and Remedies Code,* and the contract, *Rule 11 and Settlement Agreement* mediated and willingly signed by his clients.

Where did learned lawyer Regan G. Pearson get the term organization? It came from THE CONSTITUTION AND BY-LAWS OF THE DESOTO GUN CLUB, amended on February 23, 1989.

Excerpt: The Constitution and By-laws of the Desoto Gun Club, *Article II-Character:*

A. The club shall be a corporate body under the laws of the state of Texas. It shall have no capital stock, and shall be a non-profit organization, organized and operated exclusively for the pleasure recreation and other non-profit purposes, no part of which will ensure to the benefit of any member thereof.

Once again, an exhibit from Defendants' Response controverted statements to the Court by Regan G. Pearson. The words *non-profit organization* are obtained from a sentence that is preceded by one that clearly states *the club shall be a corporate body under the laws of the state of Texas*. It's in their Bylaws.

The *Articles of Incorporation of DeSoto Gun Club* were filed with the Texas Secretary of State on June 24, 1966. If I could obtain a copy, so could the attorneys for the ECSC. Treasurer Rusty Porter, registered agent of record, signed the *Periodic Report of a Nonprofit Corporation* required by the Secretary of State.

I also discovered the gun club is identified as Desoto Gun Club, Inc. on the Ellis County Appraisal District (Ellis CAD) tax rolls. The *Property Summary Report* identifies the property as a *golf course*. I'm surprised Pearson didn't make an argument the ECSC was a golf course, not a live-fire shooting facility, even though most everyone in a golf cart on the property is armed.

Before filing a lawsuit, my attorney ascertained the legal status of the ECSC. It's in my original petition. In response to my attorney's objection regarding the Bylaws, this is what Regan G. Pearson told the Court.

Excerpt: Court Transcript,

MR. PEARSON: We think that's clearly proper to be used here at the summary judgment hearing to show that the Gun Club is organized as a nonprofit organization. As usual, Regan G. Pearson had no affidavit from his client, ECSC, to support his arguments.

Here's the kicker. In *Defendant Desoto Gun Club d/b/a Ellis County Sportsmans Club's Responses to Plaintiff's Request for Disclosure*, dated February 1, 2019, the ECSC was required to provide; *The correct name of the parties to the lawsuit.* ECSC Treasurer Rusty Porter responded; *Desoto Gun Club, Inc. is the Defendant's complete corporation name.* The "Big Dog," J. Richard Harmon, received a copy of *Defendant Desoto Gun Club d/b/a Ellis County Sportsmans Club's Responses to Plaintiff's Request for Disclosure.*

This legal document, identifying the correct legal status of Defendant Desoto Gun Club d/b/a Ellis County Sportsmans Club as a corporation was signed and submitted by none other than Ronald E. Bunch, attorney of record for Defendant Desoto Gun Club d/b/a Ellis County Sportsmans Club. Obviously, co-counsel Ronald E. Bunch knew the ECSC was a corporation.

Yet, as attorney of record for ECSC, Ronald E. Bunch went right along with his co-counsel, Regan G. Pearson, and the "Big Dog," J. Richard Harmon's false representation of ECSC's legal status. Ronald E. Bunch signed Defendants' Response.

Furthermore, Waxahachie attorney Ronald E. Bunch, as an officer of the Court, sat or stood in a courtroom, listening to his co-counsel, Regan G. Pearson, falsely assert to the Court that the gun club wasn't a corporation. Ronald E. Bunch remained silent.

How could anyone rationalize or excuse such misrepresentation by Regan G. Pearson, J. Richard Harmon, and Ronald E. Bunch? Once again, these learned lawyers, as officers of the Court, misled the 443rd Ellis County District Court with a false fact that had far-reaching legal consequences regarding the disposition of my case.

On 12/28/2020, my attorney filed *Plaintiff Anita Dickason's Supplement to Motion for New Trial* with the 443rd Ellis County District Court. Attached to my motion was a *Certificate of Fact* from the Office of the Texas Secretary of State, certifying the Desoto Gun Club was a domestic non-profit corporation. This was a document any attorney competently representing his client should, could, and would easily obtain.

Unbelievably, Defendant ECSC and their attorneys would continue this misrepresentation in another court filing to the 443rd Ellis County District Court, in their *Appellees' Brief* before the Court of Appeals, Tenth District of Texas, and in a filing before the 40th Ellis County District Court.

E as in Egg

Chapter Seventeen

Regan G. Pearson's misrepresentation to the Court didn't stop with his client's legal status.

Excerpt: Court Transcript,

MR. PEARSON: In addition, Plaintiff's prior counsel should have contacted defense counsel before drafting an unnecessary motion for summary judgment and incurring nearly $6,000 in attorney fees.

Regan G. Pearson's statement to the Court was refuted by another email in the twenty-five emails in Defendants' Response. On July 12, 2019, my first attorney emailed Regan G. Pearson, notifying him of my intention to file a motion for summary judgment.

Excerpt: July 12, 2019, email from my first attorney,

The Rule 11 agreement requires that any issues arising out of the terms of the agreement would be taken up first in a phone conference with the mediator then with an additional mediation if the phone conference is unsuccessful. It was my understanding from previous emails that your side is not willing to do this. Please confirm this. We will be filing a motion to enforce the Rule 11 agreement and I am sure one of the first questions the judge will ask at our hearing is whether we complied with that requirement.

On August 14, 2019, over a month later, my attorney filed my *Motion for Summary Judgment* to force Defendants to comply with the terms of the *Rule 11 and Settlement Agreement* they mediated and willingly signed. Still no settlement check.

During the hearing, my attorney informed the Court that Defendants had failed to send the check stipulated by the contract, *Rule 11 and Settlement Agreement*. This was Regan G. Pearson's response.

Excerpt: Court Transcript,

MR. PEARSON: *Plaintiff's counsel has kind of made repeated indications that we breached the settlement agreement point blank because we didn't have a check to them May 2nd. Your Honor, we didn't even have a - - have known about Plaintiff's objections to the language in the settlement agreement until May 24th, so clearly we didn't have a signed settlement release. Typically in civil litigation, we'll have a check, and we will send it to Plaintiff's counsel as soon as we have a signed settlement release; otherwise, we are not properly protecting our client.*

After studying transcripts for two hearings, I noted a generalization throughout Pearson's arguments, using terms such as *typically, nearly every*, or *every*. Where were the details of the cases that allowed Pearson to make such statements? Each case must be judged on its own merits. It appeared to me Pearson acted on assumptions, perhaps what he had gotten away with in the past, rather than acting on the facts.

In my case, the contract, *Rule 11 and Settlement Agreement* his clients mediated and willingly signed, expressly stipulated I was to receive the settlement check on or before May 2, 2019. I didn't. I also wasn't required to sign another document.

When I finally got out of Ellis County, the Court of Appeals, Tenth District of Texas, agreed with my attorney. The Court of Appeals stated, *However, what is not in dispute is that Hunt and ECSC did not make the $15,000 payment by the May 2, 2019 deadline.* According to the Court of Appeals, this constituted the first breach of the contract.

Here was another fact. Pearson stated; *As soon as we have a signed settlement release.* Pearson already had a *signed settlement release*. It was the contract, *Rule 11 and Settlement Agreement*. Defendants would admit this fact in a subsequent filing with the 443rd Ellis County

District Court. I've often wondered how Regan G. Pearson expected his contradictory arguments, *misrepresentations*, and *miscites of facts* to the Court to be construed as *properly protecting our client.*

The following is what I asked the Court to do. It's straightforward, not complicated. Simply enforce the agreement Defendants signed.

Excerpt: ***Plaintiff's Amended Motion for Summary Judgment,***

VII. Request for Relief: WHEREFORE, Plaintiff requests that, for the reasons above and foregoing, her Motion for Summary Judgment be granted in all respects, that Defendants be compelled to comply with the terms of the Settlement Agreement, that Plaintiff be awarded $15,000.00 under the terms of the Settlement Agreement, including pre-judgment and post-judgment interest from the date of the breach, and her attorney fees and costs described herein, and for any and all further relief that Plaintiff has shown herself justly entitled to receive.

The following is what Defendants requested the Court do.

Excerpt: *Defendants' Response to Plaintiff's Amended Motion for Summary Judgment to Enforce Rule 11 Settlement Agreement,*

Defendants Dan Hunt and Desoto Gun Club d/b/a Ellis County Sportsman's Club request that the Court deny Plaintiff's Amended Motion for Summary Judgment to Enforce Rule 11 Settlement Agreement, or, alternatively, enforce the settlement agreement under the terms agreed to by the parties at mediation without awarding attorney's fees or, alternatively, rescind the settlement agreement and for such other and further relief to which Defendants may show themselves justly entitled.

In Defendants' Response, there were three distinct options. There was a second if the Court didn't like the first option. How about a third one if the first two didn't work for the Court? It was now multiple choice for the 443rd Ellis County District Court. Just pick one.

1) Deny Plaintiff's motion to enforce the *Rule 11 Settlement Agreement* or,

2) Enforce the *Rule 11 Settlement Agreement under the terms agreed to at mediation*, but don't award my attorney fees or,

3) Throw out the *Rule 11 Settlement Agreement.*

However, what Regan G. Pearson asked the Court wasn't an option in Defendants' Response. To understand what transpired, these were the exhibits within Defendants' Response.

Exhibit A: *Rule 11 and Settlement Agreement* signed at mediation by all parties on April 17, 2019. The reason for the court hearing.

Exhibit B: Defendants' first version of their new contract, *Settlement and Release Agreement.*

Exhibit D: Defendants' second version of their new contract, *Settlement and Release Agreement.*

Exhibit E: Defendants' third and final version of their new contract, *Settlement and Release Agreement.*

Excerpt: Court Transcript,

MR. PEARSON: *We believe the Court should deny Plaintiff's motion and enforce the settlement agreement reached at mediation without awarding attorney's fees.*

And, in the alternative, Your Honor, we have two arguments in the event the Court elects not to enforce the settlement agreement and not – or award attorney fees.

THE COURT: *Can I ask you, which settlement agreement? B, D?*

MR. PEARSON: *A, which is - -*

THE COURT: *A.*

MR. PEARSON: *-- the Rule 11 that was signed at mediation.*

MR. BUNCH: *She means which of the documents you want enforced.*

MR. PEARSON: *Oh. The last one, Your Honor, yes. That would be – the copy we sent over that removed the disparagement, and we thought at the time had – there should have been no argument as to that one because we had acquiesced to all of Plaintiff's wishes, and I think that is Exhibit E.*

THE COURT: *Okay,*

MR. BUNCH: *E as in egg.*

MR. PEARSON: *E as in egg, yes, Your Honor.*

THE COURT: Okay. So I see Exhibit A, I guess, is where the mediator wrote down things?

MR. PEARSON: Right, Your Honor --

THE COURT: Okay. I see it, yeah. Okay.

MR. PEARSON: -- that is kind of the standard, the mediators have you sign it.

THE COURT: Yeah.

Pearson's first statement clearly stated; ... *deny Plaintiff's motion and enforce the settlement agreement reached at mediation without awarding attorney's fees.* When the Court asked which exhibit, Pearson again indicated: *A ... the Rule 11 that was signed at mediation.*

Then Ronald E. Bunch jumped into the middle of it, interpreting for the Court. It resulted in Pearson switching gears. Regan G. Pearson now asked the Court to enforce *Exhibit E*, the third version of Defendants' new contract. Pearson asked the Court to replace a signed contract reached at mediation with a new agreement, one I had not signed. Enforcing *Exhibit E* was not an option in Defendants' Response.

This exchange emphasized the Court's unfamiliarity with my case or the *Rule 11 and Settlement Agreement reached at mediation.* It should be noted my Motion had been filed with the Court for over two months. A document that included the *Rule 11 and Settlement Agreement.* My case was about to be decided by a judge who apparently knew nothing about a *Rule 11 and Settlement Agreement.* There was no recognition from the Court that the document was a valid, binding contract. According to the Court, it was; *I guess, is where the mediator wrote down things?*

In my opinion, Regan G. Pearson displayed the same lack of recognition regarding the validity of a legally binding, mediated contract, *Rule 11 and Settlement Agreement.* Pearson agreed with the Court's trivialization; *that is kind of the standard, the mediators have you sign it.*

Regan G. Pearson wasn't finished. Next, he started on his *alternative arguments.*

[228]

Excerpt: Court Transcript,

MR. PEARSON: And, your Honor, the alternative arguments - - in the alternative, we believe the Court should deny Plaintiff's motion because there was no meeting of the minds between the parties at mediation, and thus, no contract was ever created. The most common reason parties fail to have a meeting of the minds is a disagreement as to one or more material terms to a contract. Here both parties attempted to add a material term to the settlement agreement following mediation. Defendants attempted to add the nondisparaging provision, and Plaintiff attempted to add more funds to the settlement amount. Because both parties sought to add a new material term to the Rule 11 agreement following mediation, there was no meeting of the minds during mediation and no valid settlement agreement ever - - was ever created. As a result and in the alternative, we would request that the Court deny Plaintiff's motion and hold that no valid settlement agreement ever existed.

Then Pearson takes a shot at it from a different direction. If the Court didn't like his arguments about *no meeting of the minds,* then this was attorney Regan G. Pearson's next option.

Excerpt: Court Transcript,

MR. PEARSON: And then our last alternative argument, Your Honor, is that the Court should deny Plaintiff's motion and allow the Rule 11 settlement agreement to be rescinded due to the mutual mistake. When a mutual mistake exists, the parties are entitled to rescind their contract and be restored to the positions they held before entering the contract. A unilateral mistake by one party acknowledging that mistake by the other party is equivalent to a mutual mistake under Texas law. There were two mutual mistakes here. Defendants believed during mediation that, one, the agreed settlement amount was for $15,000, and, two, the final settlement agreement would contain a nondisparagement provision due to the claims asserted in the lawsuit, the defamation claim specifically. Plaintiff agreed at mediation that 15,000 would settle all of her claims against Defendants, yet, later attempted to add the balance of *her shooting card to the settlement amount. Because the amount of the settlement is clearly a material term, the Court should rescind the agreement due to a mutual mistake as to the settlement amount. Defendants also reasonably believed that the final settlement agreement would contain antidisparagement language due to the defamation claims. Plaintiff either knew or reasonably should have known that Defendants would anticipate that such language would be included in the final agreement, and as a result, the Court should also rescind the settlement agreement due to a mutual mistake relating to the inclusion of the nondisparagement provision.*

Defendants wanted to throw out the settlement agreement because there was *no meeting of the minds* or *mutual mistake*. Both options hinged on a false fact; my intentionally stolen $48 they claimed I tried to add to the settlement amount. I didn't.

Regan G. Pearson's arguments to the Court confirmed my suspicion there was an agenda behind Pearson and Harmon's persistence about my stolen $48. The "Big Dog," J. Richard Harmon's adamant protest in his May 29, 2018, email regarding the $48 never made any sense. The email was attached as an exhibit to the Defendants' Response.

Regan G. Pearson also used my intentionally stolen $48 as another threat in another email to my first attorney.

Excerpt: Regan G. Pearson email dated June 24, 2019,

Our clients insist that Ms. Dickason's $48 shooting card balance is included in the $15,000 settlement. If your client cannot agree then our position will be that there was "no meeting of the minds" at the mediation, no valid agreement was reached and we will continue to litigate this case. It should be noted that this email was included as an exhibit in Defendants' Response.

As a reminder, my stolen $48 was never brought up in mediation and wasn't even mentioned in the *Rule 11 and Settlement Agreement.* My stolen money was first mentioned in Defendants new contract,

Settlement and Release Agreement. I was informed the settlement amount now included my stolen $48.

On January 14, 2019, the ECSC Board voted to refund the balance on my shooting card. The Board's vote was confirmed in a letter from ECSC Secretary Shannon Edwards. I received a third confirmation at the Ambush, membership appeal meeting, when local Waxahachie banker and ECSC President Mike Lee promised to send me a refund check for the balance, my $48. I expected the Board to honor their commitment by sending the check. They didn't. Instead, the Board again reneged and intentionally stole my money. As I previously identified, it was a win-win for the ECSC. By trying to include my $48 in the settlement amount paid by their 830-plus billion-dollar French insurance conglomerate, they got to keep my money.

From statements made to the Court by Defendants' attorneys, Regan G. Pearson and Ronald E. Bunch obviously believed they could add new provisions to the contract, *Rule 11 and Settlement Agreement* their clients mediated and willingly signed. When it didn't work, was the fallback plan to have the *Rule 11 and Settlement Agreement* thrown out using my intentionally stolen $48 as the reason? Without my stolen $48, Defendants and their attorneys had no basis to argue *no meeting of the minds,* or *mutual mistake.*

We had a meeting of the minds the day we signed the contract, the *Rule 11 and Settlement Agreement.* I didn't change my mind. Defendants did. They didn't like the contract they mediated and willingly signed. Again, Pearson wants to argue about assumptions, claiming I should have known. I've got news for attorney Regan G. Pearson. If it wasn't in the contract I signed, it didn't exist. No assumptions.

If Pearson's arguments about *no meeting of the mind* didn't work, let's make it all about *mutual mistake.* In my opinion, any mistakes made were by Defendants and their attorneys, not me. If their new provisions were so crucial, they should have been addressed during mediation. If the *Rule 11 and Settlement Agreement* was thrown out, we'd start over. Was this another tactic to extend the litigation, causing me further financial hardship and adding billable hours for Pearson's law firm?

Pearson wasn't finished. He was back to the *E as in Egg Exhibit,* an option that wasn't in Defendants' Response.

Excerpt: Court Transcript,

MR. PEARSON: So to kind of wrap up our response to the summary judgment, Your Honor, we believe – we would like the Court to just enforce the Exhibit E, the settlement agreement that we acquiesced all of Plaintiff's wishes on and not award any attorney's fees. But in the alternative, if the Court - - if the Court elects not to do that, we would request that the Court hold that there was never a contract due to no meeting of the minds or that the contract should be rescinded due to mutual mistake.

Attorney Regan G. Pearson again asked the 443rd Ellis County District Court to replace a valid contract, *the Rule 11 and Settlement Agreement,* a contract his clients mediated and willingly signed, with Defendants' new contract, the third version of their *Settlement and Release Agreement* that I refused to sign.

Pearson told the Court; *We would like the Court to just enforce the Exhibit E, the settlement agreement that we acquiesced all of Plaintiff's wishes on and not award any attorney's fees.*

As I have already pointed out, Pearson misled the Court. *Exhibit E,* the third version of Defendants' new contract, *Settlement and Release Agreement,* still included Shawn as a party to the lawsuit, requiring him to sign the new contract.

After studying the transcript, it appeared that Regan G. Pearson was desperate to win at any cost as he tossed option after option at the Court. Did Pearson believe if he threw enough options at the Court, one of them would finally stick?

Opposing counsel wasn't finished. Ronald E. Bunch had to add his two cents' worth. In reading Bunch's comments, it was apparent he was ignorant of the contents of Defendants' Response bearing his name. Based on what I read in the transcript, it appeared to me Ronald E. Bunch was in court to put a good ol' Ellis County, local boy spin on Defendants' case.

Excerpt: Court Transcript,

MR. BUNCH: We have been trying to enforce this settlement agreement since mediation in April of -- 17 in 2019. As a matter of fact, two days after the mediated settlement agreement, Mr. Pearson sent over the first draft of the settlement agreement. So, you know we weren't practicing delay or doing anything but trying to enforce this agreement. And if you look at Paragraph 6 of the settlement -- the mediated settlement agreement, it says the parties agree to cooperate with each other in drafting.

THE COURT: Is that Exhibit A?

MR. BUNCH: Pardon?

THE COURT: Is this Exhibit A?

MR. BUNCH: Is it?

MR. PEARSON: Yes.

MR. BUNCH: Yes.

THE COURT: Okay. Okay.

MR. BUNCH: And "parties agreed to cooperate with each other in the drafting and execution of such additional documents." And we certainly have been cooperative and as Mr. Pearson said, we sent over one, and they sent back some corrections or edits: we made them, sent it back. Then eventually they said they didn't want Mr. Shawn George to sign the agreement, and the reason he was put in there was because he was -- he was part of this from the beginning all the way through. He was present at mediation, and he signed the mediation agreement. And so we - - but we acceded to that and took him out.

Regan G. Pearson had to tell Ronald E. Bunch that *Exhibit A was the mediated settlement agreement.* Bunch then miscited the excerpt. Bunch left off the first three words; *It is contemplated.* Plus, the contract his client signed did not stipulate I was required to sign another document.

Then Ronald E. Bunch pulled, what appeared to me, was his good ol' boy routine in referring to Shawn. "He was part of this from the beginning all the way through."

A vindictive cop and ECSC leagues manager, Dan Hunt was the reason Shawn was *part of this from the beginning all the way through.* It started with Hunt's so-called investigation of the scoring dispute, Hunt's aggressive, threatening behavior toward Shawn, Hunt's whining pity email, *Immediate resignation,* Hunt's false accusations to the Board, followed by Hunt's malicious, vindictive false accusations in Defendants' Response.

Bunch used the term *enforce,* not once but twice. What was to enforce if Defendants abided by the contract *Rule 11 and Settlement Agreement* they mediated and willingly signed? Nothing.

Unbelievably, Ronald E. Bunch wasn't finished with his *misrepresentations, mischaracterizations, misquotes,* and *miscites of facts.* He parroted Regan G. Pearson's assertion Shawn was removed from the third version of their new contract, *Settlement and Release Agreement,* their *E, as in Egg Exhibit.* Ronald E. Bunch stated, *but we acceded to that and took him out.* What Ronald E. Bunch told the Court was false. Shawn was still listed as a party and required to sign. Evidently, Bunch never read his *E, as in Egg Exhibit.*

With their threats, bullying, and holding my check hostage, they tried to force me to sign a document that didn't reflect the agreement of the parties. For approximately four months, Defendants refused to remove their new provisions, *those provisions which have not been agreed upon,* as stipulated in *The Texas Lawyer's Creed.* Defendants clearly refused, in writing, to abide by the dispute provision in the *Rule 11 and Settlement Agreement* Defendants mediated and willingly signed. Yet, this was what Ronald E. Bunch defined as *cooperative.*

Excerpt: Court Transcript,

MR. BUNCH: And then they wanted the nondisparagement stuff taken out which was interesting because not only is - - is part of their cause of action, a defamation case, but there is a confidentiality requirement in the mediated settlement. I think it's number - - Paragraph Number 8, it's checked, is the settlement confidential, so the nondisparagement went right along with that.

Bunch's good ol' boy litigation style put a new spin on changing a signed contract. Again, I have to ask. Why bother suffering through intolerable hours of mediation, spending thousands of dollars to hammer out a settlement agreement that all parties signed? Why bother, if after the fact, the attorneys could add whatever they wanted, based on an assumption their new provision, *nondisparagement went right along with that?* If it did, why wasn't it part of the mediation?

The more Regan G. Pearson and Ronald E. Bunch tried to justify their actions with Defendants' new contract, *Settlement and Release Agreement*, it seemed to me that they were steering clear of the fact their clients mediated and willingly signed a valid contract, *Rule 11 and Settlement Agreement*.

Even the Court viewed the *Rule 11 and Settlement Agreement* as nothing more than: *So I see Exhibit A, I guess, is where the mediator wrote down things?*

Exhibit A, the *Rule 11 and Settlement Agreement*, was why we were in Court. This was the contract I requested the Court enforce in my motion, *Plaintiff's Amended Motion for Summary Judgment to Enforce Rule 11 Settlement Agreement*. Yet, the Court believed this document, which cost me over $3200 and signed by all parties, was just a piece of paper; *I guess, is where the mediator wrote down things?* Defendants' lawyers were assuming. The 443rd Ellis County District Court was guessing.

Excerpt: Court Transcript,

MR. BUNCH: So, the nondisparagement went right along with that. But clearly the Plaintiff wants to continue to defame the Defendants through social media, and that's why she didn't want that out.

Ronald E. Bunch's statement was a fabrication, a way to defame me before the Court. His argument, *wants to continue,* informed the Court I had already defamed Defendants on social media. Ronald E. Bunch had no proof, no affidavit, not a single social media post to support his false accusation, but as an officer of the Court, that didn't stop Ronald E. Bunch and his thirty-seven years of lawyering from misleading the Court.

Ronald E. Bunch's false accusation was just another I never had a chance to refute. Was this how Ronald E. Bunch justified his presence in Court? Was this how Ronald E. Bunch justified his billable hours by falsely attacking an innocent woman?

Perhaps I should have requested Defendants' attorneys sign a non-disparagement agreement before they were allowed to address the Court. But then, it would seem the *Order* by the *Supreme Court of Texas, The Texas Lawyer's Creed* had already addressed the issue.

II. Lawyer to Client: 6. *I will treat adverse parties and witnesses with fairness and due consideration.*

Shawn told that vindictive Duncanville cop and leagues manager Dan Hunt during the July 2, 2018, board meeting, "I triple dog dare you to make the call." I'd say the same to Ronald E. Bunch. "I triple-dog dare you to produce the evidence." Once again, I was falsely accused of something I did not do, this time by Waxahachie attorney Ronald E. Bunch.

Ronald E. Bunch's defamatory comments only highlight what I believe were Regan G. Pearson's and Ronald E. Bunch's real purpose during the hearing. To intentionally and maliciously use a breach of contract hearing to taint court records and unduly influence the Court. There seemed no end to the false facts and malicious accusations from Defendants and their attorneys. Ronald E. Bunch wasn't finished.

Billing invoices from my attorneys had been included in my motion. It was what I was charged. It was what I paid. Yet Ronald E. Bunch disagreed, claiming I was *unreasonable.* Bunch told the Court:

which shows how unreasonable the Plaintiff has been all along. Then, Bunch again labels me as *unreasonable.* This time alluding to his irrelevant, false facts about my lawsuit.

Excerpt: Court Transcript,

MR. BUNCH: And the facts that Mr. Pearson went through about the lawsuit and what happened, the Plaintiff doesn't want that part of this hearing because it shows how unreasonable the Plaintiff has been all along.

Ronald E. Bunch's support of Pearson's comments only highlights opposing counsels' malicious attempts to unduly influence the Court. I have already detailed Pearson's false facts and false accusations *about the lawsuit and what happened.* It was irrelevant to why we were in Court. Yet, Ronald E. Bunch continued to pound the table.

Dan Hunt detailed his defamatory, malicious, false accusations in the *Background* of Defendants' Response. There was no reprisal or fear of exposure. Regan G. Pearson did the same while addressing the Court. Who was going to contradict him? Every time my attorney objected, the Court overruled his objection. Why should Ronald E. Bunch's unprincipled conduct be any different? After all, Ronald E. Bunch didn't have to worry about me taking the witness stand and exposing his defamatory statements or the unprincipled conduct of his client. All the false statements, accusations, and defamation occurred during a breach of contract hearing with no signed, notarized affidavits from Defendants, especially Ronald E. Bunch's client—ECSC.

You might say Bunch's job was to defend his client. Here was the issue. There was the truth, and then there were the false statements. After studying the transcript, it appeared to me that Ronald E. Bunch chose to *misrepresent, mischaracterize, misquote and miscite,* all *to gain an advantage.* Ronald E. Bunch chose to further defame me, my reputation, and my credibility. Ronald E. Bunch couldn't attack with the truth. Then Ronald E. Bunch declared my actions were not good sportsmanship. Seriously?

This next excerpt from Ronald E. Bunch's comments was a doozy.

Excerpt: Court Transcript,

MR. BUNCH: I understand the legal arguments at the end of Mr. Pearson's presentation about lack of mutual mistake and unilateral mistake, I'm not in favor of that because it would be a colossal waste of the Court's time if you - - if you set aside this agreement. We - - then we'd be back in court eventually. There's been no hearings in this case up until today. There has been no depositions, nothing has happened really except mediation, and all the things that we've attached to our response.

Regan G. Pearson had given a lawyerly, lengthy, detailed, though seriously flawed explanation to convince the Court to throw out the *Rule 11 and Settlement Agreement.* Pearson even gave the Court two options, *no meeting of the minds* or *mutual mistake.* Attorney Regan G. Pearson had asked the Court to throw out the *Rule 11 and Settlement Agreement,* not once but several times.

Ronald E. Bunch then informed the Court what his co-counsel requested was a *colossal waste of the Court's time.* Ronald E. Bunch argued that's not what we want. Bunch didn't want the Court to *set aside this agreement.* Bunch wasn't in favor of *we'd be back in court eventually.* After studying the transcript, to me this was like an old Abbott and Costello routine of *Who's on First.*

Ronald E. Bunch certainly wasn't on the same page as his co-counsel. These two learned lawyers, representing the same client, argued against each other in a hearing before the 443rd Ellis County District Court. These two supposedly experienced attorneys couldn't agree on what they wanted the Court to do. Pearson wanted the Court to throw out the *Rule 11 and Settlement Agreement.* His co-counsel, Ronald E. Bunch, protested: *I'm not in favor of that because it would be a colossal waste of the Court's time if you - - if you set aside this agreement.*

Why did Ronald E. Bunch, a Waxahachie attorney with thirty-seven years of legal experience, wait until he got before the Court to object? Did Bunch not know what Defendants' Response stated? Ronald E. Bunch signed it. Did he even read it?

Excerpt: *Defendants' Response to Plaintiff's Amended Motion for Summary Judgment to Enforce Rule 11 Settlement Agreement,*

Defendants Dan Hunt and Desoto Gun Club d/b/a Ellis County Sportsman's Club request that the Court, rescind the settlement agreement.

Ronald E. Bunch's client, Defendant ECSC, requested the Court *rescind* the *Rule 11 and Settlement Agreement.* Yet, local Waxahachie attorney Ronald E. Bunch stood before the 443rd Ellis County District Court, arguing against his co-counsel, his client, and Defendants' Response that he, Ronald E. Bunch, signed.

Since Bunch obviously wasn't on board about tossing out the *Rule 11 and Settlement Agreement,* why wasn't this discussed between co-counsel Regan G. Pearson and Ronald E. Bunch before they appeared before the Court? Talk about a *colossal waste of the Court's time.* If there was no *meeting of the minds* or *mutual mistake,* it was obviously between these two supposed learned lawyers.

Why would Ronald E. Bunch be so concerned that *we'd be back in court eventually?* Was it because the ECSC's culpability would finally be exposed? ECSC leagues manager Dan Hunt's bogus charge of cheating, Vice President DVM Chris Rose's recorded phone call, the unchanged scoresheet, their clandestine meeting, Porter's enhancement of my suspension, violation of Texas law, and all the false facts they fed the Court would come to light in front of a jury.

Add Dan Hunt's failure to adhere to the stipulations for a leagues manager, as cited by Treasurer Rusty Porter, during Hunt's so-called investigation of the scoring dispute. An investigation in which Hunt failed to adhere to the club's rules. The ATA rules the Board clearly emphasized governed their trap leagues.

Then add Hunt's misconduct with weapons, Hunt's false accusations as recorded in the July 2, 2018, board meeting minutes, and Hunt's vicious, libelous, whining pity email, *Immediate resignation,* sent to nearly one hundred unsuspecting men, women, and even children—

a nefarious act committed in Hunt's official capacity as a representative of the ECSC. Add ECSC condoning Hunt's bogus accusation of assault rifle intimidation in Defendants' official court document.

Then, add the gun safety infractions and mixing guns, alcohol, and children on club property. What I believe was the real reason for the wrongful suspension of my paid membership rights to participate in club-sponsored events. Porter and his cronies tried to silence me.

All that would be a doozy to explain, before a jury, under oath, with perjury rules in effect. Why would anyone be surprised Bunch didn't want a trial?

Another point. Bunch was quick to protest to the Court that he didn't want to throw out the contract, the *Rule 11 and Settlement Agreement*. Not once did Ronald E. Bunch speak out, correcting Regan G. Pearson's false statements to the Court that the ECSC, Bunch's client, wasn't a corporation. As an officer of the court, Ronald E. Bunch never corrected the false representation of his client's legal status to the 443rd Ellis County District Court. As a reminder, Ronald E. Bunch signed and submitted a court document stipulating the ECSC was a corporation.

Excerpt: Court Transcript,

MR. BUNCH: The settlement check was tendered, and as a matter of fact, it was tendered and referenced in the emails, it was tendered as -- you know, as soon as you sign the documents, we got the money. We will send it to you. And it took so long that the settlement check had to be cancelled and reissued which was reflected in the emails as well.

Ronald E. Bunch clearly admitted they were holding my settlement check hostage. No check until I signed their new contract. Unfortunately for Ronald E. Bunch and his thirty-seven years of experience, the Court of Appeals, Tenth District of Texas, disagreed. The Court of Appeals clearly stated, and I quote: *What is not in dispute is that Hunt and ECSC did not make the $15,000 payment by the May 2, 2019 deadline.*

Excerpt: Court Transcript,

MR. BUNCH: You know, the - - these terms and the provisions of the settlement agreement were negotiated and went back and forth, and I've been a party to a lot of settlements over 37 years, and this is just part of it. The lawyers get together whether it's after a settlement between the parties or a mediation, that's just part of it. That's finishing the job is going back and forth about what's going to be included in the settlement agreement. And that doesn't mean when - - when one party is dissatisfied with how the negotiation is going that they can run to Court and ask for their attorney's fees that have been incurred after the settlement. It's just part of it. It's part of finishing the job.

What a good ol' boy speech. Did Bunch not read what his client, ECSC, signed? All the back and forth was over. That took place in mediation, costing me over $3200. Negotiations ended when his client willingly signed the contract, *Rule 11 and Settlement Agreement*. I have to wonder if what Ronald E. Bunch described about his settlements over 37 years was what the *Supreme Court of Texas* wanted to stop with *The Texas Lawyer's Creed*.

III. Lawyer to Lawyer: 4. *I will attempt to prepare documents which correctly reflect the agreement of the parties. I will not include provisions which have not been agreed upon or omit provisions which are necessary to reflect the agreement of the parties.*

If you follow Ronald E. Bunch's logic, why would anyone bother with mediation? Why would anyone put themselves through mediation and the expense, sign a contract, only to have the attorneys decide what will be included in the settlement agreement after the fact?

I believe all the rhetoric and table pounding by Regan G. Pearson and Ronald E. Bunch to convince the Court it was acceptable behavior to add provisions to a signed contract, to threaten and bully, and then hold hostage the settlement check was nothing but a flagrant violation of *The Texas Lawyer's Creed, A Mandate for Professionalism*. Mulligans are not alluded to in *The Texas Lawyer's Creed*.

Ronald E. Bunch adds; *when one party is dissatisfied with how the negotiation is going that they can run to Court and ask for their attorney's fees that have been incurred after the settlement.*

Ronald E. Bunch's, *they can run to Court,* comment was offensive and insulting. Another defamatory remark that I believe was intended to prejudice the Court. I filed a legal motion to enforce the *Rule 11 and Settlement Agreement* after Defendants refused to abide by the terms of the contract they mediated and willingly signed.

Excerpt: Court Transcript,

MR. BUNCH: Plaintiffs - - I mean the Defendants have incurred attorney fees as well in this matter, but we are not here asking for it because we believe that's just part of finalizing the settlement agreement.

What a flagrantly false, self-serving statement to the Court. Another misrepresentation of the facts. What Ronald E. Bunch, local Waxahachie attorney, didn't tell the 443rd Ellis County District Court was Defendants were barred from collecting their attorney fees by the contract, *Rule 11 and Settlement Agreement* they signed.

When the "Big Dog," J. Richard Harmon, arrogantly ordered my prior attorney in his June 5, 2019, email, *Do not contact Judge Fifer, and I can guarantee you that there will not be another mediation,* the "Big Dog" breached the dispute clause in the *Rule 11 and Settlement Agreement* Defendants mediated and willingly signed.

Harmon's email was another attachment to Defendants' Response that evidently Bunch didn't read. Either that or Bunch didn't read the contract, *Rule 11 and Settlement Agreement* signed by his client.

My attorney's statements to the Court throughout the approximately fifty-seven (57) minute hearing were professional, articulate, precise, and truthful. My attorney didn't take any cheap shots at Dan Hunt or the ECSC. My attorney didn't disparage or defame them. My attorney stuck to why I was in Court, the *Rule 11 and Settlement Agreement.* His every attempt to keep the hearing on track was overruled.

Excerpt: Court Transcript,

MY ATTORNEY: I renew my objections of everything else and the reason I renew those, Your Honor, because I knew they would come in here and give a whole backdrop speech when they had absolutely no affidavits. They are using the Rules of Civil Procedure as this is a final jury trial for evidence.

The Court allowed Defendants' attorneys to run the hearing as if it were a trial of my lawsuit without the necessity of producing witnesses, evidence or any signed, notarized affidavits. Defendants' attorneys introduced false facts and accusations controverted by the very emails opposing counsel attached to Defendants' Response. Defendants' attorneys misquoted and miscited Defendants' Response while addressing the Court. Before the 443rd Ellis County District Court, Regan G. Pearson and Ronald E. Bunch actually argued against one another. The Court now had dueling co-counsel. Studying the transcript, I couldn't help imagining music from a guitar and a banjo.

In reading the transcript, the root of the problem appeared to be a Court unknowledgeable in civil proceedings and lacking any familiarity with the court filings. Otherwise, why would the Court have allowed Defendants and their attorneys to enter false, malicious, disparaging, and defamatory statements that damaged my reputation and Shawn's into the court record? All without any evidence, signed, notarized affidavits from any witnesses or Defendants. Was it intentional?

Based on what I read in the transcript, it's my belief an unknowledgeable Court relied on opposing counsels' *misrepresentations, mischaracterizations, misquotes and miscites of facts* in reaching a decision.

It took over two months for the 443rd Ellis County District Court to rule on my two motions. On March 30, 2020, the Court denied both *Plaintiff's Amended Motion for Summary Judgment to Enforce Rule 11 Settlement Agreement* and *Plaintiff's Motion to Strike Facts not in Evidence and Exhibits contained in Defendants' Response to Plaintiff's Amended Motion for Summary Judgment to Enforce Rule 11 Settlement Agreement.*

[243]

About-Face

Chapter Eighteen

When the Court denied my motions, it meant I was headed back to court, this time for a trial. On April 6, 2020, my attorney requested a trial date with the 443rd Ellis County District Court. After what transpired during the January 16, 2020, hearing, I was even more concerned about a fair trial, though I had no other option. My attorney advised that a change of venue was still not warranted. I was still stuck in Ellis County.

A few weeks later, my attorney received a letter from Regan G. Pearson. Included was a check issued by *Sedgwick CMS as Agent for T.H.E. Insurance Company* dated April 14, 2020.

Excerpt: Regan G. Pearson's April 28, 2020, letter,

This check represents full and final settlement of the claims made by Anita Dickason in the above-captioned suit as specified in the settlement agreement reached by the parties at mediation. As you know, the court has denied Plaintiff's Amended Motion for Summary Judgment to Enforce the Rule 11 Settlement Agreement, effectively ruling that your client is not entitled to attorney's fees related to enforcement of the settlement. In the spirit of good faith, our clients have agreed to have the settlement agreement signed at mediation by the parties serve as the full and final settlement agreement in this case.

Regan G. Pearson's notification that his *clients have agreed to have the settlement agreement signed at mediation by the parties serve as the full and final settlement agreement in this case,* reinforced my opinion of Defendants' unwarranted conduct and opposing counsels' multiple violations of *The Texas Lawyer's Creed.*

II. Lawyer to Client: 7. *I will advise my client that we will not pursue conduct which is intended primarily to harass or drain the financial resources of the opposing party.*

II. Lawyer to Client: 8. *I will advise my client that we will not pursue tactics intended primarily for delay.*

III. Lawyer to Lawyer: 4. *I will attempt to prepare documents which correctly reflect the agreement of the parties. I will not include provisions which have not been agreed upon or omit provisions which are necessary to reflect the agreement of the parties.*

For months, opposing counsel attempted to force me to sign Defendants' new contract, *Settlement and Release Agreement,* with threats of legal action, bullying, and holding my check hostage. Regan G. Pearson stood before the 443rd Ellis County District Court, pounding the table about why his clients were justified in revising a contract, *Rule 11 and Settlement Agreement,* Defendants mediated and willingly signed. Pearson justified his behavior using twenty-five attorney-to-attorney emails as evidence.

Pearson even requested the Court throw out the signed contract, *Rule 11 and Settlement Agreement,* and replace it with their *E as in Egg Exhibit,* the third version of Defendants' new contract, *Settlement and Release Agreement* I had not signed.

Opposing counsels' manipulation created a financial hardship for me, adding even more stress. It wasn't a problem for Defendants. They had an 830-plus billion-dollar French insurance conglomerate paying their attorney fees. It certainly appeared to be a lucrative source of revenue for opposing counsel. Since April 17, 2019, the date Defendants mediated and willingly signed a contract, *Rule 11 and Settlement Agreement,* I wonder how many hours the "Big Dog," J. Richard Harmon and Regan G. Pearson, billed to the 830-plus billion-dollar French insurance conglomerate to finalize a lawsuit that was already settled. I knew what I paid for the unwarranted, unnecessary extended litigation.

If Defendants' attorneys could send the check in April 2020, without their *Settlement and Release Agreement* they demanded I sign, they could have done the same *on or before May 2, 2019.*

Their comment, *In the spirit of good faith,* was another insult. Nothing Defendants or their attorneys did could be categorized as; *In the spirit of good faith.* They had destroyed my and Shawn's reputation and credibility. Furthermore, Defendants continued their malicious false accusations and defamation in a court document and opposing counsels' statements before the 443rd Ellis County District Court. That vindictive Duncanville cop, ECSC leagues manager Dan Hunt, along with Porter and his cronies wouldn't know the meaning of, *In the spirit of good faith,* if it bit them in their backsides.

As it turned out, their *In the spirit of good faith* was nothing but a self-aggrandizing statement. Their check was another underhanded tactic to stop me from going to trial. The threat was in the second paragraph of Pearson's letter.

Excerpt: Regan G. Pearson's April 28, 2020, letter

Please be advised that if your client refuses to accept this settlement check and dismiss the lawsuit, we will be moving forward with a motion for summary judgment seeking a determination from the court that the case is settled as a matter of law, in addition to requesting our reasonable and necessary attorney's fees related to the motion.

If I accepted their settlement check, it was over. There wouldn't be a trial. I couldn't recover my attorney fees or interest on the long overdue settlement amount. If I refused, I would be hit with a lawsuit, which meant another hearing in front of the same Ellis County judge, not a trial with a jury.

If I've learned anything about Defendants' attorneys, it was to carefully read their documentation. In the header of the check, it stated; *Full and final settlement of any and all claims.* According to Defendants and their attorneys, the settlement amount now represented all claims, including any that arose after the *Rule 11 and Settlement Agreement* was signed. Sneaky, sneaky, sneaky.

Paragraph 4 of the contract, *Rule 11 and Settlement Agreement* stipulated an *as of this date* for the settlement of claims. The *Rule 11 and Settlement Agreement* and the $15,000 settlement amount only covered claims as of April 17, 2019, when all parties signed the contract. My second breach of contract lawsuit against Defendants was filed on July 29, 2019. The claims from my second breach of contract lawsuit were a new issue, not part of the original settlement amount.

The settlement check with its new provision attached as a condition of acceptance was another breach of the contract, *Rule 11 and Settlement Agreement.* My attorney refused to accept the check.

On June 3, 2020, Defendants filed *Defendants' Motion for Summary Judgment.* I was headed back to Court for another hearing. Once again, unfortunately, in Ellis County.

On October 14, 2020, a hearing was held before the 443rd Ellis County District Court. Most of the approximately forty-nine (49) minute hearing was a repeat of the January 16, 2020, hearing. In fact, most of the *Background* within Defendants' new motion was nearly word-for-word the same as in their January 9, 2020, filing, *Defendants' Response to Plaintiff's Amended Motion for Summary Judgment to Enforce Rule 11 Settlement Agreement.* The same twenty-five (25) attorney-to-attorney emails were attached as an exhibit. I still wondered if opposing counsel had ever read them.

This time, once Regan G. Pearson started with all the irrelevant *Background* as Pearson had done in the first hearing, irrelevant details the Court had already heard, my attorney immediately asked for a running objection. The Court overruled my attorney's request, just as the Court did with every other objection from my attorney during the hearing. This was essentially the same song and dance, with one major exception.

In Defendants' new filing, *Defendants' Motion for Summary Judgment* and subsequent hearing, Defendants and their attorneys did a complete about-face on the validity of the *Rule 11 and Settlement Agreement.* Defendants and opposing counsel now asked the same Court and the same judge to enforce the *Rule 11 and Settlement Agreement.* By the way, Defendants now wanted their attorney fees.

Quite frankly, this was unbelievable. In *Defendants' Response to Plaintiff's Amended Motion for Summary Judgment to Enforce Rule 11 and Settlement Agreement,* filed on January 9, 2020, Defendants requested the Court throw out the agreement. Pearson even offered numerous arguments for throwing out the *Rule 11 and Settlement Agreement* based on *no meeting of the minds,* thus no contract was formed, or because of a *mutual mistake,* rendering the contract invalid.

Now, in a second motion and hearing, Defendants and their attorneys did their about-face. They asked the Court to grant their motion for summary judgment to enforce the same *Rule 11 and Settlement Agreement* that I had asked the Court to enforce, which was denied. The same agreement Defendants and opposing counsel now wanted the Court to enforce was the same agreement they didn't want the Court to enforce or to award my attorney fees in January 2020. The same agreement opposing counsel argued multiple times to have invalidated.

On October 14, 2020, the same day as the hearing, the 443rd Ellis County District Court granted Defendants' Motion. After the first hearing, the Court denied my motion to enforce the same *Rule 11 and Settlement Agreement.* It took over two months to obtain a ruling. Yet, the Court granted Defendants' Motion and signed the court order the same day the hearing was held. What's wrong with this picture? Evidently a lot, since the Court of Appeals, Tenth District of Texas ultimately overturned the ruling by the 443rd Ellis County District Court.

Just as with their January 9, 2020, filing, *Defendants' Motion for*

Summary Judgment still lacked any evidence and signed, notarized affidavits from Defendants to support their false facts and defamatory accusations. Once again, the 443rd Ellis County District Court would allow the misrepresentations, mischaracterizations, misquotes, and miscites of facts to stand within an official court document. As in the first hearing, the Court allowed Defendants' attorneys to blather about irrelevant, false facts that had nothing to do with why we were in court. Regan G. Pearson and Ronald E. Bunch would pound the table just as they had done in the first hearing.

Excerpt: Court Transcript,

MR. PEARSON: I would like to start with some background because I think it's important that the Court understand how the parties got to this point.

Regan G. Pearson was about to repeat the same irrelevant, false details to the 443rd Ellis County District Court and the same judge as in the first hearing. In my opinion, there was only one reason for Pearson regurgitating the same false story. After all, the Court heard all of it the first time around. It wasn't to inform the Court. I believe the hearing was another opportunity to get Defendants' false and malicious defamatory statements into another court record. Defendants' Motion and hearing were another opportunity to try the settled lawsuit in court without the necessity of providing witnesses, signed, notarized affidavits, or evidence.

After reading the second transcript, my opinion of who was driving the bus in the hearing didn't change from the first hearing. It was Defendants' attorneys, Regan G. Pearson and local Waxahachie attorney Ronald E. Bunch, and the Court allowed it.

Using false facts and accusations, rank hearsay, embellishments, unsupported by any signed, notarized affidavits to such, downtown Dallas attorney Regan G. Pearson and Waxahachie attorney Ronald E. Bunch, led the 443rd Ellis County District Court, right where they wanted the Court to go. The Court granted their motion on the same day.

Pearson started with the false, irrelevant details of what happened on the final night of the trap league, just as he did in the first hearing. We were in court for a hearing on the contract, *Rule 11 and Settlement Agreement*. Yet, Regan G. Pearson still argued about two irrelevant points that had nothing to do with my lawsuit, or why we were in Court. Nothing different from the first hearing. I still believed Regan G. Pearson's false facts and false accusations violated *The Texas Lawyer's Creed*, an *Order* by the *Supreme Court of Texas*.

IV. Lawyer and Judge: 6. *I will not knowingly misrepresent, mischaracterize, misquote or miscite facts or authorities to gain an advantage.*

Once again, all my attorney could do was object, which he did, but he couldn't stop the damaging, false statements any more than he could in the first hearing. The Court overruled my attorney's every objection.

Excerpt: Court Transcript,

MR. PEARSON: So, we met with (plaintiff's attorney) *introduced him to the case and it - - you know, that fact that these additional attorney's fees that Plaintiff was claiming was discussed, and it was made clear that Defendants had no intention of paying Plaintiff any additional money for this new claim for alleged attorney's fees incurred during the negotiations of the settlement agreement language.*

It was the same false information Regan G. Pearson told the Court in the first hearing. Attorney Regan G. Pearson was still just as oblivious to his so-called evidence, twenty-five emails that refuted many of his statements. In an email dated September 19, 2019, Pearson informed my new attorney; *As we discussed, I spoke with my adjuster regarding your client's claims for attorney's fees and whether she would be willing to offer anything on the fees. She advised that she is not inclined to pay on the attorney's fees.*

It wasn't the Defendants refusing to pay, it was Pearson's other client, the 830-plus billion-dollar French insurance conglomerate that had hired the downtown Dallas, multi-state law firm.

Excerpt: Court Transcript,

MR. PEARSON: And this Court held an oral hearing back on January 16th of 2020, and following that hearing, Your Honor, this Court denied Plaintiff's Motion for Summary Judgment ruling that Plaintiff is not entitled to any additional attorney's fees as a matter of law.

When the Court denied my motion, it meant I was headed for trial. It would be up to a jury to decide on the attorney fees. As I previously stated, my attorney promptly requested a trial date. Evidence could be submitted in a trial, and I could testify about what happened. I believe this was why Defendants pulled their underhanded stunt with the check. It was to avoid going to trial—another way to silence me.

If I accepted their check, I couldn't pursue further legal action, and their 830-plus billion-dollar French insurance conglomerate didn't have to worry about a jury awarding my attorney fees or interest on the long overdue settlement amount. If I didn't, then I was back in another hearing where they could get a ruling in their favor. Either way, I believe it was a win-win for Defendants and opposing counsel. No trial.

Excerpt: Court Transcript,

MR. PEARSON: So as a result, Your Honor, Defendants were forced to file this motion and incur approximately $4,817 of their own attorney's fees in an effort to enforce the settlement and the Court's prior ruling.

Pearson's statement was another misrepresentation to mislead the Court. Billing invoices from Pearson's law firm, Exhibit F, in *Defendants' Motion for Summary Judgment,* were sent to XL Catlin Insurance America, Inc., a division of AXA, the 830-plus billion-dollar French insurance conglomerate. Once again, attorney Regan G. Pearson's statements were controverted by Defendants exhibits. Defendants were not paying the attorney fees.

Excerpt: Court Transcript,

MR. PEARSON: And I can just tell the Court, really, our requests for attorney's fees aren't that big of an issue in this case. We're - - we're willing to eat those fees if we can get this case resolved. At this point, our clients just believe they're entitled to those fees because we had to draft this motion and - - and do all this work attempting to enforce the Court's prior ruling. But really, we would be willing to eat those fees, just to get this matter fully and finally resolved.

What a self-serving statement, considering it was highly likely that the 830-plus billion dollar French insurance conglomerate had already paid the invoices attached to Defendants' Motion. In Regan G. Pearson's signed, notarized affidavit included in Defendants' Motion, Pearson stated:

Excerpt: Regan G. Pearson Affidavit,

Since March 20, 2020, Defendants have incurred attorney's fees and costs in the approximate amount of $3817.00 from work performed by me and/or other attorneys and staff at my law firm Thompson, Coe, Cousins, & Irons, LLP. I anticipate Defendants will incur an additional approximate $1000.00 in reasonable attorney's fees to prepare for and attend the hearing on their Motion for Summary Judgment.

When dealing with opposing counsels' documents, I found it behooved a person to read their exhibits—carefully.

Excerpt: Regan G. Pearson Affidavit,

The associate hourly rate is $170.00 per hour and the partner hourly rate is $200.00 per hour on this case, which is in my experience is consistent with attorney rates being charged for an attorney of my skill and experience in North Texas, including Ellis County.

What garnered my attention was Pearson's low hourly rate, as well as the *partner* (the "Big Dog," J. Richard Harmon), especially for such a large, extensive, multi-state law firm. It wasn't consistent with my experience with attorney fees. It didn't make sense until I read an additional rider in Pearson's affidavit. The words that struck me were; **on this case.** Was there a different hourly rate depending on his firm's client? What would Pearson's massive, multi-state law firm have charged me, not being an 830-plus billion-dollar French insurance conglomerate with their oh-so-deep pockets and lots of business to hand out? It seemed to me this was another example of Pearson's manipulation to unduly influence the Court and malign my attorney fees. I paid what I was charged.

Excerpt: Court Transcript,

MR. PEARSON: This case involves a settlement - - essentially involves a settlement which took longer than anticipated to finalize due to objections by Plaintiff to traditional nondisparagement language that you see in every settlement agreement for defamation cases.

This wasn't what Regan G. Pearson told the Court in the first hearing. Pearson, once again, embellished. In the first hearing, Regan G. Pearson said *that **in nearly all** defamation settlements,* Now, Pearson informs the Court *in **every** settlement agreement for defamation cases.*

Pearson was just as prone to exaggeration as his client, Dan Hunt. His statements were another attempt to mislead the Court. If, as Pearson stated, the *traditional nondisparagement language* is now applied to ***every*** *settlement agreement for defamation cases,* why wasn't it brought up during mediation and stipulated within the *Rule 11 and Settlement Agreement* his clients mediated and willingly signed?

Excerpt: Court Transcript,

MR. PEARSON: Your honor, to the extent that Plaintiff contends that the Defendants delayed the finalization of this settlement, for whatever reason, we would show that any delay was - - due Plaintiff - - or Plaintiff's prior counsel's own actions.

Once again, Regan G. Pearson sang the same song. This time, his statements to the Court are controverted by his letter dated April 28, 2020, in which Pearson wrote; *In the spirit of good faith, our clients have agreed to have the settlement agreement signed at mediation by the parties serve as the full and final settlement agreement in this case.*

There was no necessity to finalize the settlement, as Pearson informed the Court. Had Pearson done the same *on or before May 2,*

2019, multiple court filings, two court hearings, an appeal to the Court of Appeals, Tenth District of Texas and another mediation ordered by the Court of Appeals that failed would never have happened.

Here's the kicker. Pearson's statement; *Plaintiff contends that the Defendants delayed the finalization of this settlement,* was controverted by the following excerpts from Defendants' motion.

Excerpt: *Defendants' Motion for Summary Judgment,*

The parties previously signed a settlement agreement and release at mediation to resolve this case for $15,000.

The settlement agreement and release signed by all parties at mediation is binding on each party that signed it.

In two separate statements within Defendants' Motion, Defendants admitted the contract, *Rule 11 and Settlement Agreement,* signed at mediation, was *a settlement agreement and release.* Defendants' new contract, *Settlement and Release Agreement,* they tried to force me to sign by holding my check hostage was unnecessary and unwarranted.

Multiple statements referencing the necessity of Defendants' *Settlement and Release Agreement* within Defendants' two court filings and arguments advanced by Regan G. Pearson and Ronald E. Bunch, page, after page, after page in two transcripts, were all now refuted by their admission in *Defendants' Motion for Summary Judgment.*

In the January 16, 2020, hearing, Regan G. Pearson told the Court; *Those e-mails, Your Honor, clearly relevant to just show the communications between the attorneys to try to finalize the settlement agreement.* Pearson referred to twenty-five attorney-to-attorney emails included in *Defendants' Response to Plaintiff's Amended Motion for Summary Judgment to enforce Rule 11 Settlement Agreement.* The same twenty-five emails were again attached as an exhibit in *Defendants' Motion for Summary Judgment.*

There was no need to finalize the settlement. There was no justifiable reason to extend the litigation. Defendants, by their own admission, already had their *settlement agreement and release at mediation.*

In my opinion, these two statements within *Defendants' Motion for Summary Judgment* showed Defendants and their attorneys wasted my time and money. They wasted the insurance company's money. Furthermore, they wasted the court's valuable time.

Defendants attorneys' rhetoric and bombastic oratory about their efforts to finalize the settlement agreement were nothing but an unwarranted attempt to justify their conduct. Their acknowledgment of the validity of the contract, *Rule 11 and Settlement Agreement*, as a *settlement and release agreement at mediation,* demonstrated what I had repeatedly stated. Opposing counsel wasn't finalizing the settlement agreement. They were changing it to get all those new provisions Defendants didn't get the first time around. Defendants wanted a new contract. Defendants wanted a mulligan.

When my attorney countered with arguments, his statements were clear, concise, truthful, and professional. There were no oratories, bombast, disparaging, or defamatory remarks as displayed by Defendants' attorneys. My attorney told the Court the truth. My attorney explained the law as it applied to my case. In my opinion, the Court wasn't interested.

Dare I say, Defendants and their attorneys made a mockery of the Texas judicial system and legal ethics? But remember, it was more billable hours into the deep pockets of the 830-plus billion-dollar French insurance conglomerate. Was this type of behavior by Ronald E. Bunch, Regan G. Pearson, and the "Big Dog," J. Richard Harmon what an *Order* by the *Supreme Court of Texas* tried to prevent when the Court mandated *The Texas Lawyer's Creed?*

Excerpt: *Defendants' Motion for Summary Judgment,*

In the agreement, Plaintiff agreed to "release, discharge, and forever hold, the Defendant(s) harmless from any and all claims, demands, suits, known or unknown . . . arising from or related to the events and transactions which are the subject of this case."

Excerpt: Court Transcript,

MR. PEARSON: In the settlement agreement signed by the parties at mediation, Plaintiff agree to release, discharge and hold Defendants harmless from any and all claims, known or unknown, arising from or related to the events and transactions which are the subject of this case. Ultimately, Your Honor, it's our position that Defendants fulfilled their obligations under the settlement agreement by tendering the $15,000.

Once again, Regan G. Pearson affirmed that Defendants had a settlement and release agreement at mediation, *Plaintiff agree to **release, discharge and hold Defendants harmless.*** However, Pearson, in my opinion, intentionally left out one very significant detail.

Excerpt: Rule 11 and Settlement Agreement,

The Plaintiff(s) agree(s) to release, discharge, and forever hold, the Defendant(s) harmless from any and all claims, demands, or suits, known or unknown, fixed or contingent, liquidated or unliquidated whether or not asserted in the about case, as of this date, arising from or related to the events and transactions which are the subject of this case.

The glaring, I believe intentional, omission of a critical detail within Defendants' Motion and what Regan G. Pearson told the Court was the ***as of this date.*** That date was April 17, 2019, when all parties signed the contract. The $15,000 settlement amount didn't include any claims after that date. The underhanded stunt opposing counsel pulled when they sent my settlement check, dated April 14, 2020, claimed the settlement amount included all claims before and after the ***as of this date.*** Again, sneaky, sneaky, sneaky.

Excerpt: Court Transcript,

MR. PEARSON: You know, Plaintiff's counsel is - - is - - keeps stating that whatever they wanted in this settlement agreement, they should have put in there from the beginning. We all know that in these cases, the - - that you sign a Rule 11 agreement at mediation and - - and you work with opposing counsel to finalize the final settlement agreement after the mediation. It happens in every single case. This is the first case that I've ever had where they are trying to hold everybody to only what was within the Rule 11 signed at mediation and no - - no other provisions are allowed in, which I will note we actually have since agreed to. We agreed to let the Rule 11 signed at mediation stand as the final settlement agreement.

Why bother with mediation? Why pay for something the attorneys would change? It appeared to me that Regan G. Pearson acted on assumptions and generalities.

Regan G. Pearson made a telling statement. *This is the first case that I've ever had where they are trying to hold everybody to only what was within the Rule 11 signed at mediation and no - - no other provisions are allowed in.*

Was this the reason the "Big Dog," J. Richard Harmon, fired off his threats to my prior attorney? Did the "Big Dog" believe he could fix the problem with threats, bullying, and withholding my settlement check?

I would again note the term stipulated by *The Texas Lawyer's Creed* was the *agreement of the parties. The Texas Lawyer's Creed* doesn't state the agreement of the attorneys. Maybe Pearson's problem was someone finally stood up to him and fought back.

The false statements and accusations, threats, bullying, and defamation by J. Richard Harmon, Regan G. Pearson, and Ronald E. Bunch were appalling. It appeared to me they wanted to win and didn't care how they did it.

Again, was I dealing with Rambo-style lawyers? The conduct of J. Richard Harmon, Regan G. Pearson, and Ronald E. Bunch, I believe, certainly seemed to fit the definition of such. If it looks like a duck, waddles like a duck, and quacks like a duck, you can pretty much bet, it's a duck. Their billable hours to the French insurance conglomerate just kept waddling along.

Then Ronald E. Bunch had to climb back on the bandwagon, interjecting his two cents' worth, which I found was worth less than it was in the first hearing.

Excerpt: Court Transcript,

MR. BUNCH: *You know, we have been trying to finalize this matter since mediation, which was a year and a half ago. We've been obstructed in it in multiple ways. I think Mr. Pearson covered all the bases, so I won't comment beyond that unless the Court has some questions.*

Evidently Ronald E. Bunch was oblivious to the contents of Defendants' Motion. A document he signed. These two statements— *The parties previously signed a settlement agreement and release at mediation,* and; *The settlement agreement and release signed by all parties at mediation is binding on each party that signed it,*—refuted every statement Bunch made, in two court hearings, about *trying to finalize this matter since mediation*

So, who was really guilty of obstruction? I give you attorneys Regan G. Pearson and Ronald E. Bunch, officers of the Court. Attorneys who admitted they wouldn't send my settlement check until I signed their new contract, *Settlement and Release Agreement.*

Excerpt: Court Transcript,

MR. BUNCH: *Just a couple of comments. The - - to me, the bottom line is that this case was settled at mediation a year and half ago. The - - the Defendants - - we promptly sent out formal settlement release documents, attempted to finalize this matter. Mr. Pearson is now offering to send a third $15,000 check again. Of course, we will do that. The other ones have expired.*

The first check expired because they held it hostage, refusing to send the check unless I signed Defendants' new contract, *Settlement and Release Agreement.* With the second check, they pulled another underhanded tactic. Even my attorney referred to their actions in his statement to the 443rd Ellis County District Court as *tricky.*

Excerpt: Court Transcript,

MR. BUNCH: *And we have - - you know, they raised objections to the settlement documents. We have compromised on every single one, save one. I think the $48, was still - - still there.*

Ronald E. Bunch thinks? The ECSC was his client, and he didn't know? Well, I'll tell him. My intentionally stolen $48 was removed, though Defendants still reneged. Shawn was still listed as a party to the lawsuit and required to sign the document. Then local Waxahachie attorney Ronald E. Bunch had to take another cheap shot.

Excerpt: Court Transcript,

MR. BUNCH: But at any rate, we compromised in an effort to finalize this matter. We've been obstructed. The first - - Plaintiff's first lawyer basically threw up her hands. Plaintiff got a second lawyer, and here we are.

Ronald E. Bunch's comment was inexcusable, unwarranted, and insulting. On what did Bunch base his insult? Did Ronald E. Bunch parrot what he heard from his co-counsel, Regan G. Pearson, who had already labeled me a *difficult client*? I believe Bunch's uncalled-for statement was another blatant attempt to prejudice the Court. One that, I viewed, characterized Bunch's lack of professionalism. It was, however, hardly surprising after Bunch's conduct before the 443rd Ellis County District Court in the first hearing.

Throughout the proceedings following mediation, in two court filings, and two court hearings, Regan G. Pearson and Ronald E. Bunch's conduct, I believe, blatantly violated multiple sections of *The Texas Lawyer's Creed*, an *Order* by the *Supreme Court of Texas*.

II. Lawyer to Client: *6. I will treat adverse parties and witnesses with fairness and due consideration.*

II. Lawyer to Client: *7. I will advise my client that we will not pursue conduct which is intended primarily to harass or drain the financial resources of the opposing party.*

II. Lawyer to Client: *8. I will advise my clients that we will not pursue tactics which are intended primarily for delay.*

III. Lawyer to Lawyer: *4. I will attempt to prepare documents which correctly reflect the agreement of the parties. I will not include provisions which have not been agreed upon or omit provisions which are necessary to reflect the agreement of the parties.*

III. Lawyer to Lawyer: *7. I will not serve motions or pleadings in any manner that unfairly limits another party's opportunity to respond.*

IV. Lawyer and Judge: *6. I will not knowingly misrepresent, mischaracterize, misquote or miscite facts or authorities to gain an advantage.*

Excerpt: Court Transcript,

MR. PEARSON: The law is clear that reasonableness of attorney's fees is a question of law for the Court to decide. It's not for a jury. It's for the Court to decide, which the Court already did.

After Defendants and their attorneys attempted to take away my First Amendment Rights, they now wanted to take away my right to a jury trial. It is my belief that this is why they pulled their stunt with the settlement check my attorney received in April 2020. It was a way to block me from going to trial.

When the Court denied my Motion on March 20, 2020, it opened the door for me to have a trial. On April 4, 2020, my attorney asked for a trial date.

On October 14, 2020, Regan G. Pearson informed the Court I didn't have a right to a trial because the Court denied my motion. *It's not for a jury. It's for the Court to decide, which the Court already did.*

Excerpt: Court Transcript,

MR. PEARSON: We request that our summary judgment be granted so we can finally put this case to bed. We will send another $15,000 check, but we would just like that the $15,000 check that we send this time to be a full final resolution of the case.

The Court: All righty.

With an *All righty,* later the same day, the 443rd Ellis County District Court signed the order granting Pearson's request to *finally put this case to bed.*

All that changed between the first and second hearing was who asked the *Rule 11 and Settlement Agreement* be enforced. When I asked, the Court refused, taking over two months to issue the Court's ruling, denying my two motions, *Plaintiff's Motion to Strike and Plaintiff's Amended Motion for Summary Judgment.*

Months later, when Defendants asked in a second filing and hearing, the Court granted *Defendants' Motion for Summary Judgment.* The Court signed the order on the same day as the hearing.

Dare I say I was right in my concerns about receiving a fair and impartial hearing in the Ellis County Court system? What the 443rd Ellis County District Court did with an *"All righty"* stopped me from having a trial. I had two choices. One, I could submit to the Ellis County Court system that Porter bragged the club had so many connections to. Second, I could spend a lot more money to get out of Ellis County by filing with the Court of Appeals, Tenth District of Texas.

I chose to appeal, believing once I got out of Ellis County, I would finally get a fair and impartial hearing.

To Breach or Not to Breach

Chapter Nineteen

The next step in the judicial process was filing an appeal with the Court of Appeals, Tenth District of Texas. Since the Court of Appeals was located in McLennan County, I hoped to get a fair and unbiased hearing based on the facts.

The appeal process meant another new attorney, an appeals specialist. After studying my case, my appeal attorney was astounded it had reached this point. My appeal attorney had the same opinion as my attorney, who handled my case before the 443rd Ellis County District Court. It should never have happened.

Yet, here I was, filing an appeal. As the Plaintiff, I filed the first brief, *Appellants' Brief*. Defendants would respond with their *Appellees' Brief*. I had the final response with *Appellants' Reply Brief*.

Twice, my appeal attorney rebuked Defendants and opposing counsel for their *unsupported, alleged, irrelevant facts* dealing with my settled lawsuit rather than the breach of contract. The first rebuke was in *Appellants' Brief.*

Excerpt: *Appellants' Brief,*

Much of Defendants' "Background" Statement in their Response to *Dickason's Amended Motion for Summary Judgment is Irrelevant and* *Unsupported by any Evidence.* *Defendants allege a series of "facts" related to alleged occurrences at the gun club prior to the settlement of the case. These "facts" are unsupported by any summary judgment evidence at all, and are totally irrelevant to the summary judgment issues at bar. Instead, these unsupported "facts" are simply designed to make Dickason look dishonest and/or unreasonable.*

Then my attorney received Defendants' twenty-eight-page response, *Appellees' Brief.* Remember, appeals were the only type of litigation my new attorney handled. He told me it took a lot to surprise him, but *Appellees' Brief* did.

Appellees' Brief dealt with the same irrelevant, false, malicious rhetoric and false trivialization of my lawsuit that characterized Defendants' two court filings to the 443rd Ellis County District Court. This time, however, Defendants and their attorneys elected to embellish their false *facts* even further.

My appeal attorney again rebuked opposing counsel. In *Appellants' Reply Brief* to the Court of Appeals, my appeal attorney wrote:

As demonstrated by both Appellant's and Appellees' Briefs, this case relates entirely to the Rule 11 Settlement Agreement (the "Rule 11 Agreement") signed by the parties at a mediation on April 17, 2019. The issues relate to whether Appellees breached that Rule 11 Agreement and if so, whether Appellant was entitled to attorney's fees that she incurred as a result of such breach. Accordingly, Sections A and B of Appellees' Statement of Fact are completely irrelevant to this case.

The alleged "facts" contained in these sections falsely accuse Appellant's boyfriend, Shawn George, of numerous bad acts such as bullying people into changing shooting scores, starting an argument and attempting to intimidate the ECSC Board with an assault rifle. These alleged "facts" are completely unsupported by any evidence. In this regard, the citations to the record in Sections A and B refer only to claims made in Appellees' Motion for Summary Judgment that are themselves unsupported by affidavits or any other type of summary judgment evidence. Accordingly, presenting such accusations as "facts" is irresponsible and not called for in an appellate brief. Appellant strongly disputes these claims, which likely have been included merely to disparage Appellant and her boyfriend, Shawn George, and to wrongfully influence the Court. Accordingly, the "facts" contained in Sections A and B should be disregarded by the Court.

Defendant Dan Hunt repeated most of his false statements and accusations about Shawn from his two filings with the 443rd Ellis County District Court. However, Hunt changed two details.

Within Defendants' court filings with the 443rd Ellis County District Court, this was Dan Hunt's statement; *Hunt explained that George was likely merely making notations at his own direction.* It's not what Dan Hunt told the Court of Appeals.

Excerpt: *Appellees' Brief,*

Hunt explained that George was likely merely keeping his own score.

A statement that once again showed Dan Hunt's ignorance of the ATA rules governing a trap league. Competitors do not keep their own score. It was another false statement by Dan Hunt, in a long list of Hunt's false statements. Hunt knew what Shawn had written. Hunt, as shoot management, issued the order to do it. Hunt had the scoresheet. Danny Garth Hunt intentionally misled the Court of Appeals, Tenth District of Texas.

This vindictive Duncanville cop and incompetent, unqualified ECSC leagues manager Dan Hunt wasn't finished. Before the Court of Appeals, Hunt went even further with his deceitful misconduct.

Excerpt: *Appellees' Brief,*

At some point during this meeting, George retrieved an assault rifle he brought to the club previously and set it on a table as some sort of apparent intimidation tactic.

This was not what Defendant Dan Hunt told the 443rd Ellis County District Court in two filings, *Defendants' Response to Plaintiff's Amended Motion For Summary Judgment to Enforce Rule 11 Settlement Agreement* and *Defendants' Motion For Summary Judgment.* Hunt falsely stated, *At some point during this meeting, Shawn George retrieved an assault rifle he brought to the club previously and set it on the table as some sort of perceived intimidation tactic.*

In *Appellees' Brief* to the Court of Appeals, Duncanville narcotics detective and ECSC leagues manager Danny Garth Hunt embellished his lie, changing *perceived intimidation* to *apparent intimidation.*

Once again, I hold Defendants' attorneys, J. Richard Harmon, Regan G. Pearson, and Ronald E. Bunch accountable for Dan Hunt's malicious, vicious, false accusation. I've added Wade C. Crosnoe, a partner in the same law firm as Pearson and Harmon, who signed and submitted *Appellees' Brief*, to my list. Combined, these attorneys are just as guilty as Dan Hunt in perpetuating the vicious defamation of an individual, who was not a party to the lawsuit, and was never allowed to defend himself against Hunt's despicable accusation. All for one purpose, to further destroy Shawn's reputation and credibility and wrongfully influence the Court of Appeals. All under the guise of a contract dispute. Danny Garth Hunt, a Duncanville cop and ECSC leagues manager was still lying, and none of it was relevant to the judicial proceedings. Yet, Dan Hunt's damaging, defamatory, false accusation about assault rifle intimidation was now part of the court record.

As I pointed out in a previous chapter, Dan Hunt willfully and maliciously lied without repercussions. No one was on the witness stand to expose Hunt's lies. Why should a brief filed with the Court of Appeals be any different? Who would hold this vindictive Duncanville cop and ECSC leagues manager accountable for his false accusations and vicious defamation of an innocent third party, an individual not a party to the lawsuit? Was this why Dan Hunt never backed up his lies with a signed, notarized affidavit?

In *Appellees' Brief,* Dan Hunt changed *Perceived,* defined as assumed or guessed, to *Apparent,* defined as clearly visible or understood, obvious, actual, or manifested. For Dan Hunt's falsely alleged *apparent intimidation tactic* to have been clearly visible, Hunt had to be present. Hunt wasn't in the room. The ECSC July 2, 2018, board meeting minutes state, *Note: Shawn George brought in an AR-15 rifle and laid it on the conference room table. Dan Hunt arrived later.*

What Dan Hunt described to the Court of Appeals was impossible. Hunt wasn't in the room.

What should be noted as missing in the July 2, 2018, monthly board meeting minutes is **assault rifle, retrieved,** or **intimidation tactic.** You will not find **perceived,** or more especially Hunt's embellishment to the Court of Appeals, **apparent.** Nor are any of these words in Dan Hunt's whining pity email, *Immediate resignation* sent to nearly one hundred unsuspecting men, women, and children less than three hours after the July 2, 2018, board meeting ended.

Though I have already identified what really occurred on the evening of July 2, 2018, in the ECSC clubhouse, it bears repeating. Before the meeting began, Shawn asked the Board for permission to bring the target rifle into the conference room as evidence against Dan Hunt. Upon permission from President Beard and Poobah Porter, with no objections from any board member, Shawn left, then returned with the inert evidence he carefully laid on the Formica table. Again, this all occurred before the start of the meeting. Dan Hunt wasn't there. Hunt didn't enter the conference room until an hour or so later.

With his lie, Danny Garth Hunt, a Duncanville narcotics detective, admitted to the Court of Appeals that as a law enforcement officer, he sat in a room and witnessed an act of intimidation with an assault rifle toward six ECSC board members—and did nothing. What's wrong with this picture? The answer—Danny Garth Hunt lied. It never happened. Danny Garth Hunt, a Duncanville narcotics detective and ECSC leagues manager lied to the 443rd Ellis County District Court in two filings. Dan Hunt perpetuated, then embellished his egregious lie to the Court of Appeals, Tenth District of Texas. Remember, Hunt threatened Shawn, "Nobody calls me a liar and gets away with it."

Dan Hunt's conduct was appalling for a law enforcement officer. In my professional opinion, Hunt is the type of individual who should never be allowed to wear a badge and gun. I believe Dan Hunt's false statements, false accusations, and embellishments make his testimony against other individuals in other courts highly questionable. Had Hunt done this before? Are there innocent people in jail because of this despicable, vindictive Duncanville narcotics detective? In his whining pity email, *Immediate resignation*, Dan Hunt told nearly one hundred unsuspecting club members, guests, and even children he had been called a liar. Are Dan Hunt's own words the proof that he is a liar?

Dan Hunt wasn't the only one to extend his false statements to the Court of Appeals.

Excerpt: *Appellees' Brief,*

However, the Rule 11 Agreement also expressly contemplated that the parties would enter into a formal agreement.

The contract, *Rule 11 and Settlement Agreement* did not stipulate a *formal agreement.*

Excerpt: *Rule 11 and Settlement Agreement,*

It is contemplated that counsel for defendants shall deliver drafts of any further settlement documentation to the other parties by April 24, 2019. The parties agree to cooperate with each other in the drafting and execution of such additional documents.

Nothing in the contract, *Rule 11 and Settlement Agreement* stipulated *parties would enter into a formal agreement.* Plus, *contemplated* is not the same as required.

Next was Defendants' statement the ECSC was *not a corporation.* I couldn't believe they would repeat this to the Court of Appeals, Tenth District of Texas. Yet, they did.

Excerpt: *Appellees' Brief,*

Furthermore, Chapter 38 allows attorney's fees to be recovered only from an "individual" or "corporation." Plaintiff cannot recover attorney's fees from ECSC under Chapter 38 because the club is organized as a non-profit organization and is not a corporation.

In their arguments, Defendants' attorneys intentionally overlooked Defendant Dan Hunt. As an individual, Dan Hunt was equally liable for attorney fees. In *Appellees' Brief,* Defendants' attorneys lumped Dan Hunt in with the ECSC, thereafter using ECSC to reference both defendants. Was this an intentional attempt to mislead the Court of Appeals?

On December 28, 2020, my attorney filed *Plaintiff Anita Dickason's Supplement to Motion for New Trial* with the 443rd Ellis County District Court. My Motion included a *Certificate of Fact* from the Office of the Texas Secretary of State, stamped with the state seal, certifying that Desoto Gun Club is a domestic non-profit corporation.

Regan G. Pearson, J. Richard Harmon, and Ronald E. Bunch received a copy of my Motion. Yet, they continued to perpetuate the false statement about the legal status of the ECSC in their filing with the Court of Appeals. Once again, Ronald E. Bunch, attorney of record for ECSC, went along with the false claim his client was *not a corporation*. Ronald E. Bunch signed *Appellees' Brief*. Ronald E. Bunch knew the ECSC was a corporation. In February 2019, Ronald E. Bunch submitted and signed a court document stipulating that the correct legal name for the ECSC— *Desoto Gun Club, Inc. is the Defendant's complete corporation name.*

****

On February 1, 2023, the Court of Appeals issued its *Memorandum Opinion and Judgment.*

Excerpt: Court of Appeals Memorandum Opinion,

Further, because the Court finds there is error in the trial court's order granting Dan Hunt and Desoto Gun Club d/b/a Ellis County Sportsman's Club's Motion for Summary Judgment signed on October 14, 2020, it is the judgment of this Court that the trial court's order granting Dan Hunt and Desoto Gun Club d/b/a Ellis County Sportsman's Club's motion for summary judgment is reversed and this proceeding is remanded to the trial court for further proceedings.

There were several notable statements within the Court of Appeals *Memorandum Opinion.* The first dealt with the check. The Court wrote; *However, what is not in dispute is that Hunt and ECSC did not make the $15,000 payment by the May 2, 2019 deadline.*

As for the breach of contract, this was what the Court wrote; *Viewing the summary-judgment evidence in the light most favorable to the nonmovant, Dickason, we conclude that material fact issues exist regarding which party first committed the first material breach of the Rule 11 agreement. From the evidence outlined above, a jury reasonably could find that Hunt and ECSC—rather than Dickason—committed the first material breach of the Rule 11 agreement, thereby excusing Dickason from further performance.*

The Court of Appeals' ruling meant my case was headed back to trial. Once again, I was seriously concerned about whether I would receive a fair and impartial trial in Ellis County. However, another new wrinkle occurred. After the Court of Appeals reversed the 443rd Ellis County District Court ruling, my case was moved to the 40th Ellis County District Court.

It wasn't the only significant change. Some two months after the Appeal Court issued its *Memorandum Opinion*, on April 19, 2023, a document was filed with the 40th Ellis County District Court removing Regan G. Pearson and the "Big Dog," J. Richard Harmon, as counsel for Defendants. They were replaced by Heather H. Phelps and Jordan Harrison, both from the same downtown Dallas multi-state law firm hired by the 830-plus billion-dollar French insurance conglomerate.

After *Plaintiff's Motion for Summary Judgment* was filed on August 14, 2019, I hired a new attorney specializing in breach of contract lawsuits. On September 4, 2019, a notice of representation for my change in attorneys was filed with the 443rd Ellis County District Court. On the same day, my new attorney contacted Regan G. Pearson. I incurred about a three-week delay in hiring a new law firm.

Yet, a change within the same law firm hired by the 830-plus billion-dollar French insurance conglomerate resulted in a delay of several months, during which my attorney repeatedly attempted to set a trial date with Defendants' attorneys.

During the October 14, 2020, hearing before the 443rd Ellis County

District Court, opposing counsel Ronald E. Bunch accused me of obstruction.

MR. BUNCH: *We've been obstructed. The first - - Plaintiff's first lawyer basically threw up her hands. Plaintiff got a second lawyer, and here we are.*

I wonder if Ronald E. Bunch would have the same comment about his co-counsels, Regan G. Pearson and the "Big Dog," J. Richard Harmon. Did they "basically" throw up their hands since they are no longer on the case?

I would ask Ronald E. Bunch, who was really guilty of obstruction?

They Actually Did It Again!

Chapter Twenty

On July 31, 2023, a hearing was held before the 40th Ellis County District Court to establish a scheduling order for a trial.

What a difference from what I had encountered in the 443rd Ellis County District Court. The new judge had obviously studied the previous filings in the 443rd Ellis County District Court and the opinion rendered by the Court of Appeals, Tenth District of Texas. This was how the Court succinctly identified the issues.

Excerpt: Court Transcript,

THE COURT: *So to be clear, at a point in time on the underlying lawsuit in the 443rd District Court was a Rule 11 Agreement believed to be a global settlement agreement as to all issues and causes of action, correct?*

MY ATTORNEY: *Yes, Your Honor. So we filed an amendment. An amendment to our motion to add breach of contract for that Rule 11 Settlement Agreement to which was filed and everybody agreed.*

THE COURT: *And you filed a Motion for Summary Judgment on the part of plaintiff; is that correct?*

MY ATTORNEY: *Yes. For that issue.*

THE COURT: *Noted. And that was denied?*

MY ATTORNEY: *That was denied.*

THE COURT: *Okay. Then the defense turned around and filed a Motion for Summary Judgment.*

MY ATTORNEY: *Yes, Your Honor. And that was granted.*

THE COURT: Okay. What happened in the appellate court then?

MY ATTORNEY: And the appellate court - - the appellate court overruled and reversed and remanded the Defendant's Motion for Summary Judgment and they set that, the final issues for trial, to be tried in front of you, Your Honor.

THE COURT: I think it's Justice Brett Busby, when he was on either the Second or Fourteenth Court of Appeals, he wrote an opinion essentially saying that the breach of the Rule 11 Settlement Agreement is a brand-new lawsuit –

MY ATTORNEY: Yes.

THE COURT: He did everything but say you're entitled to another jury trial.

MY ATTORNEY: Yes.

THE COURT: So I think that's the implication. So we start from ground zero as though it's a brand-new lawsuit, right?

The Court had an interesting comment regarding attorney fees.

THE COURT: Well, these verdicts from a jury, they're never predictable, but the last one we had two weeks ago awarded nearly $200,000 in attorney fees to the plaintiff. A regular, ordinary couple that had to borrow money and pay money out of pocket, et cetera, et cetera. But they awarded every single dollar requested by plaintiff's attorney.

The Court also queried opposing counsel about Defendants' attorney fees. Jordan Harrison, Defendants' latest attorney of record, responded.

Excerpt: Court Transcript,

THE COURT: And so there's no basis for you to recover any attorney fees on your own, correct?

MR. HARRISON: That's correct, Your Honor.

Yet, less than three months later, Defendants and their attorneys did another *About-Face*. This time, it was to the 40th Ellis County District Court. On October 20, 2023, Defendants filed *Defendants' Second Amended Answer and Counter-Claim*. They asked for their attorney fees.

Excerpt: *Defendants' Second Amended Answer and Counter-Claim,*

Defendants seek reasonable and necessary attorney's fees under Chapters 37 and 38 of the Texas Civil Practice and Remedies Code. TEX. CIV. PRAC. & Rem. Code 38.001.

It wasn't the only issue in Defendants' new filing. Defendants Dan Hunt and Desoto Gun Club d/b/a Ellis County Sportsmans Club sued me for breach of contract.

Excerpt: *Defendants' Second Amended Answer and Counter-Claim,*

Pursuant to TEX. R. CIV. P.97, Defendants file this Counter-Claim against Plaintiff for Breach of Contract. Defendants incorporate the preceding paragraphs and assert that Plaintiff has breached the Rule 11 Agreement by failing to cooperate in the drafting and execution of the formal settlement and Release Agreement, failing to dismiss this lawsuit, and/or failing to accept the settlement check in the amount of $15,000 that Defendants tendered to her. In conjunction with this Counter-Claim, Defendants seek a declaration from the Court under Chapter 37 of the Texas Civil Practice and Remedies Code that the settlement agreement previous(ly) signed by the parties at mediation is binding on all parties, and that all of Plaintiff's claims asserted in this lawsuit are hereby settled in exchange for the previously agreed settlement of $15,000.

Basically, Defendants used the same arguments about my *failing to cooperate* that Defendants used in their previous motions filed with the 443rd Ellis County District Court and argued by Defendants' attorneys in two hearings. To further support their claim for breach of contract, Defendants' Motion included my refusal to accept their settlement check. What Defendants and their attorneys ignored was the ruling by the Court of Appeals, Tenth District of Texas. Did they even read it?

On October 14, 2020, the 443rd Ellis County District Court ruled in favor of *Defendants' Motion for Summary Judgment.*

On February 1, 2023, the Court of Appeals, Tenth District of Texas, issued their *Memorandum Opinion and Judgment,* reversing the October 14, 2020, ruling by the 443rd Ellis County District Court.

Excerpt: Court of Appeals Memorandum Judgment,

Further, because the Court finds there is error in the trial court's order granting Dan Hunt and Desoto Gun Club d/b/a Ellis County Sportsman's Club's motion for summary judgment signed on October 14, 2020, it is the judgment of this Court that the trial court's order granting Dan Hunt and Desoto Gun Club d/b/a Ellis County Sportsman's Club's motion for summary judgment is reversed and this proceeding is remanded to the trial court for further proceeding.

The Court of Appeals was most emphatic when it came to the check.

Excerpt: Court of Appeals Memorandum Opinion,

However, what is not in dispute is that Hunt and ECSC did not make the $15,000 payment by the May 2, 2019 deadline.

The referenced check in *Defendants' Second Amended Answer and Counter-Claim* was not issued until April 14, 2020. It included another provision not stipulated by the *Rule 11 and Settlement Agreement.*

Furthermore, this was what the Court of Appeals wrote regarding the first breach of the contract.

Excerpt: Court of Appeals Memorandum Opinion,

Pursuant to the Rule 11 agreement, Hunt and ECSC were required to pay Dickason a sum of $15,000 to settle Dickason's claims by May 2, 2019. Rather than pay the $15,000 by the May 2, 2019 deadline, Hunt and ECSC made revisions to the Rule 11 agreement to include a non-disparagement clause, a clause requiring Dickason to release her right to any balance on her ECSC "target card," and a requirement that George sign the agreement. Then on May 3, 2019, counsel for Dickason responded with revisions to the agreement. Dickason also refused to dismiss her lawsuit against Hunt and ECSC. And because the parties *disputed several terms of the Rule 11 agreement, Dickason insisted that pursuant to the terms of the Rule 11 agreement, the parties were required to participate in mediation to resolve the terms of the settlement agreement. Hunt and ECSC refused to mediate.*

Viewing the summary-judgment evidence in the light most favorable to the nonmovant, Dickason, we conclude that material fact issues exist regarding which party first committed the first material breach of the Rule 11 agreement. From the evidence outlined above, a jury reasonably could find that Hunt and ECSC—rather than Dickason—committed the first material breach of the Rule 11 agreement, thereby excusing Dickason from further performance.

Once Defendants breached the contract by failing to tender the check *on or before May 2, 2019,* anything I did or didn't do from that point forward was moot.

Unbelievably, Defendants and their attorneys, Heather H. Phelps and Ronald E. Bunch, did it again. They falsely asserted the Desoto Gun Club d/b/a Ellis County Sportsmans Club was **not a corporation.** Defendants again referenced their Bylaws.

Ronald E. Bunch signed *Defendants' Second Amended Answer and Counter-Claim* filed on October 20, 2023, with the 40th Ellis County District Court. A document that, once again, misrepresented the legal status of his client.

Excerpt: ***Defendants' Second Amended Answer and Counter-Claim,***

While denying that Plaintiff is entitled to any attorneys' fees from Defendants, Defendants affirmatively plead that Plaintiff is not entitled to attorney's fees from Defendant Desoto Gun Club d/b/a Ellis County Sportsman's Club under Chapter 38 of the Texas Civil Practice and Remedies Code because the club is organized as a non-profit organization and is not a corporation. See Club Bylaws attached as Exhibit "C"; see also Fleming & Assoc., L.L.P. v. Barton, 425 S.W.3d 560,

576 (Tex. App.—Houston [14th Dist.] 2014. pet. denied) (holding that Chapter 38 does not authorize recovery of attorney's fees against a limited liability partnership because it is not a corporation); 8305 Broadway, Inc. v. J & J Martindale Ventures, L.L.C., 04-16-00447-CV, 201, WL 279 1322, *5 (Tex. App.—San Antonio, June 28, 2017, no pet. h.) (holding that Chapter 38 does not apply to a limited liability company because it is not a corporation).

IV. Lawyer and Judge: 6. *I will not knowingly misrepresent, mischaracterize, misquote or miscite facts or authorities to gain an advantage.*

Did opposing counsel plan to stand before an Ellis County jury and deny what the Bylaws actually stated? *The club shall be a corporate body under the laws of the state of Texas.*

In two previous filings before the 443rd Ellis County District Court, Defendants cited the same cases for an LLC or LLP to justify their arguments. Did opposing counsel now plan to stand before an Ellis County jury in the 40th District Court and convince them the ECSC was a limited liability partnership (LLP) or a limited liability company (LLC)?

On February 1, 2019, Ronald E. Bunch signed and submitted *Defendant Desoto Gun Club D/B/A Ellis County Sportsmans Club's Responses To Plaintiff's Request For Disclosure,* stipulating *Desoto Gun Club, Inc. is the Defendant's complete corporate name.* Did opposing counsel plan to ignore this document again?

Did opposing counsel plan to ignore the *Certificate of Fact* filed with the 443rd Ellis County District Court on December 28, 2020? This document, carrying the Texas state seal and signed by the Secretary of State, stipulated the Desoto Gun Club is a not-for-profit corporation.

Did opposing counsel actually plan to stand before an Ellis County jury and mislead them into believing the ECSC is *not a corporation*, and the Texas Secretary of State didn't know who is and isn't a corporation in the State of Texas? If Defendants' attorneys could blow off the Court of

Appeals, Tenth District of Texas, why not do the same to the Texas Secretary of State?

Could it be any clearer? Yet repeatedly, Defendants and their attorneys, in two filings and a hearing before the 443rd Ellis County District Court, *Appellees' Brief* filed before the Court of Appeals, Tenth District of Texas, and now in their filing to the 40th Ellis County District Court, asserted the ECSC is *not a corporation*. Not only did Defendants and their attorneys mislead, dare I say outright lie to three Courts, but they also intentionally ignored Defendant Dan Hunt, an individual who was equally responsible for my attorney fees.

In response to *Defendants' Second Amended Answer and Counter-Claim*, on October 27, 2023, my attorney filed:

Plaintiff Anita Dickason's Trial Witness List

This is a list of individuals my attorney planned to put on the witness stand under oath before an Ellis County jury. The list included Dan Hunt and Defendants' attorneys, Ronald E. Bunch, J. Richard Harmon, Regan G. Pearson, Heather H. Phelps, and Jordan Harrison.

Plaintiff Anita Dickason's Trial Exhibit List

A list of forty-five (45) documents my attorney planned to submit as evidence during the trial. The list included Defendants' court filings, court transcripts, attorney-to-attorney emails, ECSC board meeting minutes, Defendants' Interrogatories, State of Texas corporation report signed by Treasurer Rusty Porter, Court of Appeals Memorandum of Opinion, Defendant ECSC Responses to Plaintiff's Request for Disclosure, ECSC insurance documents, ECSC emails, Dan Hunt's emails, including his July 2, 2018, *Immediate resignation,* and more. Danny Garth Hunt's whining pity email was coming home to roost. It should be noted that the *Trial Exhibit List* included nearly all the referenced or quoted documents within this book.

Item #32 on the list was the *Certificate of Fact* with the Seal of Texas, signed by the Texas Secretary of State, stipulating the Desoto

Gun Club was a not-for-profit corporation.

The 40th Ellis County District Court wasn't finished with the Court's summation. At the conclusion of the hearing, the Court stated:

Excerpt: Court Transcript,

THE COURT: And the only other thing I would say is if there is a breath of fresh air is to say that I've had my fair share of dealings with the Tenth Court of Appeals, the Supreme Court over the years, so I'm just glad that I was not a party to this one. We'll see you. We're in recess.

The *party* wasn't over. It would seem opposing counsel planned to continue to pound the table as they had done throughout nearly five years of unnecessary, unwarranted litigation.

"If you have the facts on your side, pound the facts; if you have the law on your side, pound the law; if you have neither the facts nor the law, pound the table."

Sleight Of Hand

Chapter Twenty-one

What was apparent to me throughout the events leading up to my lawsuit and during the judicial process was Dan Hunt, a vindictive Duncanville narcotics detective and ECSC leagues manager, didn't hesitate to embellish his false accusations or outright lie. Not once did Dan Hunt back up his false accusations with evidence or signed, notarized affidavits.

In two court hearings, Regan G. Pearson made a production of *how the parties got to this point.*

Excerpt: January 16, 2020, Court Transcript,

MR. PEARSON: Your Honor, I would like to start with some background because I think it's particularly important in this case that the parties understand now—or that the Court understand how the parties got to this point.

Excerpt: October 14, 2020, Court Transcript,

MR. PEARSON: I would like to start with some background because I think it's important that the Court understand how the parties got to this point.

Regan G. Pearson regurgitated Dan Hunt's false statements and false accusations to the 443rd Ellis County District Court, not once but twice. In my opinion, to wrongfully influence the Court in hearings where Hunt's falsely alleged details were irrelevant. Regan G. Pearson's renditions of *how the parties got to this point* were based on Dan Hunt's latest version of events within the *Background* of Defendants' filings. It was a version not supported by evidence or signed, notarized affidavits from Defendant Dan Hunt or witnesses.

How the parties got to this point wasn't because of two points, as Regan G. Pearson claimed. It was due to Regan G. Pearson's client, Dan Hunt, a Duncanville, Texas, self-aggrandizing, lying cop and incompetent, unqualified ECSC leagues manager's libelous, whining pity email, *Immediate resignation.* An email Hunt sent to nearly one hundred unsuspecting men, women, and children at thirty-four minutes preceding midnight on July 2, 2018.

Defendants' counsel had Dan Hunt's self-serving document, his whining pity email. On February 1, 2019, Ronald E. Bunch signed and submitted *Defendant Desoto Gun Club d/b/a Ellis County Sportsmans Club's Responses to Plaintiff's Request for Disclosure.* The respondent was Treasurer Rusty Porter. The "Big Dog," J. Richard Harmon, received a copy of this document. A copy of Dan Hunt's July 2, 2018, *Immediate resignation* email was included. Defendants' counsel couldn't deny they didn't know about Hunt's libelous email.

Yet, in the *Background* of two Defendants' filings, statements of attorney Regan G. Pearson in two court hearings before the 443rd Ellis County District Court, then Defendants' *Appellees' Brief* to the Court of Appeals, Tenth District of Texas, Dan Hunt's malicious *Immediate resignation* email was never mentioned. Nor was there any mention of the dozen or so false accusations Hunt spread to nearly one hundred unsuspecting club members, guests, and even children. Nor was Hunt's whining pity email attached as an exhibit to Defendants' filings.

What I found truly curious was Dan Hunt's omission in his court filings about Shawn calling him a liar. During the July 2, 2018, ECSC board meeting, Dan Hunt lunged from his chair, charging toward the table as he threatened Shawn. "Nobody calls me a liar and gets away with it."

Dan Hunt was so incensed that at 11:26 p.m. that same night, he launched his cowardly attack in the form of his vicious, libelous

Immediate resignation email, including his *grievance* at being called a liar, to nearly one hundred club members, guests, and children. Hunt wrote; *I was directly accused by Shawn George of being a liar.* Yet, not once did Dan Hunt include his *grievance* that Shawn called him a liar in his future court filings. Was this omitted because Danny Garth Hunt truly was a liar?

During Regan G. Pearson's telling of Dan Hunt's latest rendition of the scoring dispute in two hearings, Pearson emphasized two emails, June 29th and July 1, 2018, Dan Hunt sent to league competitors. Yet, Pearson did not mention Hunt's third email, July 2, 2018, that Dan Hunt sent to nearly one hundred club members, guests, and even children. Pearson never brought forth any of Dan Hunt's accusations contained within Hunt's whining pity email, *Immediate resignation.*

Since Dan Hunt's July 2, 2018, whining pity email, *Immediate resignation* was the result of an ECSC board meeting earlier that evening, I believe a reasonable, prudent individual would expect Regan G. Pearson's rendition about *how the parties got to this point* would include Dan Hunt's whining, pity email and his lengthy list of falsely alleged grievances.

It should be noted Hunt's whining pity email didn't include the false accusation of assault rifle intimidation, though Dan Hunt certainly added his vicious lie to his later court filings. It was a vicious defamation of an innocent individual who wasn't a party to the lawsuit or even connected to the reason I was in Court. It was an act condoned by Dan Hunt's learned lawyers. There was no evidence or a signed, notarized affidavit from Dan Hunt attesting to the truthfulness of his malicious, libelous accusation. Instead, Regan G. Pearson, the "Big Dog," J. Richard Harmon, and Wade C. Crosnoe used Dan Hunt's lie to unduly influence the court. Why? In my opinion, it was to gain an advantage.

I believe Defendants' attorneys, like Hollywood directors, wanted to get the "gun on camera" and clearly make it visible within their filings to the Courts. How could anyone, let alone Defendants' supposedly learned lawyers, see Hunt's vicious intimidation lie as relevant in a *Rule 11 and Settlement Agreement* contract dispute? There could only be one answer—to prejudice the Court.

Defendants' attorneys spread Hunt's false accusation within two court filings to the 443rd Ellis County District Court and within their *Appellees' Brief* to the Court of Appeals, Tenth District of Texas. Hunt's attorneys never produced any evidence or a signed, notarized affidavit from their client or witness.

One other note of importance. Why and how did the word *perceived,* which is to assume or guess, get changed to *apparent,* which is clearly visible or understood, obvious, actual or manifested within *Appellees' Brief* to the Court of Appeals, Tenth District of Texas?

Did opposing counsel Wade C. Crosnoe get a phone call, text or email from Danny Garth Hunt telling him to change *perceived* to *apparent?* Did Dan Hunt have an epiphany before his filing to the Court of Appeals, causing him to change *perceived* assault rifle intimidation to *apparent* assault rifle intimidation? Or did attorney Wade C. Crosnoe take it upon himself to up the ante on his own? It is a question that begs to be answered. Whoever did it, lied. Lied to wrongly influence the Court of Appeals, Tenth District of Texas, and once again libel an innocent victim of a vindictive cop from Duncanville, Texas, ECSC leagues manager Dan Hunt. The assault rifle intimidation was an egregious lie. I believe it defines this Duncanville cop as a bald-faced liar.

Since Dan Hunt and his attorneys didn't hesitate to include all the false rhetoric about assault rifle intimidation, why wasn't Dan Hunt's whining pity email, sent out some three hours following the July 2, 2018, board meeting, not included in Defendant Dan Hunt's *Background* or Regan G. Pearson's statements to the Court? Defendants' attorneys didn't hesitate to condone Dan Hunt's vicious lie about assault rifle intimidation in Defendants' motions, blackening the name of an innocent third party. Why didn't Dan Hunt's attorneys use all those libelous accusations in Hunt's whining pity email to add to their defamation? It was another opportunity to wrongfully influence the Court.

It was as if Dan Hunt's whining pity email never existed. All those false, vicious, libelous statements Dan Hunt declared to nearly one hundred club members, guests, and even children were just to be ignored, including Hunt's grievance that Shawn called him a liar.

Perhaps Hunt's late-night, false accusations while claiming mental whatever, following *intense and severe exposures at work,* had become a liability. Was it ignored because Dan Hunt's email, *Immediate resignation* would define Hunt's character as a vindictive, deceitful individual?

Considering it was Dan Hunt's libelous, whining pity email that exposed both Hunt and the ECSC to a lawsuit, its significant omission in *how the parties got to this point* certainly raised a valid question. Why was it missing?

In the event Danny Garth Hunt has forgotten or misplaced what he wrote, here again is Dan Hunt's near midnight, malicious, libelous, whining pity email sent less than three hours following Dan Hunt making a fool of himself before the Ellis County Sportsmans Club Board of Directors on July 2, 2018.

From: Ellis County Sportsmans Club Leagues <ecscleagues@gmail.com>
Sent: Monday, July 2, 2018, 11:26:07 PM CDT
Subject: Immediate resignation

On 7/2/18 I responded to a short notice request to speak before the ECSC board regarding grievances brought forth by Shawn George and Anita Dickason as a result of alleged conduct during the 2018 Spring trap league. These grievances stemmed from my volunteer service as the manager of the skeet and trap leagues at ECSC. During this board meeting I was directly accused by Shawn George of being a "liar" and to endangering STCP, 4H, and club shooters. The dispute was directed and intended solely as a character assault. In addition, Shawn George repeatedly invoked the name of my son as an involved party. The basis of these accusations are wholly and completely unfounded. However, I have no reason that I can determine, that would lead me to withstand such ridiculous abuse at the hands of such individuals.

I have attempted to instill a high level of quality enjoyment with accountability for all of those participating in the leagues that I have directed. That has been my main focus and direction while performing this volunteer function. I can no longer justify continued volunteer service, to my family or myself, while enduring ridicule, slanderous allegations, and outright misconduct allegations through no fault of my own.

I have participated in the last few leagues simply to fill teams or to assist other shooters who were new to the sport or who needed guidance. This has been met with biased attacks on my own credibility and has placed my family in a position of discomfort.

This sport allowed me an opportunity to relax and to enjoy good company after intense and severe exposures at work. Since that is no longer the case, I feel no need to continue with the leagues. I hereby resign any responsibilities or commitments related to the ECSC leagues that I have previously committed to. This includes any past, present, or future events. I cannot justify participation in these events to the detriment of my well being or the well being of my family. Any monies or data possessed by me will be transferred to the board as soon as possible. I apologize for any discomfort or inconvenience.

Having said that, any and all false allegations or slanderous events will be met with legal action.

Thank you and shoot well,

Dan Hunt

Porter's Hypocrisy

Chapter Twenty-two

Hypocrisy
The practice of claiming to have moral standards or beliefs to which one's own behavior does not conform.

On December 20, 2018, ECSC Treasurer and Grand Poobah, His Excellency Russell Alvin (Rusty) Porter, Jr., assault-style rifle builder of Ovilla, Texas, filed charges against me with his ECSC Board of Directors. The purpose of Porter's formal complaint was to terminate my membership. In his formal complaint, His Excellency wrote; *In my opinion a member suing the club, costing the club money and taking action detrimental to the club's mission of fostering good fellowship among its members and guests constitutes grounds for cancellation of the membership.*

The Grand Poobah, Rusty Porter's concept of *Fostering Good Fellowship* was to condone the inappropriate misbehavior with guns within the membership, the malicious misconduct of leagues manager Dan Hunt, and the unprincipled conduct of the ECSC leadership that resulted in *taking action detrimental to the club's mission of fostering good fellowship.* Porter and his cronies had one set of rules for themselves—another set of rules for everybody else.

I have often wondered if Porter fully understood the hypocrisy of his concept of *Fostering Good Fellowship.* Dan Hunt and the ECSC leadership were the club members responsible for the lawsuit. It happened because of Dan Hunt's false accusations, the unprincipled conduct of the ECSC Board of Directors, and the Board's willful disregard for their fiduciary responsibility, and Texas laws. I did everything I could to resolve the issues without resorting to litigation. Porter and his cronies stonewalled me.

Porter's concept of *Fostering Good Fellowship* was to destroy the reputations and credibility of two rightfully concerned, innocent individuals who did nothing wrong. They wanted to silence us. Stop us from talking about gun safety infractions and mixing guns, alcohol, and children at the Ellis County Sportsmans Club.

Porter's concept of *Fostering Good Fellowship* ignored the inherent danger to club members, family members, guests, and even children from the lack of sound gun safety procedures, misconduct with firearms by members, guests, their leagues manager Dan Hunt, along with the lack of qualified, competent management of the trap leagues.

Porter's concept of *Fostering Good Fellowship* ignored the actions of leagues manager Dan Hunt. Hunt kicked another competitor out of an earlier trap league because of complaints from the man's fellow team member, ECSC instigator Sherrie Lewis.

Shoot management Dan Hunt badmouthed his expelled league competitor and bragged about getting rid of him. There was no reason for Hunt's uncalled-for behavior. Hunt just liked to brag.

Porter's concept of *Fostering Good Fellowship* allowed their misbehaving, unqualified leagues manager, a Duncanville cop, to aggressively charge toward Shawn and verbally threaten Shawn during a board meeting.

Porter's concept of *Fostering Good Fellowship* allowed Director Jerry Jay Gage, to abuse me with a lengthy, wildly gesticulating tirade. An action no one on the Board attempted to stop.

Porter's concept of *Fostering Good Fellowship* condoned their leagues manager, Dan Hunt's use of the ECSC email address and members list to send a malicious, vindictive, whining pity email,

Immediate resignation, to nearly one hundred unsuspecting club members, guests, and even children at thirty-four minutes before midnight. An email that wasn't in the club's best interest, as defined by the ECSC *2010 Rules* **Polices** & *Operating Guidelines.* An email detrimental to the club's mission of fostering good fellowship among its members and guests.

Porter's concept of *Fostering Good Fellowship* condoned the rancor a vindictive Duncanville cop and leagues manager Dan Hunt maliciously spread to nearly one hundred club members, guests, and even children while violating a confidentiality agreement some three hours earlier. Shawn and I expected the Board to be as outraged over such an egregious, unwarranted, malicious attack as we were. After all, Dan Hunt acted in his official capacity as ECSC leagues manager when he used the club's email address and ECSC competitor list to spread his lies about fellow club members. Hunt's use of the club's email address gave his cowardly, libelous attack credibility.

What action would the Duncanville Police Department have taken if narcotics detective Danny Garth Hunt had done the same, using an official email address for the Duncanville Police Department? I don't believe they would have ignored Hunt's questionable behavior. Porter and his cronies pacified Hunt, condoning his deceitful conduct and misbehavior with firearms. What can you expect? It's Grand Poobah Porter's Ellis County Sportsmans Club.

Porter's concept of *Fostering Good Fellowship* condoned Dan Hunt's false accusations of cheating as recorded in the ECSC July 2, 2018, board meeting minutes. This was later reported to me during the recorded phone call from Vice President DVM Chris Rose. Dan Hunt's malicious, whining pity email, *Immediate resignation,* exposed the ECSC to a lawsuit. Yet Porter and his cronies condoned Hunt's actions.

Porter's concept of *Fostering Good Fellowship* was a clandestine ECSC kangaroo court. I was denied knowledge of the meeting and false accusations. I was denied an opportunity to defend myself against their bogus charge. I was charged, tried, convicted, and sentenced in secret. They wrongly suspended my paid membership rights to participate in club-sponsored events.

Porter's concept of *Fostering Good Fellowship* was to ignore a vote of the ECSC Board of Directors by adding stipulations to my wrongful suspension.

Porter's concept of *Fostering Good Fellowship* was to take my money, libel me, then stonewall me.

Porter's concept of *Fostering Good Fellowship* was to refuse to provide club documents in response to a legal request from my attorney. Documents that, as a paying member, I had a right to obtain, according to Texas law.

Porter's concept of *Fostering Good Fellowship* was to ignore a vote of the Board to refund the $48 balance on my shooting debit card. They lied to me and intentionally stole my money.

Porter's concept of *Fostering Good Fellowship* was to renege on a signed contract, *Rule 11 and Settlement Agreement* mediated and signed by Waxahachie banker, ECSC President Mike Lee. The ECSC didn't like the contract's provisions, so they wrote a new one. It contained another gag order. It was okay for Dan Hunt and the ECSC Board to destroy my reputation, but god forbid if I spoke out in my defense. The Ellis County Sportsmans Club, a Texas gun club, was after my First Amendment Rights.

Porter's concept of *Fostering Good Fellowship* condoned the malicious, false accusation spread by instigator Sherrie Lewis. Sherrie Lewis spread a vicious, false accusation that Shawn slammed an assault rifle onto a Formica tabletop to intimidate the Board.

In examining the totality of events, I found a common thread, instigator Sherrie Lewis, especially when people got kicked out of the leagues. After receiving complaints from Sherrie Lewis, Dan Hunt bragged about throwing another competitor out of the leagues.

Sherrie Lewis was one of the six individuals identified by Dan Hunt and Rusty Porter about who complained the night I filed my valid ATA protest.

Porter's concept of *Fostering Good Fellowship* condoned Dan Hunt's false accusation about assault rifle intimidation within Defendants' court filings before the 443rd Ellis County District Court and Court of Appeals, Tenth District of Texas. Porter knew Hunt's accusation in Defendants' filings was false. Before the meeting, Porter himself gave Shawn permission to bring the target rifle into the conference room as evidence against Hunt. Rusty Porter knew it wasn't an assault rifle.

Porter's concept of *Fostering Good Fellowship* condoned Director Sherrie Lewis and Dan Hunt's assault rifle intimidation lie for one reason, to destroy Shawn's reputation and credibility and wrongfully cast doubt about his behavior. Duncanville narcotics detective, and ECSC leagues manager Dan Hunt made good his threat to Shawn during the board meeting on July 2, 2018. "Nobody calls me a liar and gets away with it." Hunt's threat drew no reaction from the 2018 ECSC Board of Directors. Instead, Hunt's cronies condoned his actions. Evidently, in Porter's skewed sense of right and wrong, it was okay for his leagues manager, Dan Hunt, to threaten a senior citizen.

Porter's concept of *Fostering Good Fellowship* condoned the arrogant actions of an ECSC Board rife with individuals having attitude problems. Shortly after I joined, we were invited to a weekly round of trap with a group of retirees. Being the new guy, Shawn was conversing with a couple of the more experienced trap shooters, simply asking questions about trap shooting. Director Don Henslee, in a belligerent tone, said to Shawn, "Don't you ever shut the fuck up?" As new members, this was our introduction to Director Don Henslee's belligerent attitude and never-ending foul language.

Shawn was putting in a lot of hours working on the club's property. Upon arriving home one day, Shawn told me about an incident with

Director Don Henslee. Shawn and Porter were standing at the doorway to the mower shed when Director Don Henslee drove up with his window down. Henslee immediately went into a lengthy, foul-mouthed tirade about something he was mad about at the club. After Director Don Henslee finally left, Porter volunteered Henslee had behaved that way in front of his wife, Judy Porter, and he didn't like it. Porter then expressed Henslee was the club potty-mouth and to pay no attention to him. According to Porter, the reason he didn't say anything to Henslee about his foul language was because he, Porter, needed Henslee around to keep the machines in running order. Porter was afraid to say anything to ECSC Director Don Henslee, fearing he'd get mad and refuse to repair the machines.

I found Henslee's continuous foul language offensive and objectionable, especially considering the number of children and women on ECSC property.

There was another incident during that first trap league in which I competed. Shawn was only there to observe and had taken pictures of numerous competitors. I wanted to send the photos to the club for use on their website. I had already obtained permission to take pictures from, at the time, ECSC league manager and President Don Williams.

Shawn had asked where the better shooters were that evening. He was told they were on field zero. To field zero, he headed. Upon arriving, the relays were changing. Shawn observed a competitor, unknown to him at the time, walking toward the firing line. Shawn was standing near the west end of the wood fence that separated field zero and field one. Shawn raised his small camera with the intent of taking a picture of the competitor's trap gun. Before Shawn had a chance to take a picture, this competitor noticed Shawn. The irate competitor yelled at Shawn to put his camera down. He yelled that Shawn was breaking his concentration. The match hadn't started, and this irate competitor wasn't even on the firing line. Shawn, new to the club, not wanting to cause any trouble, returned to the trap field where I was competing.

Shawn later told me in all his decades as a competitor, then managing live fire shooting events, both law enforcement and civilian, he had never encountered a competitor needing to concentrate to find the firing line. This was Shawn's introduction to *Fostering Good Fellowship* in the trap league by a belligerent ECSC trap competitor. Shawn later learned the irate competitor was ATA registered trap shooter David C. McDaniel.

In 2018, McDaniel was elected to the ECSC Board of Directors. McDaniel was named by Porter and Hunt as a competitor who complained after Dan Hunt changed my scores.

On the evening of June 28, 2018, Director David McDaniel complained about something he had no first-hand knowledge of. Director David McDaniel had no first-hand knowledge of my official ATA protest. McDaniel wasn't present on our trap field. McDaniel didn't witness the intentional misbehavior of Larry Degal, Barbara Parks, and Susie Thompson. From my observations of Director David C. McDaniel over the years, I can assure you he would have been much less tolerant of Degal's misbehavior than Shawn.

Porter's concept of *Fostering Good Fellowship* by a Director would extend into the July 12, 2018, clandestine *Board Meeting-Emergency Meeting,* kangaroo court.

Director David McDaniel wasn't present at the monthly board meeting on July 2, 2018, to hear Dan Hunt's false accusation and threat toward Shawn. Nor did Director David McDaniel witness Director Jerry Jay Gage's gesticulating, lengthy verbal assault on me. Director David McDaniel was, however, present at the July 12, 2018, clandestine kangaroo court and voted to suspend my paid membership rights and throw me and Shawn out of the league.

On July 12, 2018, David McDaniel had no first-hand knowledge when he made a motion and then voted to suspend me from club sponsored events. Director David McDaniel either relied on Dan Hunt and other board members' false statements or was still annoyed because his team came in second. Perhaps it was both.

Think about that. David McDaniel became irritated at Shawn, the new guy at the time, for simply standing to the side of the trap field attempting to take a photo for the club website. An action that didn't disrupt a match. A match that hadn't even started. Yet, Director David McDaniel, a registered ATA trap shooter, condoned the blatant violations of ATA rules and procedures by the misbehaving scorekeeper in the match I protested. Misbehavior that indeed disrupted a match. David McDaniel, out of sheer ignorance of the ATA rules and procedures or with malicious intent, went along with so-called ECSC rules expert, Porter's club potty-mouth, Director Don R. Henslee and his seriously skewed, so-called expert opinion of ATA rules. McDaniel found no problem with the laughing, belligerent, unsafe and out-of-position misbehavior of Larry Degal, Barbara Parks, and Susie Thompson.

Porter's concept of *Fostering Good Fellowship* ignored the *club's rules, policies, and bylaws*. ATA rules that governed the trap leagues, as stipulated by the July 12, 2018, board meeting minutes were never enforced. As shoot management and leagues manager, Dan Hunt was never held accountable or responsible for enforcing the *club's rules, policies, and bylaws*. The intentional violations of the ATA rules by league competitors were never corrected. The dangerous misbehavior of competitors with firearms during the trap leagues was never addressed, including the continuous, intentional misconduct by shoot management Dan Hunt.

It's difficult to judge who *taking action detrimental to the club's mission of fostering good fellowship among its members and guests* is more worthy. Let's take a look at the cast of characters I had to draw upon.

Danny Garth Hunt was at the center of the controversy and throughout the judicial proceedings. Hunt was a threatening, highly vindictive Duncanville narcotics detective and unqualified, misbehaving ECSC leagues manager. In his whining pity email to nearly one hundred club members, guests, and children, Dan Hunt, acting in his official capacity as leagues manager, falsely accused Shawn and me of abusing him and causing harm to his family.

In Dan Hunt's own words, he was suffering from mental whatever *after intense and severe exposures at work.* This was the individual who, on the late evening of July 2, 2018, most likely placed his family in a *position of discomfort.* A Duncanville cop and ECSC leagues manager hid behind his innocent family, his work, his near midnight defamatory email, and the judicial system to carry out a systematic, malicious, defamatory attack on me and Shawn for one purpose, "Nobody calls me a liar and gets away with it." Dan Hunt, an individual who, based on his own words and malicious behavior, I came to believe was unstable and unfit to carry a badge and gun.

Or is it the former council member and past mayor of Cedar Hill, Texas? That self-proclaimed "straight-up" kind of guy, ECSC Vice President DVM Christopher Lyons Rose, who presided over a clandestine *Board Meeting-Emergency Meeting,* kangaroo court. A meeting in which I was falsely accused, wrongly tried, wrongly convicted, and wrongly sentenced. It was all done behind my back. Later, when challenged, Rose cowardly asserted in his recorded phone call, "No. I really don't want to get in the middle of it." What an outstanding Cedar Hill former council member and past mayor. Yet, don't forget, Cedar Hill DVM Chris Rose is a straight-up kind of guy. Just ask him.

I can't overlook the belligerent woman berating, wildly gesticulating ECSC Director Jerry Jay Gage. An individual who declared their misbehaving, incompetent leagues manager was the deity. Jerry Jay Gage who stated of Danny Garth Hunt, "This man is God. What he says is the law." Jerry Jay Gage then ranted, saying I had no right to protest. All because Jerry Jay Gage had absolutely no idea what the ATA rules and procedures actually state.

A.L. Dickason

Or should it be Director Don Henslee? The club potty mouth as described by his fellow board member Poobah Porter. Don Henslee, their so-called ATA rules expert, who simply chose to ignore sections of the ATA rules and procedures that didn't agree with his so-called expert clarification. In the future, ECSC Director Don Henslee might find it more helpful if he were to take his own advice as he gave to a new member. To quote ECSC Director Don Henslee, "Shut the fuck up."

Then there is ECSC instigator Sherrie Lewis, Dallas Safari Club Life Member and purported Diva Wow firearms instructor, who was so alarmed by a small clinking plastic container. The ECSC instigator who intentionally and viciously made up the false accusation about assault rifle intimidation. A lie Dan Hunt used in his malicious attack on Shawn in two court filings and a filing to the Court of Appeals, Tenth District of Texas.

Let's not overlook local Waxahachie banker, ECSC President Mike Lee, who reneged on his promise to refund the balance on my debit card, $48, then proceeded to renege on the *Rule 11 and Settlement Agreement* he mediated and willingly signed. The person I believe fits that classic line from a Bret Maverick episode, "If you can't trust your banker, who can you trust?" In my opinion, ECSC President Mike Lee's integrity was worth a measly 48 bucks. The $48 ECSC President Mike Lee and his Board of Directors intentionally stole from me.

And last, but by no means least, Mr. Fostering Good Fellowship himself, Treasurer Russell Alvin (Rusty) Porter, Jr., the ECSC self-styled, *alleged* registered agent and assault-style rifle builder of Ovilla, Texas. An individual to whom Texas laws, or a vote of his own Board of Directors had no meaning.

Grand Poobah Porter decided he didn't have to abide by the Board's vote and added stipulations, including a gag order to my suspension. From what I ascertained from club documents, it's my belief Porter was the individual responsible for altering the minutes of two critical board meetings.

As a paying member of the ECSC, what I endured due to Porter and his cronies *Fostering Good Fellowship* was appalling. I tried to rectify the gun safety issues, and the use of alcohol, I believe, represented a danger to all club members and guests. Consider what could happen if a club member, guest, or child was injured or killed due to negligent, incompetent, and unqualified individuals like Dan Hunt, who didn't hesitate to lie, or ECSC leadership willing to go to any lengths to hide their culpability. It's what they did to me, with their false accusations, deceit, coverups, violations of Texas law, misrepresentation of ATA rules and procedures, and a clandestine kangaroo court. All because I tried to address their mixing guns, alcohol, and children. Had Hunt, Porter, Rose, and their arrogant cronies done this to others in secret? After the July 2nd meeting, President Beard told me, "Don't worry about it. We deal with this all the time."

Let's not forget my thought-to-be friend Robert D. Fournerat of Irving, Texas. I find that with friends like Fournerat, who needs enemies?

What Emergency?

Chapter Twenty-three

The 2018 Ellis County Sportsmans Club Board of Directors titled the minutes of their clandestine kangaroo court, *Board Meeting-Emergency Meeting.* I titled my book—*What Emergency?*

It's my belief the *Emergency* at the Ellis County Sportsmans Club on July 12, 2018, was to bury the truth about the dangers of mixing guns, alcohol, and children, along with repetitive firearms safety infractions Shawn and I attempted to address. I believe the purpose behind their *Board Meeting-Emergency Meeting* was to silence me. To keep me from speaking out about the liabilities to the club as a whole, along with its members, and guests from the unsafe handling of firearms and alcohol consumption.

From my personal experiences and professional training, I believe mixing guns, alcohol, and children at a shooting facility is unwarranted, foolhardy, downright dangerous, and negligent. I believe these are legitimate concerns and topics of public interest. Every competitor or parent of a child participating in events at a gun club allowing the use of alcohol, gun safety infractions, and unqualified shoot management has a right to voice their concerns and, in my opinion, a moral obligation. What type of message did the gun safety infractions and alcohol consumption send to the inordinate number of youths using the facilities?

How the 2018 ECSC leadership could ignore the dangerous liabilities, then punish a competent, experienced, knowledgeable member for attempting to raise their awareness was beyond my comprehension.

Once I informed the Board I would file a formal complaint at the next meeting, the Secret 7 rushed to hold their *Board Meeting-Emergency Meeting.* During their clandestine gathering, they wrongly found me guilty of cheating, according to none other than the "straight-up" guy who presided over their clandestine meeting. After I filed my lawsuit, exposing their bogus cheating charge, ECSC leadership tried to justify their wrongful suspension of my paid membership rights to participate in club-sponsored events with another false accusation. This time, an incompetent Board of Directors wrongly alleged an ATA *clear scoring violation,* which didn't hold water any more than their bogus charge of cheating. Were they now grasping at straws?

Let's not forget the identities of the Secret 7. Voting was Director David C. McDaniel, 11,950 ATA registered targets to his name, yet he had no idea what the ATA rules stated. Voting was Jerry Jay Gage, 2400 ATA registered targets, their gesticulating, woman berating ECSC Director, just as clueless as McDaniel. Voting was Don R. Henslee, with a mere 200 ATA registered targets, their continuous foul-mouthed ECSC Director, and according to the minutes, their ATA rules clarifier, obviously clueless. Voting was Director Wayne Johnston, with 3800 ATA registered targets, and like McDaniel, Gage, and Henslee, just as clueless concerning the ATA rules. Four ATA registered shooters with 18,350 registered targets to their names, yet in combination, still clueless. Voting was Sherrie A. Lewis, club instigator, lying about assault rifle intimidation, which she knew first-hand never happened. Voting was Treasurer Rusty Porter, to whom a vote of his own Board and Texas law were irrelevant. Last, but by no means least, voting was the former mayor of Cedar Hill, Texas, Vice President DVM Christopher Lyons Rose, who, while presiding over a kangaroo court, convicted an innocent woman behind her back, all the while espousing he was a "straight-up" kind of guy, who stated, "I really don't want to get in the middle of it."

In their infinite wisdom, these surreptitious individuals decided to support Dan Hunt, their unqualified, incompetent leagues manager, an individual who most likely placed his family in *a position of discomfort*. A Duncanville cop who told nearly one hundred unsuspecting individuals, some children, he suffered from mental whatever *after intense and severe exposures at work*. In my opinion, a hothead who clearly resigned at thirty-four minutes before midnight following his resignation some three hours earlier in front of the Board. A children's shooting coach, who continuously misbehaved like a clowning buffoon with a loaded weapon in front of parents and children, was again placed in charge of forty-armed individuals, some with little to no experience with firearms and most of whom were oblivious to the ATA rules.

This book exposed what I believe is the truth behind their clandestine *Board Meeting-Emergency Meeting*, kangaroo court. The unprincipled leadership of the ECSC wanted to silence me, to stop me from speaking out about the dangers of mixing guns, alcohol, and children, along with other gun safety infractions at the ECSC.

I believe the gun safety infractions I observed and the ECSC policy allowing the consumption of alcoholic beverages, especially with the inordinate number of youths using the ECSC facility, should be a matter of public interest. As long as you allow the consumption of alcoholic beverages, you cannot control the dangerous consequences of someone drinking beer or hard liquor on a gun club's property. I have attempted to make these crucial safety issues known to the public.

This book exposed the false accusations from a vindictive Duncanville cop, incompetent, unqualified leagues manager Danny Garth Hunt. Within these pages is the evidence their false accusation of cheating was bogus. Within these pages is the proof leagues manager Danny Garth Hunt, along with Rose, Porter, and their cronies, willfully and maliciously ruined my reputation and credibility, all to silence me.

They held their clandestine kangaroo court and denied me the right to defend myself. *This book is my defense.*

Aftermath

Chapter Twenty-four

In the Preface, I wrote: *This is a book every member of a gun club, guest, or parent of a child participating in events sponsored by a gun club should read. First, to raise awareness of the critical importance of club leadership's duty to its members by implementing sound gun safety policies and procedures, then recognizing the importance of appointing qualified, competent individuals to oversee live-fire shooting events. Second, to understand what can happen when a club member is intentionally harmed by another club member's misbehavior and false accusations, and such misconduct is intentionally condoned by club leadership.*

Throughout the events described within this book, Duncanville narcotics detective and ECSC leagues manager Dan Hunt and the ECSC Board of Directors demonstrated an inexcusable pattern of contempt for their Bylaws, Texas laws, a mediated, signed contract, and First Amendment Rights. I detailed the misconduct of five attorneys representing Dan Hunt and the ECSC, citing multiple violations of *The Texas Lawyer's Creed, A Mandate for Professionalism*, signed by the Justices of *The Texas Supreme Court* and *The Court of Criminal Appeals*.

As I pointed out numerous times within this book, Danny Garth Hunt's misconduct raised serious questions regarding his veracity as a law enforcement officer. Were people convicted based on Danny Garth

Hunt's propensity to lie and embellish? This question was and is still valid.

I filed an official complaint with the Dallas County District Attorney, John Creuzot, regarding Danny Garth Hunt's misconduct and lies in the events leading to my lawsuit and within the judicial proceedings. I provided District Attorney Creuzot with a copy of my book, *What Emergency? Guns! Alcohol! Children!*, which detailed the evidence of Danny Garth Hunt's culpability. I requested that every criminal case where a person was convicted and incarcerated based on Danny Garth Hunt's testimony be reopened and examined. I also recommended the attorney of record for the defense in these cases be notified of Danny Garth Hunt's lack of veracity.

I filed similar complaints with the Duncanville City Manager, Douglas E. Finch, Assistant City Manager, Robert D. Brown, and Interim Duncanville Police Chief, Matthew Stogner. Each was provided with a copy of my book. Again, I recommended that any case where an individual was convicted and incarcerated due to the testimony of Danny Garth Hunt should be investigated. In addition, a letter outlining the misconduct of a sworn Duncanville police officer was sent to each member of the Duncanville city council.

It should be noted that Assistant City Manager Robert D. Brown was the Duncanville Police Chief during nearly six years of judicial proceedings involving Danny Garth Hunt. To the best of my knowledge, Robert D. Brown allowed an officer named a defendant in a lawsuit where he was accused of lying to continue arresting and testifying in criminal cases. Furthermore, some six months earlier, Dan Hunt was served with a *Cease and Desist Notification* from my attorney at the Duncanville Police Department. The notice outlined Dan Hunt's malicious, defamatory conduct. See *Stonewalled, Chapter 4*. I was never contacted regarding any investigation by the Duncanville Police Department into Dan Hunt's misconduct. Dan Hunt subsequently refused service of my lawsuit at the police department. Instead, Dan

Hunt requested he be served at the Ellis County Sportsmans Club facility.

I attempted to purchase advertising space in a local Waxahachie, Texas newspaper, *The Daily Light*, with an unexpected, disturbing result. I had provided a complimentary copy of my book to the editor. I was subsequently informed, *"Our director along with our upper management team feels it's best to politely decline running your ad."* The reason cited was that my book *"portrayed items we are unable to associate with our publications."*

My book was based on approximately forty-five documents. Many were obtained through judicial proceedings. These include multiple court filings and transcripts from the 443rd and 40th Ellis County District Courts and filings to the Court of Appeals, Tenth District of Texas. In addition, my book is based on my extensive law enforcement experience and training, most specifically, the adverse effects of the consumption of alcoholic beverages. I took a stand on gun safety and the unwarranted, dangerous policy to allow the consumption of alcoholic beverages at the Ellis County Sportsmans Club, a local gun range. I paid a heavy price. I believe my reputation was intentionally and maliciously destroyed to stop me from speaking out. It took a lawsuit, nearly six years of judicial proceedings, and tens of thousands of dollars in attorney fees to obtain the proof the elected officers of the Ellis County Sportsmans Club and their leagues manager, Dan Hunt, lied and why they lied.

Within this book, I addressed the dangers of mixing guns, alcohol, and children at the Ellis County Sportsmans Club. Many high school youth teams utilize the gun club weekly. I wrote: *"Legitimate concerns every participant and parent of any child participating in events at a gun club allowing the consumption of alcoholic beverages has not only, in my opinion, a right to express, but a moral obligation."* Yet, this was an *"item"* the local newspaper, *Waxahachie Daily Light* was *"unable to associate with their publications."*

I would simply ask, when did the safety of the children of their Ellis County readership become something the *Waxahachie Daily Light* could not associate with in their publication?

Based on my experiences and professional training, the mixing of guns, alcohol, and children at a shooting facility is unwarranted, foolhardy, downright dangerous, and negligent. These are legitimate concerns and should be topics of public interest. Yet, such safety issues were an *"item"* the *Waxahachie Daily Light* was *"unable to associate with their publications."*

I attempted to raise the public's awareness of the infractions of basic gun safety that I found presented a danger and liability to club members, guests, and the many children at the ECSC. This wasn't soccer night at a local high school stadium. Balls weren't being kicked around. Loaded guns were being used. Dangerous machines were in play. Yet, such safety issues were an *"item"* the local newspaper, *Waxahachie Daily Light,* was *"unable to associate with their publications."*

I attempted to raise the public's awareness of the ECSC Board of Directors and their incompetent, hothead, grandstanding league's manager and Duncanville police officer's contempt for Texas law and club bylaws, even to the extent they lied in their court filings. Such misconduct was a liability to every club member. Yet, this was an *"item"* the *Waxahachie Daily Light* was *"unable to associate with their publications."*

The position taken by the *Waxahachie Daily Light* director and management team, in my opinion, condoned the ECSC's actions. I had to wonder if the newspaper had the same policy regarding drinking and driving. Had they never witnessed the devastation of a fatality automobile crash caused by a drunk driver? I have. I certainly didn't want to see a similar scenario involving guns played out at a gun range that allowed members and guests to consume alcoholic beverages.

I also wondered if the individuals who refused to advertise my book were Ellis County Sportsmans Club members or affiliated with the club. Within this book, I raised the issue of the club's influence within the Ellis County legal community, even questioning whether I would get a fair trial. I repeatedly asked my attorney if I could request a change of venue. Each time, I was told there was insufficient evidence to support such a request.

And now, the local Waxahachie newspaper refused to allow me to purchase an ad to advertise my book. The position taken by the *Waxahachie Daily Light* certainly reinforced my beliefs regarding the club's influence and added weight to the concerns I encountered throughout the judicial process. After the *Waxahachie Daily Light* refused to run my paid ad, I purchased an ad in the *Dallas Morning News*.

As the conduct of Texas lawyers is governed by the *Texas Disciplinary Rules of Professional Conduct* and *The Texas Lawyer's Creed*, my next step dealt with the Texas Judicial System. Within Chapters Thirteen to Twenty, I detailed the violations of *The Texas Lawyer's Creed* by the five attorneys, J. Richard Harmon, Regan G. Pearson, Wade C. Crosnoe, Heather H. Phelps, and Ronald E. Bunch for Defendants Dan Hunt and the Desoto Gun Club d/b/a Ellis County Sportsmans Club. From my observations and analysis of the many court documents, their conduct made a mockery of the Texas Judicial System. The following is an excerpt from *The Texas Lawyer's Creed*:

THE TEXAS LAWYER'S CREED—A MANDATE FOR PROFESSIONALISM.
ORDER OF THE SUPREME COURT OF TEXAS AND THE COURT OF CRIMINAL APPEALS

The conduct of a lawyer should be characterized at all times by honesty, candor, and fairness. In fulfilling his or her primary duty to a client, a lawyer must be ever mindful of the profession's broader duty to the legal system.

A.L. Dickason

The Supreme Court of Texas and the Court of Criminal Appeals are committed to eliminating a practice in our State by a minority of lawyers of abusive tactics which have surfaced in many parts of our country. We believe such tactics are a disservice to our citizens, harmful to clients, and demeaning to our profession.

The abusive tactics range from lack of civility to outright hostility and obstructionism. Such behavior does not serve justice but tends to delay and often deny justice. The lawyers who use abusive tactics, instead of being part of the solution, have become part of the problem.

The desire for respect and confidence by lawyers from the public should provide the members of our profession with the necessary incentive to attain the highest degree of ethical and professional conduct. These rules are primarily aspirational. Compliance with the rules depends primarily upon understanding and voluntary compliance, secondarily upon re-enforcement by peer pressure and public opinion, and finally when necessary by enforcement by the courts through their inherent powers and rules already in existence.

These standards are not a set of rules that lawyers can use and abuse to incite ancillary litigation or arguments over whether or not they have been observed.

We must always be mindful that the practice of law is a profession. As members of a learned art we pursue a common calling in the spirit of public service. We have a proud tradition. Throughout the history of our nation, the members of our citizenry have looked to the ranks of our profession for leadership and guidance. Let us now as a profession each rededicate ourselves to practice law so we can restore public confidence in our profession, faithfully serve our clients, and fulfill our responsibility to the legal system.

I am a lawyer; I am entrusted by the People of Texas to preserve and improve our legal system. I am licensed by the Supreme Court of Texas. I must therefore abide by the Texas Disciplinary Rules of Professional Conduct, but I know that Professionalism requires more than merely avoiding the violation of laws and rules. I am committed to this Creed for no other reason than it is right.

II. Lawyer to Client: 6. *I will treat adverse parties and witnesses with fairness and due consideration.*

II. Lawyer to Client: 7. *I will advise my client that we will not pursue conduct which is intended primarily to harass or drain the financial resources of the opposing party.*

II. Lawyer to Client: 8. *I will advise my clients that we will not pursue tactics which are intended primarily for delay.*

III. Lawyer to Lawyer: 4. *I will attempt to prepare documents which correctly reflect the agreement of the parties. I will not include provisions which have not been agreed upon or omit provisions which are necessary to reflect the agreement of the parties.*

III. Lawyer to Lawyer: 7. *I will not serve motions or pleadings in any manner that unfairly limits another party's opportunity to respond.*

IV. Lawyer and Judge: 6. *I will not knowingly misrepresent, mischaracterize, misquote or miscite facts or authorities to gain an advantage.*

This document was signed by the Justices of the Supreme Court of Texas and the Justices of the Court of Criminal Appeals. The operative words are: ***These rules are primarily aspirational. Compliance with the rules depends primarily upon understanding and voluntary compliance, secondarily upon re-enforcement by peer pressure and public opinion, and finally when necessary by enforcement by the courts through their inherent powers and rules already in existence,*** and within the attorney's oath, ***I am committed to this Creed for no other reason than it is right.*** In other words, there are no sanctions for violations of *The Texas Lawyer's Creed.*

Attorneys are licensed by the *Supreme Court of Texas* as stipulated in *The Texas Lawyer's Creed.* I filed a grievance with Chief Justice Nathan L. Hecht regarding the multiple violations of *The Texas*

A.L. Dickason

Lawyer's Creed—A Mandate for Professionalism by five attorneys, J. Richard Harmon, Regan G. Pearson, Wade C. Crosnoe, Heather H. Phelps, and Ronald E. Bunch. As evidence, I provided a copy of my book: *What Emergency? Guns! Alcohol! Children!* I directed Chief Justice Hecht's attention to the chapters dealing with the judicial procedures, where I identified the violations, 'chapter and verse' from multiple court filings to the 443rd and 40th Ellis County District Courts and the Court of Appeals, Tenth District of Texas, the attorney emails submitted as evidence to the courts, and transcripts of three court hearings.

Judge Cindy Ermatinger, 443rd Ellis County District Court, and Judge Bob Carroll, 40th Ellis County District Court, received a copy of my book: *What Emergency? Guns! Alcohol! Children!* Once again, I directed the Courts' attention to the chapters addressing the judicial proceedings and the multiple violations of *The Texas Lawyers Creed* within their respective courts.

The second document governing the conduct of Texas lawyers fell under the jurisdiction of the Texas State Bar. The following is an excerpt.

TEXAS DISCIPLINARY RULES OF PROFESSIONAL CONDUCT

Preamble: A Lawyer's Responsibilities

1. A lawyer is a representative of clients, an officer of the legal system and a public citizen having special responsibility for the quality of justice. Lawyers, as guardians of the law, play a vital role in the preservation of society. The fulfillment of this role requires an understanding by lawyers of their relationship with and function in our legal system. A consequent obligation of lawyers is to maintain the highest standards of ethical conduct.

Rule 3.01. Meritorious Claims and Contentions

A lawyer shall not bring or defend a proceeding, or assert or controvert an issue therein, unless the lawyer reasonably believes that there is a basis for doing so that is not frivolous.

1. The advocate has a duty to use legal procedure for the fullest benefit of the client's cause, but also a duty not to abuse legal procedure. The law, both procedural and substantive, affects the limits within which an advocate may proceed. Likewise, these Rules impose limitations on the types of actions that a lawyer may take on behalf of his client. See Rules 3.02-3.06, 4.01-4.04, and 8.04. However, the law is not always clear and never is static. Accordingly, in determining the proper scope of advocacy, account must be taken of the law's ambiguities and potential for change.

2. All judicial systems prohibit, at a minimum, the filing of frivolous or knowingly false pleadings, motions or other papers with the court or the assertion in an adjudicatory proceeding of a knowingly false claim or defense.

3. A filing or contention is frivolous if it contains knowingly false statements of fact. It is not frivolous, however, merely because the facts have not been first substantiated fully or because the lawyer expects to develop vital evidence only by discovery. Neither is it frivolous even though the lawyer believes that the client's position ultimately may not prevail. In addition, this Rule does not prohibit the use of a general denial or other pleading to the extent authorized by applicable rules of practice or procedure. Likewise, a lawyer for a defendant in any criminal proceeding or for the respondent in a proceeding that could result in commitment may so defend the proceeding as to require that every element of the case be established.

Rule 3.02. *Minimizing the Burdens and Delays of Litigation*

In the course of litigation, a lawyer shall not take a position that unreasonably increases the costs or other burdens of the case or that unreasonably delays resolution of the matter.

Rule 3.03. *Candor Toward the Tribunal*

(a) A lawyer shall not knowingly:

(1) make a false statement of material fact or law to a tribunal;

(2) fail to disclose a fact to a tribunal when disclosure is necessary to avoid assisting a criminal or fraudulent act;

Factual Representations by a Lawyer

2. An advocate is responsible for pleadings and other documents prepared for litigation, but is usually not required to have personal knowledge of matters asserted therein, for litigation documents ordinarily present assertions by the client, or by someone on the client's behalf, and not assertions by the lawyer. Compare Rule 3.01. However, an assertion purporting to be on the lawyer's own knowledge, as in an affidavit by the lawyer or a representation of fact in open court, may properly be made only when the lawyer knows the assertion is true or believes it to be true on the basis of a reasonably diligent inquiry. There are circumstances where failure to make a disclosure is the equivalent of an affirmative misrepresentation. The obligation prescribed in Rule 1.02(c) not to counsel a client to commit or assist the client in committing a fraud applies in litigation. See the Comments to Rules 1.02(c) and 8.04(a).

Misleading Legal Argument

3. Legal argument based on a knowingly false representation of law constitutes dishonesty toward the tribunal.

IV. NON-CLIENT RELATIONSHIPS

Rule 4.01. Truthfulness in Statements to Others

In the course of representing a client a lawyer shall not knowingly:

(a) make a false statement of material fact or law to a third person; or

(b) fail to disclose a material fact to a third person when disclosure is necessary to avoid making the lawyer a party to a criminal act or knowingly assisting a fraudulent act perpetrated by a client.

Rule 4.04. Respect for Rights of Third Persons

(a) In representing a client, a lawyer shall not use means that have no substantial purpose other than to embarrass, delay, or burden a third person, or use methods of obtaining evidence that violate the legal rights of such a person.

8.04 Misconduct

(a) A lawyer shall not:

(1) violate these rules, knowingly assist or induce another to do so, or do so through the acts of another, whether or not the violation occurred in the course of a client-lawyer relationship;

(2) commit a serious crime or commit any other criminal act that reflects adversely on the lawyers honesty, trustworthiness or fitness as a lawyer in other respects;

(3) engage in conduct involving dishonesty, fraud, deceit or misrepresentation;

(4) engage in conduct constituting obstruction of justice

I filed a formal grievance against attorney J. Richard Harmon, Regan G. Pearson, Wade C. Crosnoe, Heather H. Phelps, and Ronald E. Bunch with the Texas State Bar. For each grievance, I provided a copy of the court filings by these individuals with the 443rd and 40th Ellis County District Courts, the Court of Appeals, Tenth District of Texas, court transcripts, and other pertinent court documents as evidence. I addressed the material facts for each grievance, providing 'chapter and verse' of the violations of *The Texas Lawyer's Creed* and corresponding *Texas Disciplinary Rules of Professional Conduct.*

Following the signing of a mediated settlement contract by the Defendants that resolved my lawsuit, J. Richard Harmon and Regan G. Pearson demanded that I sign a new contract. Their new contract included provisions not discussed during mediation, nor were they part of the original contract signed by the Defendants. J. Richard Harmon, Regan G. Pearson, and Ronald E. Bunch refused to issue the settlement check according to the provisions stipulated in the original contract until I signed their new contract.

J. Richard Harmon, Regan G. Pearson, and Ronald E. Bunch refused to honor the dispute clause in the original contract. In an email to my attorney, J. Richard Harmon emphatically refused to re-enter mediation. Their threats and demands resulted in an unnecessary extension of the litigation for nearly five years. Their unwarranted manipulation created a financial hardship of tens of thousands of dollars in attorney fees I had to expend to enforce the original contract.

While the unwarranted extension of the judicial proceedings was a heavy financial burden for me, nearly five years of added billing was, in my opinion, a windfall for J. Richard Harmon and Regan G. Pearson. In addition to Dan Hunt and ECSC, their third client was the insurance company, an 830-plus billion-dollar French insurance conglomerate, who had hired the law firm.

To force Dan Hunt and ECSC to comply with the contract they willingly mediated and signed, I had to file a summary judgment motion with the 443rd Ellis County District Court. Within my motion for summary judgment, I requested my attorney fees. Per the original contract, I was legally entitled to recover my fees. Since J. Richard Harmon had ordered my attorney in an email, *Do not contact Judge Fifer, and I can guarantee you that there will not be another mediation,* Defendants were barred from recovery of attorney fees. The contract's dispute clause stipulated that any party who refused to re-enter mediation in the event of a dispute could not recover attorney fees to enforce the contract.

To prevent my recovery of attorney fees to which I was legally entitled, J. Richard Harmon, Regan G. Pearson, and Ronald E. Bunch lied to the 443rd Ellis County District Court. They again lied, along with Wade C. Crosnoe, to the Court of Appeals, Tenth District of Texas. Heather H. Phelps and Ronald E. Bunch subsequently lied to the 40th Ellis County District Court. These five attorneys, within documents filed with three courts, informed said courts that I was not entitled to attorney's fees under Chapter 38 of the Texas Civil Practice and Remedies Code because the ECSC is *not a corporation.* They even went so far as to cite other cases that had no relevance to the legal status of the ECSC. In previous chapters, I referenced numerous documents establishing that ECSC was registered with the Texas Secretary of State as a non-profit corporation. I provided these documents within my grievances filed with the Texas State Bar.

During the January 16, 2020, hearing before the 443rd Ellis County District Court, Regan G. Pearson reiterated the lie, explaining to the Court why his client was not liable for attorney fees. Ronald E. Bunch, Waxahachie attorney of record for ECSC, was present during this hearing. I have already presented court records identifying Ronald E. Bunch's complicity in allowing his co-counsel to mislead the Court. The liability of ECSC for attorney fees was a material fact. In my opinion, the lies by five attorneys to three courts had one purpose: to defraud me of tens of thousands of dollars in attorney fees.

In addition, I addressed the unwarranted, defamatory accusations in documents submitted by J. Richard Harmon, Regan G. Pearson, Wade C. Crosnoe, and Ronald E. Bunch in the grievances I filed with the Texas State Bar. The unwarranted, malicious defamations were not pertinent to the matter before the Bar, a hearing on a breach of contract.

J. Richard Harmon, Regan G. Pearson, Wade C. Crosnoe, and Ronald E. Bunch had used Defendants' court filings to enter into public records not only false details regarding events that led to my lawsuit but also malicious, false accusations toward an individual who wasn't even a party to my lawsuit. None of which were supported by any factual evidence, Defendants' or witness affidavits. It's my belief the misrepresentations, false details, and vicious accusations violated *The Texas Lawyer's Creed* and the *Texas Disciplinary Rules of Professional Conduct.*

Based on the irrelevancy and lack of evidence, my attorney filed a motion to strike the misrepresentations, false details, and vicious accusations in Defendants' filing, which Judge Cindy Ermatinger denied.

Throughout the hearing, Regan G. Pearson and Ronald E. Bunch embellished the lies they reiterated to the Court. My attorney informed the Court that opposing counsel was attempting to try the case as if it was a jury trial, albeit without evidence, which was unwarranted and inappropriate for a hearing on a breach of contract. Despite my attorney's multiple objections to the hearsay and irrelevancy of such statements, Judge Cindy Ermatinger denied every objection. In fact, not once did Judge Ermatinger sustain an objection by my attorney during two court hearings.

But then, what can I say about her role in the proceedings? This was the same judge who didn't realize she was missing a sixty-one-page document that my attorney had referenced at the start of the hearing until some fifteen minutes later. Evidently, the missing document wasn't important until opposing counsel referred to their document. This was the same judge who viewed an exhibit contained in Defendants' filing, the mediated, signed contract, and the reason for the court hearing as "I guess, is where the mediator wrote down things?" The three words that come to mind regarding Judge Ermatinger's actions are incompetent, unknowledgeable, and biased.

Following Judge Cindy Ermatinger's denial of my motion to enforce summary judgment, Defendants' attorneys did a one-eighty. They filed the same motion I had filed for summary judgment and asked for their attorney fees. They now reversed their arguments from the first hearing. Instead of throwing out the contract, they now asked the court to enforce it. Once again, their filing contained the same misrepresentations, false details, and vicious accusations. They got away with it the first time; why not do it again? Their new motion gave them another opportunity to falsify another court document. This time, Judge Ermatinger granted Defendant's motion. I was still unable to recover my attorney fees. I appealed.

Appellees' Brief filed with the Court of Appeals by Wade C. Crosnoe contained the same lies regarding the legal status of their client, *Desoto Gun Club d/b/a Ellis County Sportsmans Club*. The Court of Appeals, Tenth District of Texas was informed the ECSC was *not a corporation*. Furthermore, their *Appellees' Brief* contained the same misrepresentations, false details, and now, an enhanced embellishment of the vicious, defamatory accusations that characterized opposing counsel's previous documents.

The Court of Appeals overturned Judge Ermatinger's second ruling and remanded the case to the lower court. Heather H. Phelps and Ronald E. Bunch subsequently filed a breach of contract lawsuit against me in the 40th Ellis County District Court.

Within their court filing, Heather H. Phelps and Ronald E. Bunch lied to the 40th Ellis County District Court, asserting that the gun club was *not a corporation* and, therefore, not liable for attorney fees. The misrepresentations, false details, and defamatory accusations against an individual who wasn't even a party to my lawsuit that characterized their earlier filings were now conspicuously missing. The omission only emphasized the malicious intent by J. Richard Harmon, Regan G. Pearson, and Wade C. Crosnoe to undermine my case and unduly influence the court with false accusations and malicious defamation irrelevant to a breach of contract before the Bar.

The insurance company for the ECSC entered the picture shortly after I filed my lawsuit against Dan Hunt and ECSC in December/2018. In January/2019, a document was filed with the 443rd Ellis County Sportsmans Club that replaced the attorney of record for Dan Hunt with two new attorneys, J. Richard Harmon and Regan G. Pearson.

At the time, I questioned why a big downtown Dallas law firm specializing in insurance litigation would represent Dan Hunt. A couple of weeks later, a second document was filed to add the same two attorneys as attorneys of record for the ECSC, in addition to Ronald E. Bunch, who was already an attorney of record. I subsequently learned that Dan Hunt was included because the gun club's insurance policy covered elected officers and club members.

While researching the law firm, I discovered a lawsuit against another Texas gun range, Alpine Shooting Range. According to court documents, Alpine had been sued by an individual injured at their facility. The lawsuit was touted as a WIN on the home page of the law firm's website. The following is an excerpt from the court records.

"Alpine Industries Inc v. Whitlock (2018): Court of Appeals of Texas, Fort Worth. NO. 02-17-00396-CV. Attorneys for Appellants: Wade C. Crosnoe, Thompson, Coe, Cousins & Irons, L.L.P., Austin, Texas, J. Richard Harmon, Heather H. Sauter & Cassie J. Dallas, Thompson, Coe, Cousins & Irons, L.L.P., Dallas, Texas.

On December 17, 2016, Benjamin Whitlock went to Alpine's shooting range in Fort Worth. He carried with him a fully-loaded .22 caliber Winchester rifle. When he arrived at the range, Whitlock stopped at the gate to have his rifle cleared before entering. While Range Safety Officer Shinogle inspected Whitlock's rifle, the weapon was accidentally discharged, and a bullet struck Whitlock's leg, injuring him."

I would note that this type of incident was one of the safety infractions I addressed in detail in *Chapter Six: Guns! Alcohol! Children!*

Additionally, it's noteworthy that three of the four attorneys hired to represent Dan Hunt and the ECSC—J. Richard Harmon, Wade C. Crosnoe, and Heather H. Phelps (Sauter)—also represented Alpine Industries. This led me to question whether the insurance company for ECSC also represented Alpine.

After I provided the Alpine case information to my primary and appeal attorneys, I was informed the case was dismissed due to a legal issue—the filing of a threshold expert report. What struck me was the similarity in tactics used by the attorneys in the Alpine case to my case.

As I identified in previous chapters, after mediation, Dan Hunt and the ECSC signed a contract agreeing to the terms and conditions of the settlement for my lawsuit. J. Richard Harmon and Regan G. Pearson subsequently submitted a new contract that added several new conditions to which I had not agreed, nor were such stipulated in the signed contract their clients willingly mediated and signed.

One new condition was to include a $48 balance on my club's debit card within the settlement amount, which the ECSC had obtained through a charge to my credit card. This was my money. It didn't belong to the ECSC. As I pointed out in previous chapters, there was never a discussion regarding my $48 balance on my debit card during mediation, nor did the contract Defendants signed stipulate such was part of the settlement amount. There was no reason to discuss it since the Board had voted to send me a refund check for the balance, then confirmed such in a letter from the club secretary and reiterated to my face by ECSC President Mike Lee—the same individual who signed the mediated contract on behalf of ECSC that settled my lawsuit.

It was merely a fabricated material fact J. Richard Harmon, Regan G. Pearson, and Ronald E. Bunch used as evidence to persuade the Court to invalidate the contract the Defendants signed, citing there was "no meeting of the minds" or a "mutual mistake." Their entire argument hinged on a fabricated material fact that J. Richard Harmon, Regan G. Pearson, and Ronald E. Bunch added to their new contract, then attempted to force me to sign by withholding the settlement check.

The ECSC's insurance company had hired the law firm that had employed four of the five attorneys for Defendants. According to Regan G. Pearson, the insurance adjuster was calling the shots. It was the adjustor who refused to pay my attorney fees, to which I was legally entitled, according to the contract Defendants had willingly mediated and signed. Had the adjustor agreed to pay my attorney fees in August/2019, it would have amounted to only a few thousand dollars. Instead, the total ran into tens of thousands of dollars I incurred.

Once my case reached the Court of Appeals, Tenth District of Texas, the Court ordered another mediation. It was a surprise to my attorneys and seemed illogical. After the first mediation, I couldn't get the court to uphold the contract. It was why my case was at the appeal level. And now, the Court of Appeals wanted another round of mediation. I knew the mediation wouldn't work and it didn't. I have often wondered if J. Richard Harmon, Regan G. Pearson, and Ronald E. Bunch told the same lie to the insurance adjustor that they told the

Courts—the ECSC was *not a corporation* and, therefore, not liable for attorney fees. I believe it was and is a valid question.

Despite the preponderance of documented evidence I submitted, court documents, transcripts, and other pertinent documents regarding the duplicity and misconduct of five attorneys, the Texas State Bar denied my grievances. I can't say I was surprised. *The Texas Lawyer's Creed* and *Texas Disciplinary Rules of Professional Conduct* certainly sound impressive. However, from my firsthand experiences, they were ineffective and worthless. It was and is still my opinion that the actions of five licensed attorneys and the 443rd Ellis County District Court made a mockery of the Texas Judicial system. Was the Texas State Bar any different?

Even in the face of documented evidence, it appeared to me that the Texas State Bar's outright dismissal of five grievances only underscored that it's acceptable for an attorney to add new conditions not stipulated in the original contract after all parties have signed. Then, demand the opposing party sign the new contract while withholding the settlement check as leverage. Such action was what Regan G. Pearson and Ronald E. Bunch argued in court—it was a standard practice for them. By their own documented words, they did it all the time.

From my perspective, the Texas State Bar's outright dismissal only underscored that it was acceptable for an attorney to refuse to abide by the stipulations in a signed contract. It's what J. Richard Harmon, Regan G. Pearson, and Ronald E. Bunch did when they refused to comply with the dispute clause. It's what these three attorneys did when they refused to send my settlement check until I signed their new contract.

From my perspective, the Texas State Bar's outright dismissal only underscored that it's acceptable for an attorney to lie to the Court in their filings to avoid their client's liability, defrauding the opposing side of tens of thousands of dollars in attorney fees, even when the attorney possessed evidence refuting his lies.

From my perspective, the Texas State Bar's outright dismissal only underscored that it was acceptable for an attorney to lie to the Court during a hearing.

From my perspective, the Texas State Bar's outright dismissal only underscored that it's acceptable for an attorney to maliciously destroy the reputations of the opposing party and a non-party to the initial lawsuit in court documents and arguments before the court without the necessity of providing evidence or signed affidavits.

The Texas Lawyer's Creed stipulated: ***Compliance with the rules depends primarily upon understanding and voluntary compliance, secondarily upon re-enforcement by peer pressure and public opinion, and finally when necessary by enforcement by the courts through their inherent powers and rules already in existence.***

From my perspective, ***understanding and voluntary compliance*** and ***peer pressure*** certainly didn't stop these five attorneys from submitting documents riddled with misrepresentations, false details, and malicious, defamatory accusations. Were their actions driven by the knowledge they wouldn't be held accountable? The Texas State Bar's dismissal of my grievances certainly supported my belief.

From my perspective, the court system's ***inherent powers and rules*** were ineffective, as evidenced by multiple objections from my attorney that Judge Cindy Ermatinger of the 443rd Ellis County District Court overruled. As I referenced earlier, not once did Judge Ermatinger sustain an objection by my attorney during two court hearings.

Furthermore, the court system's ***inherent powers and rules*** were ineffective, as evidenced by Judge Ermatinger's refusal to grant my motion to strike the misrepresentations, false details, and malicious, defamatory statements made without any supporting evidence or affidavits from the Defendants or a witness. Instead, Judge Ermatinger allowed the misrepresentations, false facts, and malicious, defamatory statements to stand within two court records and in two court transcripts. The Court of Appeals, Tenth District of Texas, ignored my appeal attorney's admonishments, instead allowing the misrepresentations, false facts, and malicious, defamatory accusations to stand within their court records.

Regarding **public opinion**—this is why I wrote my book, *What Emergency? Guns! Alcohol! Children!* This is why there is a *Second Edition* of *What Emergency? Guns! Alcohol! Children!*

The Texas Lawyer's Creed stipulated: *The Supreme Court of Texas and the Court of Criminal Appeals are committed to eliminating a practice in our State by a minority of lawyers of abusive tactics which have surfaced in many parts of our country. We believe such tactics are a disservice to our citizens, harmful to clients, and demeaning to our profession. The abusive tactics range from lack of civility to outright hostility and obstructionism. Such behavior does not serve justice but tends to delay and often deny justice. The lawyers who use abusive tactics, instead of being part of the solution, have become part of the problem.*

My lawsuit was settled on April 17, 2019. However, due to what I viewed as abusive tactics by five attorneys, my case was dragged through two Ellis County District Courts and the Court of Appeals, Tenth District of Texas for almost five additional years. The damage they caused can never be eradicated.

"The conduct of a lawyer should be characterized at all times by honesty, candor, and fairness."
The Texas Lawyers Creed—A Mandate for Professionalism

"A consequent obligation of lawyers is to maintain the highest standards of ethical conduct."
Preamble –Texas Disciplinary Rules of Professional Conduct